Acclaim for URI SAVIR's

THE PROCESS

"*The Process* is an insider's story of how bitter contenders for the same tiny patch of parched land struggled to disentangle their mutual hatreds, grievances and claims. . . . There is another process here, a far deeper and more human one. This is the process by which the Israelis and Palestinians involved in the intense negotiations . . . rose above their deep resentments and hatreds . . . to achieve if not always friendship, then at least a recognition of a partnership in a common predicament."
—*The New York Times Book Review*

"In *The Process*, Savir tells how the tissue of togetherness was woven with patriotism and empathy, passion and patience." —*The Washington Post*

"Fascinating and engaging." —*Tikkun*

"A nuts and bolts look at how Israeli and Palestinian leaders struggled to end their 100 years' conflict. . . . Disappointed believers in the Oslo process will read this book not only as a recounting of what was but also as a tantalizing hint of what might have been." —*The New Leader*

"Savir reveals the drama and details behind the scenes in three years of negotiations. . . . Many of the particulars are reported here for the first time." —*Jewish Week*

URI SAVIR
THE PROCESS

Uri Savir was Israel's chief negotiator with the PLO
from 1993 to 1996. He was the first Israeli official to negotiate secretly with a senior representative of the PLO.
From their first meeting up until the signing of the
Interim Agreement in September 1995, he and his
Palestinian counterpart, Abu Ala, spent approximately
thirty-five hundred hours in negotiations. In 1994-95,
Savir headed Israel's delegation for talks with Syria and
permanent status negotiations with the Palestinians. He
was Israel's consul general in New York between 1988
and 1992 and director-general of Israel's Foreign Ministry from 1993 to 1996. Today, he heads the Peres
Center for Peace in Tel Aviv.

THE PROCESS

THE
PROCESS

1,100 Days That Changed the Middle East

URI SAVIR

Vintage Books / A Division of Random House, Inc. / New York

FIRST VINTAGE BOOKS EDITION, JULY 1999

Copyright © 1998 by Uri Savir

All rights reserved under International and Pan-American Copyright
Conventions. Published in the United States by Vintage Books, a division
of Random House, Inc., New York, and simultaneously in Canada
by Random House of Canada Limited, Toronto. Originally
published in hardcover in the United States by
Random House, Inc., New York, in 1998.

The Library of Congress has cataloged
the Random House edition as follows:
The process : 1,100 days that changed the Middle East/Uri Savir.
p.   cm.
Includes index.
ISBN 0-679-42296-X
1. Savir, Uri. 2. Arab-Israeli conflict—Peace—1993– 3. Israel.
Treaties, etc. Munaẓẓamat al-Taḥrīr al-Filasṭīnīyah, 1993 Sept. 13.
I. Title.
DS119.76.S78   1998
956.04—dc21   98-10940

Vintage ISBN: 0-679-74561-0

www.vintagebooks.com

Printed in the United States of America
10 9 8 7 6 5 4 3 2 1

To Leo and Henni Savir

Contents

Introduction

On May 29, 1996, Shimon Peres narrowly lost an election to Binyamin Netanyahu, bringing to a close an era of experienced leadership and a bold and active Israeli peace policy. In June 1996 I resigned from my positions as director-general of the Israeli Foreign Ministry and Israel's chief peace negotiator. For the previous three years, almost to the day, I had been intensely involved in negotiating with Israel's former archenemy, the PLO. Entrusted by Yitzhak Rabin and Shimon Peres to head the Israeli negotiating teams, I was privileged to witness and participate in a series of dramatic turning points in the history of the Middle East. Driven by a need to express what I had internalized over a thousand days and four thousand hours of negotiations, I have decided to write this book while my impressions are still powerful and fresh.

Peacemaking is a gradual revolution that moves from hostility to a desired conciliation, a collection of moments in which a new trend is set in motion. This book is an attempt to capture and understand components of the Middle East peace process as they occurred. For despite the persistence of conflict and mistrust, the process initiated at Oslo will ultimately determine a new future for the Middle East. Change is often best perceived in the immediate drama of its occurrence, before new routines have set in. In responding to change, society tends to linger in a kind of psychological jet lag as long-standing perceptions resist the impact of new ideas and realities. Peacemaking tries to reset perceptional clocks.

This is a story about people—above all, the three people whose courage made the process possible: Yitzhak Rabin, who paid for his beliefs with his life, Shimon Peres, and Yasser Arafat. It is also about the people who were charged with crafting the agreements and, in the course of doing so, developed new and surprising relationships. And it is equally about the people for whom the agreements were designed—Israelis and Palestinians.

Not everyone trusted our motives. The opposition to the process was fierce on both sides. Some were even prepared to kill in order to undo what they regarded as an ill-conceived and dishonest peace. As a result, the peace process is not only a test of the relations among Israel, the Palestinians, and the Arab states; it also tests the identity and general will of the entities involved in the process. The ability to make peace—to compromise and coexist—will determine our ability to resist religious fundamentalism and nationalist fanaticism. This dichotomy became painfully clear during the negotiations of 1993–1996.

Having played an active role in the Oslo process—minute by minute, day and night—I have described it from a personal vantage point. I have not attempted to offer a comprehensive view of all the events—or, for that matter, an objective one. Rather than resist subjectivity, I have embraced it as both unavoidable and necessary for drawing my own conclusions while telling the story as honestly as I could.

By sharing my experience, I hope to contribute in a small way to the fulfillment of this process. I believe that the historic change that occurred between 1993 and 1996 has charted the course that Israel, the Palestinians, and the entire region must follow. After countless hours of negotiation and difficult decisions, and despite the violent opposition to peace on both sides and deep political fluctuations, the Middle East will not revert to what it was before the secret channel opened in Oslo at the beginning of 1993.

Translating these feelings and experiences into a cogent narrative was a daunting task. It could not have been accomplished without the guidance and assistance of good friends. Jason Epstein, a brilliant and thoughtful editor and the one person I know who takes virtually nothing for granted, guided and inspired me with wise counsel and sharp challenges. Ina Friedman helped me more than anyone else to find words, not only with her superb linguistic skills but with her deep understanding of people and peace. Avi Gil is the one Oslo veteran I consulted for both his broad knowledge of the facts and his acute and honest appraisal of their significance. Esther Newberg, my agent at ICM, gave generously of her acumen and empathy, born of deep conviction.

I also want to thank those who helped me to sharpen sensitivities, extend the research, and turn thoughts into legible copy: Joy de Menil of Random House, Maya Yaul, Aviva Meir, Ivry Verbin, Idit Zeltenreich, Meital Rubin, Margo Farley, and Ravit Bar-Av.

To thank my wife and daughter, Aliza and Maya, for their encouragement, shared passion, and endless patience does not do justice to their involvement. They were simply with me all along the way.

Finally, I wish to express my gratitude to Shimon Peres, the man who made the Oslo process possible and whose trust enabled me to take part in this most rewarding of experiences. During the years of negotiation, I wrote him many long, personal accounts that have served me, along with what I have stored away in memory and feeling, as the main source for this book.

Israel is turning fifty this year. I firmly believe that for all it has achieved, the Oslo process is the true test of its maturity as a strong, modern nation able to coexist with former enemies.

I

Breakthrough

1

A FIRST ENCOUNTER

FOR ME, IT ALL BEGAN ON MAY 14, 1993, A BALMY SATURDAY AFTER-
noon, when my boss, Israel's Foreign Minister Shimon Peres, asked
me to his official residence in Jerusalem. (He had recently appointed
me director-general of the Foreign Ministry, an appointment that
caused a commotion since I was only forty at the time.) Dressed in a
British cardigan, Peres was relaxed as I entered his living room. Avi
Gil, his wise chief of staff, was already seated on one of the comfortable sofas. I sat down opposite him.

"A glass of wine?" Peres asked. I nodded, he poured, and as he
handed me the glass he asked dryly, "How about a weekend in Oslo?"
as though he were offering cheese and crackers.

"Excuse me?" I mumbled, straining to suppress my excitement. I
knew that Oslo meant a first official talk with the PLO. For five
months, two Israeli academics, Yair Hirschfeld and Ron Pundak, had
been secretly and informally talking with three senior PLO officials:
Ahmed Qurei (Abu Ala), Hassan Asfour, and Maher al-Kurd, all close
associates of Yasser Arafat. These secret talks had been initiated by Israel's deputy foreign minister, my close friend Dr. Yossi Beilin, an ardent peace advocate. In mid-1992 Beilin had joined forces with Terje
Larsen, a Norwegian social scientist who headed FAFO, a major European peace research institute. Larsen was conducting a study of
Palestinian living conditions in the occupied territories. He and
Beilin had set up the informal talks between the two professors and

the three PLO men, which had begun in Norway on January 20. Their aim was to draft an informal document on the basic principles for future peacemaking between Israel and the Palestinians.

In these talks, the Palestinians—especially Abu Ala, their senior representative—advanced some surprisingly flexible positions, far more practical than the legalistic tangles created by the "non-PLO" delegation in Washington, made up solely of Palestinians from the occupied territories, which had been holding formal negotiations with us since the 1991 Madrid Peace Conference. These Washington talks had been going nowhere for months. At one point Avi Gil sent Peres, Beilin, and me a collection of reports on the Washington talks with the dates whited out. Because the talks had gone around in circles, none of us could put them in order. Later, in Oslo, Abu Ala would emphasize two key elements for our secret talks that impressed us: a pragmatic progression from easier to more difficult issues, which would allow for the development of trust between the parties; and Palestinian-Israeli cooperation, mainly in the economic field. The contrast between the two styles suggested that Arafat was sending us a definite message: the Washington talks would grind on endlessly, but in Oslo, where the PLO was officially represented, he was prepared to compromise. We believed, therefore, that the time had come to risk a test.

Peres sat down next to Avi Gil and began to describe his most recent conversations on the subject with Prime Minister Yitzhak Rabin.

"I told Yitzhak that the peace process is in danger of collapsing, even though the ground is fertile for progress," he said.

We had often discussed this paradox. The Middle East had changed in the previous five years. The Soviet Union, a longtime patron of various radical Arab rulers, had disintegrated. Moreover, the Arab world itself had fragmented after the Iran-Iraq war. Religious fundamentalism, which thrives on poverty, was now a serious threat to most of the regimes in the region—especially in the case of Iran, which was exporting terror and developing nonconventional weapons. As a result, economic development had become more important to those Arab governments than traditional strategic considerations. The United States was being courted by almost every country in the area, and a demonstration of stability was the only way to attract serious economic investment and American political involvement.

Many Arabs had begun to view Israel as a potential partner in their endeavors. The Palestinians understood that years of terrorism and the intifada (the violent uprising in the West Bank and Gaza Strip that started in 1987) had brought them neither political nor economic gains. The PLO, in fact, seemed on the verge of bankruptcy. Now that the Gulf War had upset regional political alignments, the next step was an Arab readiness to negotiate with Israel. This led to the 1991 Madrid Peace Conference and the subsequent Washington negotiations.

Yet the talks were stalled. The ideologically and politically rigid Syrians were moving very slowly if at all. The Jordanians had signaled that until a breakthrough had occurred with the Palestinians, they too would continue to wait. And so the Palestinians, the weakest link in the chain, were the key to peace. The problem in Washington was that Faisal Husseini, the West Bank leader, and the rest of his delegation lacked a mandate to negotiate. Every point we raised with them had to be referred back to the PLO leadership. Though we would never admit it openly, we were engaged in a charade. In Washington, we were actually negotiating with Yasser Arafat by fax!

"It's clear who's running the Palestinian show there," Peres continued. "I've told Rabin that I'm prepared to go to Oslo, meet secretly with their envoys, and test the PLO's true intentions. We're committed to moving this forward, and it's pointless to waste time in Washington by pretending that the PLO isn't there.

"Rabin, too, seems fed up with the Washington talks," Peres told me, "but he feels that it's premature for a minister to become involved with the PLO. He prefers that a senior official go to Oslo, and we decided you'd be the man."

I leaned forward to reply, but Peres said, "Wait, there's more. Rabin insists on two conditions: absolute discretion and the resumption of the talks in Washington, which must remain the main channel of negotiations. You're to send this message to the Palestinians through the Norwegian mediators. Be sure to stress that if word of the meeting is leaked, the Oslo channel will come to an end."

As for matters of substance at Olso, Peres authorized me to raise three issues. "Above all, the Palestinians must agree that Jerusalem will not be included in any autonomy arrangement; otherwise, further progress will be impossible," he said. "Second, they must drop their traditional demand that all outstanding questions be referred to binding international arbitration. We don't want to introduce another Security Council mechanism. The point is to learn to solve our problems on our own. Finally, there's the notion of creating autonomy in Gaza first and possibly moving the PLO leadership there."

Peres had long been in favor of testing Palestinian autonomy in Gaza before extending it to the West Bank. In November 1992 he had already raised such a proposal with President Hosni Mubarak of Egypt, who passed it on to Arafat. The PLO seemed amenable to the idea in principle, but Arafat wanted the addition of Jericho and control of the passage over the Jordan River: in other words, a foothold on the West Bank and a direct link with Jordan. Rabin, however, was reluctant to add Jericho to the first phase and absolutely refused to relinquish control of the bridge over the Jordan (or the border passage between Gaza and Egypt, for that matter). Everything relating to the external security of Israel and the territories, he insisted, must remain in Israeli hands. Israel must have complete control of its current borders.

"So you should certainly air the idea of 'Gaza first,'" Peres told me, "but don't commit us to the addition of Jericho. As to the draft of a declaration of principles drawn up with Pundak and Hirschfeld, you may explore the issues, but don't start negotiating the document itself. We'll decide how to proceed after you return. Is everything clear?" he asked with uncharacteristic sternness.

I nodded.

"Then good luck," he said, which was even less characteristic; Peres preferred to leave nothing to luck.

Within two days the Norwegians sent word that our two conditions for holding the next meeting in Oslo—absolute secrecy and the resumption of the Washington talks—had been accepted by the PLO, and I was studying the existing material on the Oslo track. On Peres's orders, I made all my travel arrangements through Beilin's bureau and told my personal staff that I would be holding economic talks in Paris and would then probably join my wife, Aliza, at the Cannes Film Festival (as the head of the Foreign Ministry's Cultural Division, she was representing our government there). I told my mother I was going abroad and elaborated no further. I did hint to my daughter, however, that this was to be no routine journey. Maya, who had just completed two years of compulsory army service, was strongly pro-peace. Since the age of four, she had been accompanying us to peace demonstrations and had adopted our belief in the desirability of a dialogue with the PLO. Though I couldn't tell her the purpose of my journey, I wanted her to sense that one of our dreams was about to come true.

"This trip is an important one," I remarked offhandedly a day or two before leaving.

"Oh?" she said, her curiosity piqued. "How important?"

"The most important," I said—and I believed she understood.

Finally I paid a private visit to Yossi Beilin at his home. Together we had looked forward to this moment ever since the days, in the mid-1980s, when Peres was first prime minister and we were jokingly known as the Blazers, five young, highly motivated aides with a penchant for dark blue sport jackets. (Yossi, who had worked with Peres since 1977, was then the cabinet secretary, and I had been plucked out of Israel's New York consulate in 1984 to serve as Peres's spokesman.) I felt uneasy that I was going to Oslo and Yossi was not. After all, he had created the secret back channel, at no small risk to his standing. Yossi assured me, however, that he was delighted. Like Peres, he was already envisioning the future.

On Friday, May 20, I boarded an El Al flight to Paris. After takeoff I made some notes to guide me in my opening statement. Then I reread some of the material from the ministry's Research Department, including a brief profile of Ahmed Qurei (Abu Ala), known as the PLO finance minister, the fifty-six-year-old man I was to meet that evening. A banker by training, he was in charge of the Palestinian bank, Samed, as well as various organs that funded economic and

Map 1: Israel, the West Bank, and Gaza, 1993

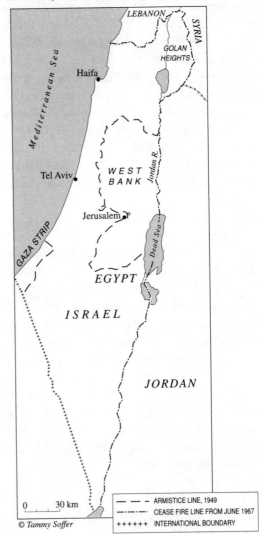

© Tammy Soffer

– – – –	ARMISTICE LINE, 1949
– · – · – ·	CEASE FIRE LINE FROM JUNE 1967
+ + + + + +	INTERNATIONAL BOUNDARY

social activities in the West Bank. He had been born in Abu Dis, just outside Jerusalem, but since the 1967 war he had lived in the Persian Gulf, Beirut, Cyprus, and Tunis. He had known Arafat for some thirty years, advised him on economic matters, and been a member of Fatah since 1968. He worked closely with Abu Mazen (Mahmoud Abbas), who for the previous five years had been in charge of the PLO's unofficial contacts with Israelis. Our analysis described Abu Ala as an astute pragmatist. He had been guiding the Palestinian involvement in the Multilateral Talks since the Madrid Peace Conference—orchestrating but not participating, since the PLO was formally excluded from the negotiations. He would sit in a hotel room and tell the "non-PLO" people what to say. But as far as we were concerned, he wasn't there.

I wondered whether this man had been directly involved in any of the PLO terror operations against Israel. The profile didn't suggest it, but I couldn't help speculating on whether he had known about the plan to kill Israeli athletes at the Munich Olympics, or about the attacks on Israeli schools in Ma'alot and Kiryat Shmonah, where scores of children had been murdered. My mind was racing with thoughts about bloodshed, the occupation, the thirst for peace, the upcoming meeting. It was proving to be a tiring journey, and I hadn't even completed the first leg.

I landed at Charles de Gaulle Airport at 11:00 A.M., to be greeted by Yitzhak Eldan, the minister in our Paris embassy. As he accompanied me to the Baltimore hotel on the Rue Kléber, I explained that I was going to Cannes to join my wife and suggested that we have dinner when I returned to the hotel on Saturday night. When he finally left me in the lobby, I dashed up to my room, rumpled the bedspread and blanket, threw some towels on the floor, and hung the *Ne pas dérangez, S.V.P.* sign on the door. Then I hurried down to the street and caught a cab back to de Gaulle. Waiting for me there, at precisely the appointed spot, stood Ron Pundak, looking conspicuously conspiratorial. Ron's short-cropped hair and John Lennon glasses give him a boyish air. He's also blessed with a mixture of typical Israeli directness and a sharp analytical mind. On the flight to Copenhagen, Ron described our Palestinian interlocutors, stressing their courage, moderation, and bonhomie. Clearly he was hoping that I would mirror all these traits, and I felt I was being tested for acceptance in an exclusive club.

In Copenhagen, where we were booked on the six o'clock SAS flight to Oslo, we ran headlong into a group of Iranians at the boarding gate. I shot Ron a cautionary glance. He looked knowingly back; then we both burst into laughter at the suspicion we Israelis carry everywhere. Not that it was mere paranoia. The threat of fundamentalist terrorism sponsored by Iran was justifiably on our minds and would become the main counterweight to the entire peace process. But since the men were speaking Parsi, without a hint of circumspection, the odds were that they were not plotting to kill us. They were simply peaceful travelers on their way to Norway.

Descending to Oslo, we were treated to an exquisite collage of deep blue sea, rugged mountains, red-tiled roofs, and lush green forests. As we filed out of the plane, at the end of the jetway stood Yair Hirschfeld, grinning broadly. With his wild brown beard, untamed hair, and bemused expression, Yair looked like a typical Viennese intellectual of the 1920s. Next to him, wearing a light overcoat and fifties-style sunglasses, stood a tall, rather dapper man in his late forties who could easily have passed for a French detective film hero but was actually Terje Larsen, a social scientist, serious intellectual, and committed humanist with a rare taste for complexity—a man, I soon discerned, of many talents. What would gratify me most as time went on, however, were his extraordinary psychological skills, which he exercised with almost saintly Norwegian patience. Even the most daunting setback usually left him unfazed, and he was to play a critical role in easing many crises ahead.

Terje went to work immediately. As he led us into the VIP room, where our passports were stamped for the only time in the three months of talks to come (thereafter, Norwegian secret service agents enabled us to dispense with the formality), he was already briefing us on procedures. We would leave the terminal through the rear exit and be driven to the "safe house" about half an hour from town where Mona Juul—Terje's wife and a successful diplomat—would bring the

Palestinians. Our car was driven by a member of the FAFO Institute staff. We enjoyed the company of two secret service escorts. Everything had been planned down to the minute.

On our way into the mountains, while I was trying to decipher Norwegian road signs, Terje was indoctrinating me into the spirit of the talks—the "Oslo spirit," he called it. He evidently considered me a staid young technocrat, perhaps too stiff for the mission at hand. He explained that humor was an important element in the talks, and that the interchange should be informal, as it had been so far with the two professors. For Terje, the essence of the Oslo channel was to come up with creative solutions by a process of free thinking, not traditional hard-nosed bargaining. He believed that the relaxed Norwegian atmosphere would have an osmotic impact on the talks and hoped we could achieve a blend between Oslo and Jerusalem.

"The Palestinians are as excited as children," he said, in an attempt to shatter stereotypes. I understood what he was doing but was far too nervous to try to convince him of that. Finally we arrived at the small Hejti Lodge, an official guesthouse. We sat for a few moments without uttering a word. Then there was a ceremonial knock on the door, and in walked Mona, carrying her femininity with disarming grace. She was followed by the three Palestinians, who filed slowly into the hallway where Yair, Ron, and I stood as if we were in an official reception line (though of the three Israelis, I was the only one wearing a dark suit and tie). Then Abu Ala was standing directly in front of me.

"Meet your Enemy Number One, Ahmed Qurei, better known as Abu Ala," said Terje.

I was surprised by the man's appearance. Comfortably middle-aged, he wore thick-lensed glasses that failed to hide his penetrating glance. He too was dressed formally and looked to me more like a European businessman than the underground leader I had expected.

"Pleased to meet you," he and I muttered, aware of the significance of our unprecedented gesture as we shook hands while eyeing each other nervously.

The room fell quiet for a second before Terje continued, "Now meet your Enemy Number Two, Hassan Asfour."

With shining eyes and an aloof, somewhat resentful expression, Asfour was a reformed Communist who had spent time in a Syrian jail and joined George Habash's radical Popular Front for the Liberation of Palestine before becoming a political adviser to Arafat's close associate Abu Mazen (who was monitoring these talks from Tunis). As I came to know him, he often seemed torn between two unshakable convictions: his certainty of Israel's abiding arrogance, and his faith in the possibility of attaining peace.

"Enemy Number Three" was introduced to me as Maher al-Kurd, a tall, forthright, yet extremely polite man who brought to mind a German schoolmaster. Indeed, he had studied at an East German university before becoming an economic adviser to Arafat.

The ice thawed a bit as Ron and Yair embraced the three Palestinians, with whom they had been partners for five months. Terje showed us into the wood-paneled lounge. Our initial exchange was a painful attempt at small talk.

"I left Tel Aviv at six-thirty this morning," I offered.

"We left Tunis yesterday," Abu Ala replied.

We could find nothing more to say.

Taking his cue from the awkward lull, Terje stood up, removed his jacket, and invited us to do the same, but this attempt to ease the atmosphere failed. It was then that Terje decided to leave us. "I'll be downstairs," he said, abruptly making for the door. "If you can't get along on your own, call me."

Thus alone in the Norwegian night, we took our places at opposite sides of a narrow wooden table. After a few strained, silent moments, I began rummaging in my briefcase for the notes I had written on the plane. Then, for the one and only time in the three years of talks that followed, I read from prepared notes. I wanted to be sure that our message reached Tunis precisely, and the Palestinians duly took down my words.

I began by expressing satisfaction that we were able to speak face to face and thanked them all for the work they had done in the preparatory talks. "The aim of Israel's elected government," I explained, "is to bring about a historic reconciliation with the Palestinian people. We have no interest in only a cosmetic change of the status quo. It is not our wish to control your lives. Our interest is in peace, in security, and, together with you, in leading the way to regional peace." The occupation, I told my listeners, had been forced upon Israel in 1967. "Our moral aim is to free ourselves from that condition in a way that will ensure the Palestinians freedom and provide Israel with security."

That much clarified, I presented the two conditions Rabin and Peres had insisted on. Above all, I stressed that Palestinian autonomy could not extend to Jerusalem. "Jerusalem is the center of our national ethos, and if that is open to negotiation, no progress can be made. As to outside arbitration, you must decide whether we are to act as partners, and solve all our differences through dialogue, or request Security Council–like arbitration and end up with a pile of resolutions that will remain no more than numbers. If you agree to these two conditions, I can recommend to Prime Minister Rabin and Foreign Minister Peres that we work to explore a declaration of principles that will be acceptable to both sides."

Finally, I explained that the guideline for the eventual negotiations should be to advance in stages and that it would be best to agree that the first political change should be effected in the Gaza Strip. I did not mention Jericho.

"For our part, the stress must be on security, and naturally the PLO will have to cease all terror operations. There is also great potential for economic cooperation, and this we must translate into deeds. This is a historic opportunity for all of us," I concluded. "It must not be wasted."

Abu Ala straightened up in his chair, readying himself to make his own opening statement. Outside, the midnight sun still cast a dim glow as he began.

"My colleagues and I, as well as our leadership in Tunis, are very pleased that our negotiations have finally reached an official stage. We have done important work with our friends Yair and Ron." (I noticed that they smiled as they continued taking notes.) "I would like you to convey to your leaders that our intentions—particularly those of our chairman, Yasser Arafat—are serious."

Upon hearing Arafat's name, so long the symbol of hostility to Israel, I felt an odd sensation—it was at first hard to think of him as a person to contend with. As though reading my thoughts, Abu Ala continued, "There's no chance of advancing toward peace without the PLO and its leaders. No one else can speak for the Palestinian people with authority and legitimacy.

"We want to live with you in peace," he said, with obvious seriousness. "We want to cooperate with you toward developing the region; encouraging the creation of a Marshall Plan for the Middle East; developing our economies, so that we can open the doors to the Arab world for you and to freedom for ourselves. The situation in the occupied territories is desperate, politically and economically. Time is running out."

Abu Ala conceded that the Washington talks were at an impasse but promised that they would go on. As to the two substantive conditions I had laid down, he explained that he would have to consult with Tunis. "But as for security," he assured us, "I have specific instructions from Arafat to accommodate you on every aspect of this matter."

He paused for a moment and then, speaking to me directly, said, "Tell me, Mr. Savir, I have heard Israel's statements that you view the PLO as an existential threat. I would like to understand. Israel is a regional power and, according to the international press, a nuclear one as well. You have the finest air force in the world, a huge number of tanks, the most effective intelligence network in the world, one of the largest and most renowned armies. You call us terrorists. We call ourselves freedom fighters and have only a few Kalashnikovs, some grenades, jeeps, and stones. Would you please explain to me how we pose an existential threat to you, and not the other way around?"

Abu Ala, having succinctly made his case—the Palestinians were David, and Israel was Goliath—smiled. In time I came to understand that the Palestinians' perception of the balance of power was much as he had described it: a dwarf facing down a giant. As in so many conflicts, each side considered itself the victim.

I reflected briefly and told him: "You are a threat, because you want to live in my home. In my house."

"Where are your from?" he asked.

"Jerusalem," I replied.

"So am I," he continued, somberly. "Where is your father from?"

"He was born in Germany."

"Mine was born in Jerusalem and still lives there."

"Why don't you ask about my grandfathers and their forebears? We could go back to King David," I said, making no effort to hide my anger. "I'm sure we can debate the past for years and never agree. Let's see if we can agree about the future."

"Fine," he said, barely above a mumble.

We had arrived at our first understanding. Never again would we argue about the past. This was an important step, for it moved us beyond an endless wrangle over right and wrong. Discussing the future would mean reconciling two rights, not readdressing ancient wrongs.

"I'd like to return to the point you raised about our security, as it stands today," I said.

I placed a sheet of yellow paper on the table and began drawing, as well as I could, a map of Israel, the occupied territories, and then, in the proper proportion, the Arab world surrounding us.

"You Palestinians have rejected our existence as a state," I continued. "From the moment of Israel's rebirth, you rallied the entire Arab world to fight us. This," I said, tapping my finger on the map, "is the true security equation."

I leaned back, satisfied that I had established who the real David was in this conflict. Abu Ala was businesslike in his reply.

"I believe we've arrived at the root of the problem," he said. "We have learned that our rejection of you will not bring us freedom. You can see that your control of us will not bring you security. We must live side by side in peace, equality, and cooperation. This is also the view of our leadership in Tunis."

"In principle, I agree," I said, attempting to establish common ground. "We need to progress in stages, forging a new context for relations in which peace, security, and economic development can evolve together. What we need is a new road map to lead us to a state of trust." I reminded Abu Ala that many Israelis despised the PLO and doubted the credibility of its leadership. "But we are serious about turning over a new leaf and gradually building trust. We can start by working on the draft prepared in your talks with Yair and Ron. But first I must have your response on Jerusalem and arbitration. And," I added, pausing for effect, "it's absolutely essential that our talks remain secret. Any leak will make this channel politically untenable."

Abu Ala laughed. "You don't have to worry about us. It's your newspapers we're concerned about. They know things before they even happen," he teased, alluding to the transparency of Israeli political life. He then suggested that we break so that he could contact Tunis and report on our conversation.

It was about four in the morning when we all stood up, shook hands, and walked downstairs to find Terje and Mona, looking tired, yet still awake and patiently waiting for us.

"So?" Terje asked warily.

"There's nothing to discuss," Abu Ala joshed. "We're going home."

"It's all over," I added with a shrug.

For a split second Terje looked uncertain about whether we were joking, but we reassured him with a laugh, the first instance of the humor that would serve us throughout the critical breaks in the long, sometimes brutal negotiations that lay ahead.

Mona and Terje invited me to stay with them in the center of Oslo. The unfamiliar view of the quiet city as Terje drove me to their home, the Scandinavian charm and warm hospitality of my hosts all stood in sharp contrast to my turbulent emotions that morning. I was aching to talk to Peres. It was he who had engineered this transition to formal talks with the PLO, part of a grand design for Middle Eastern peace and prosperity that was his obsession. But the need for secrecy prevented me from calling Jerusalem. Instead, I walked onto the terrace and gazed out at Oslo as it began to awaken. I wanted to reflect on the significance of the past hours while their impact was still fresh. Instead, my thoughts drifted to my late father.

An ardent Zionist and brilliant intellectual, Leo Savir was a born diplomat and one of the founders of Israel's foreign service. From its start, he regarded the occupation of the West Bank and Gaza as a disaster that would erode Israel's moral fiber and humanity—both of which were critical for Jewish survival. As far back as the late seventies, he had called for a dialogue with the PLO. He didn't romanticize the movement. He regarded it as the true representative of Israel's greatest enemy. But he felt that talking to the enemy was a test of Israel's maturity, that our inability even to contemplate such meetings arose from fear that led to demonization. (Menachem Begin was known to compare Arafat to Hitler.)

My father believed that Israel was strong enough to talk to its enemies. If we feared doing so, we would undermine the essence of Zionism as a historic attempt to move beyond the psychology of the ghetto. The Jewish tendency to see anti-Semitism everywhere was a disease, he believed. The Jews needed a strong state, in his opinion, not just for the sake of survival but to change traditional attitudes toward Jews, including the feelings of Jews toward themselves. The need to normalize our relations with the world was my father's credo as a diplomat. He deplored those leaders, like Golda Meir, who dwelled on the historic antagonism toward us. Though few nations had ever enjoyed the international support that flowed to Israel in 1948 and 1967, many Israelis continued to think of themselves as eternal victims. Talking to the enemy and influencing his attitudes, my father held, would not only cure this enmity but help us heal ourselves.

A year before he died in 1986, my father had published an article to this effect in the *Jerusalem Post*, and I carried it with me in my briefcase. He had been the person closest to me, and as I stood on that terrace, I suddenly felt great sadness that I couldn't tell him that I had just done the very thing that he had urged for so long; that as the official representative of the State of Israel I had just talked to the enemy in an attempt to find common ground. We had closed a circle, my father and I. He would have been proud and pleased.

As for the meeting itself, I felt that I had just visited the unknown. Our talks, while on the surface not unlike many first diplomatic encounters, had embodied both our deepest fears and our highest hopes. We were beginning at last to emerge from a century-long conflict over the same land. Both sides had denied each other's right to exist as a nation. Both had sustained a terrible toll in lives and human suffering. Our meeting had highlighted the fact that the Israeli-Palestinian dispute lay at the heart of Israel's differences with the entire Arab world. Among the Arabs, no people had a stronger motive to oppose Israel than the Palestinians. A historic compromise between Israel and the Palestinians would be the key to peace in the entire region. Gradually it would deflect the nationalists, the fundamentalists, the extremists of all kinds. We could bestow legitimacy on each other in return for freedom of national expression and freedom from war and violence.

I was elated by the great opportunity and at the same time dismayed by how difficult the road ahead would be. In fact, I had no idea how arduous the journey would prove: what obstacles lay ahead, what tragedies would occur, how often the process would verge on collapse.

Suddenly I felt Terje's hand on my shoulder, drawing me out of my reverie. He suggested I get some sleep. "Remember, you have a meeting with your new friends in the morning."

"Well," I said wearily, arching an eyebrow at him, "at least they are my future neighbors."

When I woke a few hours later, Terje and Mona were already in the dining room eating a hearty breakfast.

"Who are you?" I boomed as I eyed them in disbelief.

"Who are *you*?" Mona laughed, gesturing for me to join them.

I did so only briefly, for I wanted to jot down some points for future reference. The key to success, I sensed, would be to effect a quick change on the ground (based on Peres's notion of "Gaza first"). At the very least, it would guarantee that this opportunity did not dissolve into endless legalistic bickering. Toward that end, I sketched out ten steps to be pursued parallel to the ongoing negotiations. They included demonstrations of mutual recognition, an end to PLO-inspired terror, and autonomy in Gaza within three months. I wanted to raise these ideas with Peres upon returning to Jerusalem, and I certainly didn't expect them to cause a problem.

Then Mona and I set out to collect Yair and Ron and return to the lodge. On the way they remarked on the "chemistry" that had developed the previous night (I had evidently been accepted into the club).

Terje mentioned it too, after arriving with the Palestinians, and suggested that Abu Ala and I might like to take a short walk in the woods. As we set out down a narrow path, Abu Ala told me that he had spent the rest of the night on the phone with Tunis, reporting his satisfaction with our meeting and his impression that our intentions were serious.

As a result, Arafat and Abu Mazen had accepted our demand that East Jerusalem be excluded from the autonomy—though it would certainly be raised again in the talks on the final settlement. I was surprised by this quick and definitive reply. It convinced me all the more that the Tunis leadership wanted to move ahead. Their other answers reinforced this impression. On the issue of outside arbitration, Abu Ala suggested that it be sought only with the agreement of both sides. He also felt there was something to be said for establishing autonomy in Gaza first but noted that Arafat continued to press for the symbolic addition of Jericho. A small foothold in the West Bank was important, so that "Gaza first" would not be perceived as "Gaza last."

Turning to climb back up the path, we caught a glimpse of Terje by the lodge, standing in the shadows, there to help in an hour of need. Then we talked about ourselves. I told Abu Ala about my family and my years with Peres. He sketched the course of his odyssey from Jerusalem to Tunis. He told me of his wife and five children—two in Tunis, two in Europe, one in the United States—and spoke of his years of work with Arafat with esteem for his indomitable leader and wry derision of his quirky work habits.

When we reached the lodge and reassembled around the small table, Abu Ala repeated in the presence of the others the answers he had received from Tunis and suggested we turn to the draft of the declaration of principles that he and his colleagues had produced with Yair and Ron. We glanced over the document together. It lacked, as I quickly pointed out, any serious reference to such key issues as security or the status of the settlements, which we would not agree to dismantle. I did speak supportively, though, of the desire for economic cooperation. Actually, I was surprised by the degree of Palestinian interest in economic ties with Israel. They saw such cooperation not just as beneficial to their economy but as a bridge to regional development. The three Palestinians proved responsive to my comments and proposed that a special addendum be written on security affairs. They had evidently concluded that this meeting was a test in the eyes of Israel's leaders, and they intended to pass it.

"We're interested in cooperating with you in all areas of life," Abu Ala stressed. "Naturally, we want our national rights and the liberty we deserve. But we realize these can best be enjoyed through cooperation with you, perhaps more than with any other neighbor."

Such cooperation was what we too were striving for. And when I described, in general terms, the need for a quick change on the ground, Abu Ala's response was particularly positive. "The situation in the territories is drastic, and it could explode at any moment," he said. "We must give our people hope."

"Absolutely," I concurred. "But that hope must be divorced from any violence toward us."

"The two are naturally related," Abu Ala said. "We can put a stop to the violence, provided we can promise a different future."

This inverse ratio between hope and violence would remain the basic equation throughout the peace process.

"The intifada must yield political gains," he continued. "You will not subdue us by force. Nor is that necessary."

"Apparently you haven't been reading the papers," I said with muted sarcasm. "Israel has today a government that doesn't want to rule over your people. Human rights and occupation don't go hand in hand. We know that. But only a change in your attitude too, especially toward the political and security situation, will allow for a profound change on the ground."

It was at this point, I believe, that Abu Ala first realized he might actually be on the threshold of tough, binding negotiations. He leaned forward and looked me hard in the eye as he said: "You should know, Savir, and you should tell your principals, that in the talks with Yair and Ron, we made major concessions—historic ones, from our standpoint—because we're interested in making a fresh start. But it will be very hard for Arafat to compromise beyond this."

"I thought we'd agreed not to start bargaining yet."

Abu Ala laughed, but his expression betrayed his relish for the negotiations that lay ahead. Then Yair intervened to raise an important point that had been introduced in the exploratory talks: the need to promote reconciliation actively between our two peoples, a "peace propaganda plan," he called it.

"You know," I warned Abu Ala, "as far as most Israelis are concerned, you're just a gang of terrorists."

"And as far as most Palestinians are concerned, you are a nation of cruel oppressors, robbing us of our lands."

We agreed, in principle, to engage our peoples in the effort of reconciliation. As it turned out, we didn't always follow through on that resolution and later had cause to regret it.

When we broke for lunch, we were joined by Jan Egeland, Norway's young deputy foreign minister, who promised to do everything possible to provide us with a discreet and relaxed setting for talks. After lunch, we appointed Terje the liaison between Tunis and Jerusalem and chose a code for our communications. Arafat was "Grandfather"; Abu Mazen, "the Holy Ghost"; Abu Ala, "Number One"; and so on down the line. On our side, Rabin was "Grandfather"; Peres, "the Father"; Beilin, "the Son"; and I was "Number One." Then we parted with warm handshakes, as Terje stood by beaming.

Later that afternoon, Mona drove me to the home of Johan Jørgen Holst, who had become Norway's foreign minister about a month earlier. He greeted me warmly and introduced me to his wife, Marianne Heiberg, who happened to be Terje's assistant at FAFO—as Mona, incidentally, was Holst's assistant in the Foreign Ministry. Holst was eager to impress on me that the PLO was serious. That was his conviction after having talked with Arafat personally. He also outlined for me his contacts with the American government on our back channel. His aides had updated Dan Kurtzer, the assistant secretary of state for the Middle East, and Holst had personally briefed Secretary of State Warren Christopher, promising a more detailed report whenever the United States asked for one. He asked that we coordinate our contacts with the Americans—so as not to prejudice Norwegian interests in Washington—and I promised him that.

"They don't know about your visit here," he warned.

"I know," I told him, promising to take the point up with Peres.

To the best of my knowledge, the Americans never asked Holst for further details about the back channel, and from Rabin they received a very reserved appraisal of its prospects. At the time they were pre-occupied with the Syrian track and left us to our own devices on the Palestinian one.

By midafternoon I was on my way back to Paris to keep my dinner date with Eldan from our embassy. The next morning I flew to Rome, where I met my wife (on her way back from Cannes) and re-played the episode down to the last detail. (Aliza was to remain in the know, as a full emotional and intellectual partner, throughout the three-year journey.) Back in Jerusalem, I had to wait a few days until Peres returned from an official visit to the Far East.

It felt strange to conceal the secret of a possible peace process break-through with the PLO. As I walked through downtown Jerusalem, I tried to guess how my fellow Israelis would react to the fact that we were talking to the PLO and possibly making a deal with Yasser Arafat.

Many, I believed, would be elated, and feel that we must talk to the PLO, that we would all be better off if our children in the army no longer had to police Palestinian children throwing stones at them in Gaza. The intifada was a rude awakening for many, probably for most, Israelis—the occupation was no longer a routine that we could safely ignore. Israelis were worn out from the conflict and wanted peace, and peace of mind.

Yet, as I looked around, I tried to guess which of the passersby would fiercely deplore our talks. No doubt some of those were very religious Israeli Jews who gravitated to the ideological right and would consider a deal with Arafat a national tragedy, and a threat to our existence. Suddenly I felt anxiety that a process in which I believed deeply would be seen by others—especially those who believed that Israel should annex the West Bank for historical reasons, notwith-standing the 2 million Palestinians who lived there—as a suicidal sur-render. Though I believed that a reconciliation with our enemy would fulfill the very idea and goal of a strong, modern Jewish state, there were many others who felt that if the walls came down, we would be vulnerable to external and internal enemies, that the coherence of Israeli society depended on resisting a common enemy and the penetration of what they saw as pernicious external influences.

Was it possible in Israel to bridge these two worlds? Probably not. Peace with the PLO would widen the abyss between those who believed in the possibility and desirability of a new relationship between a strong Israel willing to face the future and its neighbors, and those who believed that eternal hostility was inherent in our situation and that Israel's interests demanded not only external vigilance but extreme suspicion of our neighbors.

Yet I believed that the majority wanted peace and that they would back us. The only question was how vehement the opposition would be. Some Israelis worried that once we and the Palestinians came to terms on the future of the West Bank, we would risk civil war. The peace that Oslo might produce would mean a struggle at home, as we would then have to answer the question that has always divided the Israeli left and right: Should modern Israel cooperate with its neighbors as David Ben-Gurion, Israel's founding father and first prime minister, had hoped, or should it continue to live within an "Iron Wall," as Ze'ev Jabotinsky, the ideologue of right-wing revisionism, insisted? If Oslo succeeded, the Iron Wall would crumble. The peace process would therefore be a crucial struggle not only with the Palestinians but with ourselves.

Palestinian society would, however, be faced with a similar predicament: reconciliation would be seen as salvation by some and as surrender by others, mainly the fundamentalists, who would probably try to continue to wage terror against us as a challenge to Arafat's "capitulation" to Israel. Peace would prove an identity struggle for the Palestinians as it would for the Israelis. Both sides would have to wage bitter internal battles for peace to succeed. Nonetheless, I deeply believed that the time had come.

I returned to my office to write two documents: one entitled "Proposed Course of Action for Continuing the Negotiations," the other a personal paper based on the ten points I had jotted down in Terje and Mona's living room.

The gist of my report was a list of recommendations for furthering the talks. As Peres had requested, I conveyed my impressions of the PLO's decision-making ability and willingness to compromise. We had an opportunity, I wrote, to improve upon the Camp David and Madrid frameworks and reach a gradual settlement starting in Gaza—while ending PLO terror activities and forging economic co-operation even before a full autonomy agreement was concluded. I therefore suggested that we pursue two parallel tracks, in Washington (primarily for appearance' sake) and in Oslo, while the Norwegians and we would keep the Americans abreast of developments. I also proposed that security arrangements be written into the proposed declaration of principles, also specifying that the settlements would remain in place. But above all, I wrote, we had to decide what to offer the Palestinians as an immediate, concrete change on the ground and what we should demand in return. I also suggested that we bring a lawyer onboard.

Peres studied the documents carefully and agreed to add a lawyer. (Shlomo Gur, Beilin's chief of staff, suggested Yoel Singer, who was working for a prestigious Washington law firm, Sidley and Austin, and had been involved in all of Israel's important treaties since Camp David.) Peres also proposed that autonomy take place first in Gaza simultaneously with the transfer of the PLO leadership there. Yossi and I questioned whether Arafat personally would be willing to accept responsibility for Gaza with its many problems. We also wondered how the idea would go down with the Israeli public. But Peres was resolute. For many years he had hoped that Jordan's King Hussein would be Israel's partner in settling the Palestinian question. As foreign minister in 1987, he had even reached an understanding in London—which came to be known as the London Agreement—with Hussein to open international negotiations similar to those held later in Madrid, in which Jordan would play an increased role. But the plan was promptly scotched by Prime Minister Yitzhak Shamir, and Hussein abandoned the Palestinian arena at the height of the intifada. Peres now saw Oslo as a historic turning point. He wanted to alter the status quo not as a political exercise but as a strategic move to create a common interest with a new partner. He was able to imagine a better future in very concrete terms, a rare and estimable gift in a nation that had become fatalistic about perpetual hostility. Fortunately, the PLO, in its weakened condition, was then ready for such a revolutionary change. The time was ripe for action. Only one more person had to be convinced of that: the prime minister of Israel.

Yitzhak Rabin and Shimon Peres had traveled a long road together in fierce competition and mistrust. They were almost perfect opposites: Rabin, a guarded analyst of the present, obsessed by details; Peres, a cosmopolitan conceptualist who sees history in terms of processes and is obsessed by the future. For two decades their contrasting natures had fueled the antagonism between these two strong-willed men. Then came Oslo, the final chapter in their relationship.

When the Rabin government was formed in the summer of 1992, Peres was assigned to deal mainly with the Multilateral Talks, while Rabin chose to direct the more important bilateral negotiations himself. They also reached another basic understanding at that time. I recall Peres saying that on a Saturday afternoon soon after the election, he paid Rabin a visit at his Ramat Aviv home to try to set their relationship on a new footing.

"Yitzhak," he said, "we're both about seventy and have been at odds with each other for most of our lives. Let's put our differences aside now and work together in the one way we can leave an indelible mark: by bringing this country peace. We can take the tough decisions required for peacemaking. We can spare our children that burden and free them to focus on the economy, on education, and social issues."

Rabin agreed, and the two lions in winter made a tacit covenant of sorts. Had they not done this, Israel couldn't possibly have attempted so controversial an undertaking as recognizing and reconciling with the PLO.

Initially Rabin was skeptical, but he was gradually convinced when he saw real change in the position of the Palestinians.

Yet Rabin was still more drawn to the Syrian process, in coordination with the United States, since the more strategic nature of its possible solution intrigued his analytical character. Peres himself had come to believe passionately in the need to reconcile with the PLO. He saw this as the only way to promote the peace process. The moment he suggested that Arafat might move to Gaza, the need for mutual recognition between neighbors became indisputable. That, in his view, would be the bridge to a comprehensive peace effort in the region based, to a large degree, on economic development.

Throughout the talks Rabin was testing the Palestinians, while Peres was trying to induce them by defining broader mutual interests. Rabin was determined to make progress, yet his mind was still attuned to conflict, while Peres was already visibly living in the post-conflict era. It was a necessary partnership. Together, they had become a tremendous force.

After their common decision to embark on official secret talks with the PLO, Rabin and Peres decided on every single word of significance in the negotiation.

Yet the process was almost derailed at the start. At their first meeting after my return from Oslo, Rabin was given the material I had prepared and immediately agreed to ask Yoel Singer, whom he respected, to come to Jerusalem for consultations. But after he had reviewed the papers, Rabin sent Peres an angry letter about my meetings in Oslo, especially my ten points, which he understood (or suspected) I had already raised with the Palestinians. At first Peres was stunned by Rabin's objection, and he immediately replied, explaining that the ten points had not been discussed in Oslo. Then, on further reflection, he was pleased by Rabin's response, for while Rabin had objected to what he assumed was my having acted without authority, he hadn't challenged the ten points themselves; he had even committed his own thoughts on the Oslo track to paper. No longer could the back channel be denied at the highest level of government. Direct talks with the PLO, though still a tightly guarded secret, had become official policy.

As if to corroborate that fact, Yoel Singer flew in and immediately went to work. An astute, seasoned, and fastidious lawyer, he had recently resigned his commission as a colonel in the army and moved to Washington. Hardly were we all seated in Yossi Beilin's office than he asked a number of questions about the proposed declaration of principles. He was blunt. He was biting. And he made an arrogant first impression.

"What's this supposed to be?" he cried, flinging the document on the table. "It's not the draft of an agreement! It's a blob of raw mush!"

Astonished by the performance, I suggested that he draw up his own draft, but he demurred. He first wanted to prepare a list of questions for the Palestinians, to clarify their positions. The list eventually included about a hundred questions and constituted the better part of the next session with the PLO.

Our return to Oslo, accompanied by Yoel Singer, was approved by Rabin and Peres in a subsequent consultation—though we had to wait until the resumption of the talks in Washington were announced. They reopened on June 16, with the Palestinians displaying a less abrasive style. Nevertheless, they had sharpened their demand to include Jerusalem in the autonomous area. Once again we sensed that Arafat was signaling us that only in Oslo, only in direct talks with the PLO, only with Abu Ala and his colleagues would it be possible to move forward.

Before returning to Oslo, I recalled my chat with Abu Ala as we walked in the woods by the lodge.

"I've heard a lot about you, Savir, and I know that you and your friends, like Yossi Beilin and Haim Ramon, speak for a new generation in Israel. We place great hope in you," he said. "Our Arab brothers have let us down, and we've reached the conclusion, Abu Mazen and I, that perhaps our Israeli 'cousins' are the best partners for progress. I want you to know that we are intertwined in what I feel will be a genuine partnership."

I had hoped for that moment for years, and I told him so.

"My friends and family have long believed that we should be talking with you," I said. "The intifada convinced many other Israelis that we can't rule over you forever. Israel is a great success story, but the occupation is corrupting our youth. We want to free ourselves from it in a way that will make us confident of our security. I hope you'll soon be able to visit Israel, meet my friends, and see this for yourself."

"My home is in Abu Dis, next to Jerusalem," he said after a short pause. "My mother is dead, and my father is ill. His lands were confiscated for one of your settlements."

"Would you like to visit your father?" I offered. "Do you want me to bring him a letter?"

"No," he said proudly and a bit roughly. "I'll go there when I can return to my home."

(Abu Ala never did see his father again. Ali Qurei died of a heart attack the following spring, after appearing in court to demand his lands back.)

"I understand," I said. "My father is already gone. But he would have been pleased to know you. I want to give you an article he wrote, back in 1985, about the need for the kind of dialogue that we're holding here."

It was then, for the first time, that Abu Ala addressed me by my first name.

"You know, Uri," he said, "I have the feeling we can bring this off."

"So do I," I confided in a hoarse whisper.

2

THE OSLO ROAD MAP

NOT THAT THINGS WENT SMOOTHLY AFTER THAT. THE NEGOTIATIONS over the next three months in Norway were long and grueling. On occasions when we reached an impasse, one side or the other halted the talks completely. From the beginning, we feared constantly that we would be discovered. When Yoel Singer and I first traveled to Oslo together on June 12, we had an unsettling moment at the Copenhagen airport. Suddenly there appeared before me the administrative officer of our Copenhagen embassy, who had come to meet Israel's National Soccer Team. He was surprised to see me (though not half as much as I was to see him) and glad of a chance for a chat.

"Where are you headed?" he asked innocently.

"Oslo," I said with as much equanimity as I could muster.

"*Oslo?*" he blurted. Whatever *for*?"

"To visit to my sister" (who happened to be in Philadelphia at the time), I said, and the matter ended there.

Still, the whole business rested on thin ice. Any leak to the press would sabotage the talks, which were being conducted without the knowledge of the Israeli government, except of course Prime Minister Rabin, Foreign Minister Peres, and Yossi Beilin. That evening another surprise awaited us. When we reached Oslo, Deputy Foreign Minister Jan Egeland showed us a report by the French wire service, Agence France-Presse, that Israeli and PLO officials were holding secret talks in Norway. The unflappable Norwegians were shaken. So were we. Fortunately, Israeli and Palestinian writers were holding a conclave in Oslo that weekend, and the resourceful Norwegians managed to deflect media attention to the seminar that was exploring the roots of the conflict but in no way proposing a solution.

The experience of June 12 forced us to be a bit more ingenious in building cover stories for our next seven trips to Oslo. Searching for a route that would reduce the odds of meeting acquaintances, we chose the Austrian Airlines' Thursday flight to Vienna and an SAS connection to Oslo, via Copenhagen. Yossi Beilin's office continued to handle the arrangements, and my devoted driver, Oded Anavim, one of the few people who knew our destination, brought us directly to the flight. The rest of the ministry's staff, except for my three secretaries, continued to believe that I was negotiating economic matters in Europe. The secretaries acquiesced in the conspiracy of silence. Of course, there were suspicious whispers in the ministry. After all, how much time could the director possibly spend abroad in the cause of economic development? People were told that I was really meeting entrepreneurs from the Persian Gulf and it was vital to keep the contacts secret. During that period we lied to colleagues, journalists, and, hardest of all, to friends and family. Yoel, who plied a biweekly route from Washington to Tel Aviv, Oslo, Tel Aviv, and back to Washington, kept his "other life" secret from his partners. But none of us doubted that the ends justified the means.

On our long flights together, Yoel and I plotted our strategy. Then, upon reaching Oslo, we regaled the Palestinians with tales of how we had each duped our respective colleagues. We felt like a club of secret agents. And as time went on, outside the negotiating room—at meals, during breaks, and on walks together—we jelled into a group that Terje, master at nourishing the bond, dubbed the "Oslo Club."

Our meetings were usually held a few hours' drive from Oslo, in comfortable lodgings and pastoral settings. The meals tended to be lavish. The woods lured us out for walks and intimate chats. As for our hosts, their greatest contribution would be their deft psychological skills, but they allotted $5 million for the logistic effort alone. Even the bodyguards were among the most sensitive and adept in the Norwegian secret service. They, too, became part of the Oslo Club.

As in a secret fellowship, we soon developed a private lexicon that harked back to memorable jokes and other remarks. An outsider would have been at a loss to fathom much of our banter. One day I happened to ask Abu Ala whether his family was with him in Tunis. "No, they're in Amman," he said. "I'm on my own." He then told a story that became part of our Oslo folklore. After fifty years of marriage, it went, a man lost his wife, to whom he had been very attached. After the funeral his house filled with dozens of mourners, and he continued to be showered with attention in the days that followed. But as time passed, fewer and fewer callers looked in on him, until one day he suddenly found himself entirely alone. Rattling around his large, silent house, the widower wailed: "I'm alone! I'm alone!" Slowly the wail became a question, and then suddenly the old man burst into laughter and emitted an ecstatic cry: "I'm alone! I'm alone! I'm alone!"

As he ended the tale, Abu Ala leapt like Zorba while singing over and over, "I'm alone! I'm alone!" The sight of him dancing that manic jig reduced us to laughter, and from then on, whenever we spoke by phone, we usually began by asking: "Are you alone?" In time the question also came to reflect our feeling that we really were alone with one another. Shimon Peres, incidentally, caught on to that nuance immediately. When I told him Abu Ala's story, to illustrate a certain side of the man, he quoted me the words of an Indian poet: "I'm alone. You're alone. / Let's be alone together."

The intimacy and humor that held our little band together did not extend to the negotiations, however. Conducted with great intensity for fifty hours or more at a time, with breaks only for two or three hours' sleep and a hearty Norwegian meal, they resembled a marathon chess game fraught with feints, bluffs, and diversions. The confrontations were often brutal, the crises close to shattering. Sometimes the tension broke in near-hysterical laughter; sometimes we pushed each other almost to the point of rage. The emotional outbursts in those sessions buffeted us between hatred and empathy. It was as if all we had felt toward each other in the past, and all we were hoping to feel in the future, gushed out to swamp us in ambivalence, on the passage from rejection to compromise. Most surprising to me were the many defenses we shared: suspicion, cynicism, defensive humor, deep feelings of historical deprivation.

"You know why we don't like you?" I asked Abu Ala one evening. "It's because you remind us of ourselves."

"Really!" he replied. "That's also my problem with you!"

"Perhaps it's because we're the sons of suffering peoples."

"And perhaps it's because we're from the same place," he said, never forgetting—or letting me forget—that we both came from Jerusalem.

To a large extent, even our negotiating strategies were similar. During two rounds of talks, on June 14–15 and July 4–6, each side subjected the other to a barrage of questions designed to clarify its positions. In his first meeting with them, Yoel asked the Palestinians the hundred or so queries he had listed in our preparations. (The most experienced operator of us all, Yoel reminisced about his earlier negotiating experiences the way most people tell war stories.) Abu Ala was not far behind. On the day Yoel badgered him with questions, in a dry, almost didactic style, he understood that he was being put to a kind of "Rabin test." He knew that Yoel had the prime minister's ear and had been asked to assess the prospects of reaching agreement with the PLO. So he replied with great patience and kept a firm hold on what I assumed were his feelings of indignation at the tone of the procedure. Even I felt that it was less an exploration than a grilling.

"Jurisdiction over the West Bank and Gaza will rest in whose hands?"

"It will gradually pass over to us."

"Have you thought about a governing mechanism? One body or two?"

"We require executive and legislative powers."

"What about the redeployments?"

"You will have to redeploy first from all our populated areas, before the Palestinian elections."

"What about further redeployments?"

"You will withdraw to specified security areas."

"And how about defining those areas? I assume you realize that the Israel Defense Forces will decide where they should redeploy," Yoel said rather sharply.

"And I assume you won't decide that the entire West Bank is a security area," Abu Ala shot back.

And so it went for two whole days, some thirty hours that helped
Yoel gauge the direction of the PLO's thinking. I was worried about
the impression he was making. Persuasion had always been my preferred method for building rapport and achieving goals. But Yoel had
his own way of doing things, and I soon found that I had been too
quick to judge it. He knew how to create rapport, but at this first
meeting, his job was to test a new partner. (That such tests are mutual
often eluded my compatriots, who took it for granted that "they"
were the ones who must pass muster.) At any rate, Yoel came away
from this round impressed by the depth and seriousness of our partners.

When the meeting ended, we flew to Vienna to report to Peres,
who was attending a UN human rights conference there. En route
Yoel told me that he was convinced there was a chance to come to an
agreement with the PLO. But he implored me repeatedly not to
show enthusiasm in front of Peres. Like many others, he thought the
Blazers were too eager to embrace the enemy—though in time he
changed his mind and considered me one of the toughest negotiators.
In Vienna we were shown up to the foreign minister's suite to wait for
him. He returned at 1:00 A.M. to find us napping in chairs.

"So what's up, Yoel?" Peres asked loudly.

I woke with a start to see Yoel's wince of confusion dissolve into a
grin.

"Shimon," he said, "if we don't come to an agreement with these
people, we're asses!"

"Good Lord!" I mumbled at him. "What do you sound like when
you *are* enthusiastic?"

Abu Ala's answers to Yoel's questions, backed by the draft worked out
with Yair and Ron, enabled Yoel to prepare the basic wording of a
proposed declaration of principles in the form of a legal agreement.
As he worked on it, I set down my thoughts on the political situation
in a report to Peres and Yossi Beilin. While I was composing it in the

coffee shop of Peres's hotel in Vienna, Farouk al-Sharaa, the foreign minister of Syria, sat down at the table next to mine. Our glances met, and we nodded at each other, though he had no idea who I was and even less that this was what I was writing:

> I have no doubt that the Palestinians' goal is the establishment of an independent state and that they would prefer a confederation with Jordan while cultivating common interests with Israel. They're interested in having Arafat come to the territories, and his aim is to disarm the Hamas. But they're wary of taking on the management of the autonomy and know that they'll be dependent on cooperation with Israel. They're very sensitive to Palestinian public opinion but show little appreciation for the local [Palestinian] leadership conducting the talks in Washington.

I made a point of sharing with Peres my impressions of the Palestinians I had met. We had all sinned, I told him, in our pretensions to being great experts on the Arabs, and the Palestinians in particular. The more time I spent with our partners, the more I discovered that we may have known a lot about them but we understood very little. It had been a great mistake for Israel to dismiss Palestinian public opinion. When we began talking to the PLO, we tended to view Palestinian society as basically nondemocratic and ready to receive Arafat's dictates uncritically. But this blinded us to the need for a people-to-people peace. Arafat is a leader and a symbol, but peace with him alone is not necessarily peace with the Palestinians. "If you obtain from Arafat, or from me, agreements that the public deems unfair, they will not hold," Abu Ala would tell me countless times. "Remember that it is the people who are your neighbors." I never knew how much he really meant that and how much he said it for tactical gain. Perhaps there was an Israeli-Palestinian "mirror effect" at work here as well. For the Palestinians always treated our claim about the deep division in Israeli society as a ploy to weaken their resolve. They knew better after November 4, 1995, of course, but it took the assassination of Rabin to make the point.

In any event, Yoel's lawyerly draft of a declaration of principles included two parts: the agreement itself and the "agreed minutes," giving a joint and binding interpretation of the more complex clauses.

He added to this his personal recommendation for a detailed agreement on mutual recognition between Israel and the PLO. Like me, he was concerned that by the very act of negotiating with the PLO, we might be legitimizing it without requiring a change in its doctrine. We were talking, after all, about the Palestinian national movement's basic policy that Israel should not exist, which was to us the crux of the Israeli-Arab conflict. So when Yoel reported to Rabin (together with Peres and Yossi Beilin), he presented his draft of the declaration and his recommendation on an agreement on mutual recognition. Rabin reacted cautiously. He approved the new draft but would allow us to extend only a "personal feeler" on mutual recognition. And on one thing he was adamant: we had to make it clear to the Palestinians that Israel would retain exclusive responsibility for safeguarding its citizens and protecting them against external threat. If they didn't accept that, they could forget an agreement.

On June 27 Yoel flew to Oslo (alone this time) to give the gist of his version of the declaration of principles orally; we knew the Palestinians would have difficulty digesting it. Yoel therefore explained our outlook with great patience and tact. Above all he wanted the Palestinians to understand that Rabin had been satisfied with his report and was now involved in the details of the negotiations. He also sounded them out on the notion of mutual recognition, but they chose to avoid the issue.

It was on our next trip to Norway, on July 4, that we presented our formal written draft of the declaration, dated July 3. It posited a three-stage process in which autonomy would be instituted first in Gaza and Jericho; then an interim agreement would be concluded on extending autonomy within the rest of the West Bank; and finally negotiations would be held on a permanent settlement of the Israeli-Palestinian conflict. The document (which bore no official symbol of the State of Israel) was given to the Palestinians to study. When they returned to the negotiating table, their response was vigorous.

"Months of work have gone down the drain, and we're starting over from zero!" Hassan Asfour fumed.

In fact, the situation was rather less drastic. In our detailed talks, the Palestinians had accepted the principle of a staged process that would start with self-rule in Gaza and Jericho. We had agreed that

Draft of July 3,
1993

DECLARATION OF PRINCIPLES ON
INTERIM SELF-GOVERNMENT ARRANGEMENTS

The Government of the State of Israel and the Palestinians,
representatives   of palestinian participation
represented by the Palestinian team in the Jordanian-
Palestinian

delegation to the Middle East Peace Conference (the "Palestinian
delegation), agree to the following principles:

Article I

PREAMBLE

1.   Israel and the Palestinians delegation agree that it is time to put an
      end to decades of confrontation and conflict and achieve
      historic reconciliation and peaceful coexistence.

2.   In order to accomplish these objectives, in line with the
      invitation to the Madrid Peace Conference the aim of the
      Israeli-Palestinian negotiations within the current Middle
      East peace process is to establish interim self-government
      authority
      arrangements for the Palestinians in the West Bank and the
      Gaza Strip for a transitional period of five years, leading
      to a permanent settlement based on Security Council
      Resolutions 242 and 338.

3.   The agreed framework for the interim self-government
      arrangements is set forth in this Declaration of Principles
      below.

-1-

Draft of the Declaration of Principles, July 3, 1993.

Jericho (referring to the city of Jericho itself) would be included in the first stage. But they feared that the autonomy we were offering was window dressing, that it did not grant them genuine powers, which contradicted the preliminary work they had done with Yair and Ron. Patiently we explained what they already knew: that the real, binding negotiations were beginning only now. The protests went on, however, until Abu Ala, an old hand at this game, decided to halt the posturing and respond to the text itself.

"I see you have placed great emphasis on security," he said. "That is acceptable to the chairman."

By invoking his highest authority for a statement of approval, he had signaled his readiness to do business. And for the next three days, through July 6, we indeed appeared to be making progress. First we agreed to insert the Palestinians' objections into the draft, in parentheses. Then we were asked to satisfy Arafat's curiosity by answering his questions. Abu Ala even showed us some papers covered with the *ra'ees*'s ("president" in Arabic) comments in red ink. We naturally deferred to Arafat's thirst for information, though I suspected the questions were really Abu Ala's reprisal for Yoel's earlier barrage.

"Who will control the border crossing?" he began.

"We will," Yoel replied.

"How large will the Jericho area be?"

"We're thinking in terms of only a symbolic enclave."

"Will Israel accept joint patrols along the Gaza-Egypt border?"

"No! External security is exclusively in Israel's hands."

"How many policemen will we be able to bring in from abroad?"

"We'll have to agree on that later, in line with security considerations."

"I understand," Abu Ala continued. "But remember, our objective is cooperation, not separation. We must also protect our economy."

"Without security, there will be no economic development," I said.

"And without economic development, there will be no security," he rejoined.

It appeared we were still at the exploratory stage—though we did have the advantage of an Israeli document, qualified by Palestinian objections, on the table.

During the next round, on July 11–12, in a hotel in Halvasbölle (in the vicinity of Oslo) that had been cleared of all other guests, the Palestinians got their turn to present their opening positions. Abu Ala began by reading a letter from Arafat in which for the first time, through us, the chairman of the PLO addressed the Israeli leadership. "The special negotiations between us are now reaching a serious stage," he wrote. "We have before us a genuine historic chance in the history of our conflict. We are both responsible for not losing this opportunity."

Most of the letter, however, was devoted to presenting new Palestinian demands. Arafat called for a prompt and significant withdrawal from Gaza and Jericho. "One must take into account Palestinian public opinion," he wrote. "Hence the presence there of the leadership from Tunis [read: Arafat] is important in order to contend with possible actions of extremist groups interested in damaging the new agreement. Elections must be held in Jerusalem, and a way must be found to give expression to the Palestinian institutions in Jerusalem." He also stressed the importance of international guarantees and outside mediation, thus reneging on the promises he had given us in May as a condition for continuing the track. I reacted sharply.

"We appreciate the chairman's message," I said, "but you are backtracking on your initial basic positions. We will not negotiate in such a way. You may convey that to the chairman immediately."

The protest had the desired effect. That night Arafat sent another message, by phone, through Abu Ala, assuring us of his intention to reach an agreement. His letter, he explained, was meant only to express his goodwill and raise some issues that were troubling him.

By July 12 we had an integrated picture of each side's demands. The basic parameters of the negotiations were also clear. Israel and the PLO were deliberating on a road map for the future of the West Bank and the Gaza Strip, respectively 2,160 and 138 square miles, which, ever since Israel had captured them in the 1967 war, had become among the most contentious places in the world.

Both sides agreed that the best formula for reshaping our future relations was to progress in stages. But the Palestinians wanted as much control as possible within the autonomous areas. In fact, they demanded full authority over them, while we insisted on retaining certain powers that could affect the shape of the permanent settlement (such as the control of water resources). Nothing was more vital to Israel, however, than security. Our problem was how to unburden ourselves of the occupation while continuing to protect our citizens—including the tens of thousands living in settlements in the territories. That is why Rabin insisted that Israel retain overall responsibility for the security of Israelis, as well as for the external security of the future autonomous areas. It would leave in Israel's hands the maximum leverage on security responsibility for present and future agreements.

Indeed, even at this early stage, each side was bent on securing advantage, with an eye to the permanent settlement. The PLO wanted us to acknowledge the national rights of the Palestinian people and promise to implement Security Council Resolution 242, which had been passed by the UN Security Council after the 1967 war and called for "withdrawal from territories" occupied in that conflict in return for a lasting peace. It wanted the autonomy council to have an executive and a legislative branch. It fought for some kind of status in East Jerusalem (such as the right of its Palestinian residents to stand for election to the council). It wanted to create a mechanism for repatriating, during the interim period, refugees from the 1967 war, and it wanted a share of control of the crossing between the West Bank and Jordan (the Allenby Bridge) so as to fix the Jordan River as the eastern border of a future Palestinian state. Finally, though committed to a shift from confrontation to cooperation, it wanted to retain the option of outside arbitration and an international presence in the territories, to guarantee that the agreement would be fulfilled.

In Israel's estimation, these were formidable and mostly unacceptable demands. Nevertheless, a joint strategic approach had definitely begun to develop, one that assumed a partnership based on mutual legitimization, reciprocal security, and economic prosperity. How were we to reconcile the issues in dispute with the basic premise of cooperation? That was the test of our negotiations. If the joint strategy prevailed, negotiations would be relatively brief; if it did not, they could drag on forever.

Oslo also fixed the basic tactical approach for the two sides to follow, beginning with the "feeler" stage, in which we were to explore our joint interests. Though not a classic stage in negotiations, it was probably critical, since it defined what we were aiming to achieve. An agreement is a compass that points to a new reality. If the direction it indicates is untenable to one of the sides, the treaty itself will be worthless. In our case, it was Peres's idea that Arafat would take Gaza first; his explorations with Mubarak on that issue in November 1992 as well as Yair and Ron's talks with Abu Ala established the direction. The negotiations on the declaration of principles began with three basic assumptions: that Israel and the PLO were entering into a historic partnership; that its first expression would be autonomy in Gaza and Jericho; and that permanent relations must be based on true reconciliation.

In the second stage each party usually chooses to display flexibility, both as a sign of goodwill and to coax the other into revealing some of its true positions. This is what occurred during the first two rounds after Yoel joined the talks.

In the third stage, the cordial atmosphere is shattered when one of the sides (in Oslo, the Israelis) puts its opening position on the table and tries to convince the other that this is its best, and only, offer. Then the other party generally reveals its opening position, and that's when the bargaining begins. At first it tends to be slow and labored, since neither side is prepared to disclose or even admit that it has fallback positions. Eventually the crises kick in, lending an element of drama to the proceedings as each party portrays the other as unreasonable, its last offer as final, and the alternative—the collapse of the negotiations—as perfectly acceptable. Crises are usually solved by invoking the trust that has developed between the sides, enabling them to reveal their true "red lines." Only then does the most meaningful bargaining begin, for in the endgame the negotiators return to cultivating their common interest and practice the art of the possible through imaginative creativity to produce an agreement that no one would have predicted at the outset.

In real life the progress of negotiations is, of course, less schematic, for the negotiators must juggle complex issues marked by varying degrees of nuance. The dynamic is also influenced by manipulation through the media, the use of third parties, feigned concessions, fake compromises, and an array of other wiles and gambits. Intricate negotiations therefore demand a precise definition of aims and long-range interests, as well as a clear grasp of what is essential and what is futile. They also require the skill and patience to think things through and manage systematic staff work. During the Oslo talks, our staff work was done by the negotiators themselves, along with Yossi Beilin, Avi Gil, and Shlomo Gur, under the baton of Rabin and Peres (who, between them, brought to the deliberations some hundred years of experience in all aspects of Israel's security).

Finally, secrecy proved to be a vital condition for the success of our endeavor. In almost three years of negotiations, leading to three successive agreements, nothing of consequence ever leaked out. Discretion is above all the key to building trust among negotiators. Ensuring privacy for creative and collaborative thinking, even during periods of great tension in the talks, makes an enormous difference to the quality of the agreements they produce.

The Norwegians were not present in the negotiating room, though they certainly encouraged us to keep going and helped out in times of crisis. This rule, established in Oslo in the spring of 1993, held through the signing of the Interim Agreement in September 1995, and it applied as well to the Americans and the Egyptians. It was a natural corollary of the belief that those who are fated to live together should decide how to do it themselves, and take responsibility for their choices.

Over the years the American government played a key role in the process, both through the conduct of its new relations with the PLO and by providing a political safety net when significant crises arose between the parties, to say nothing of extending financial aid. During the seven months of secret talks in Norway, the United States placed little stock in the Oslo track. The conventional wisdom in Washington held a breakthrough with Syria to be more likely and, strategically speaking, more valuable. The American peace team, headed by Dennis Ross, also tried to advance the talks going on in Washington; on June 28 it even issued its own draft for a brief declaration of principles. But the proposal was shallower than what we thought we could achieve in the Oslo talks, and a number of its points (relating to the permanent settlement) were problematic for us.

Another party that had a detailed picture of what was happening in Oslo was Egypt. We briefed President Mubarak and his aides from time to time (Osama el-Baz, Mubarak's close adviser, visited Prime Minister Rabin in June, Foreign Minister Peres met with Mubarak at the beginning of July), and Arafat consulted with them regularly. In fact, the Egyptians served as something of a big brother to the Palestinians. After talking with the prime minister during his visit to Israel in June, for example, Osama el-Baz was able to assure the Palestinians that Rabin was committed to the Oslo track.

During this middle stage of the Oslo talks, however, it was our Norwegian hosts who not only served as "environmental architects" but advanced the process itself. On July 12, Norway's foreign minister, Johan Jørgen Holst; his wife, Marianne Heiberg; Terje Larsen; and Mona Juul set off on a trip to Tunis defined as a "working visit" to be followed by a "private vacation." Their main purpose was to meet with Arafat, and after a long talk with him Terje and Mona flew to Israel to meet with Peres. They had with them a letter from Holst that described the meeting with Arafat.

At first, in the presence of his advisers, the chairman had laid on a grand performance, flaying the United States for its pro-Israel bias. But in a more intimate meeting (with only Abu Ala at his side), the Norwegians met a different, quite realistic Arafat, who spoke with satisfaction of the progress made in the Oslo talks and praised his guests' contribution. He showed them a map detailing the autonomous area of Gaza, a very generous rendering of Jericho, and the proposed passage between them. He also sketched in their presence his vision of the Jericho enclave on a map that was later given to us. To justify the receipt of so much territory around Jericho, he stressed that there were no Jewish settlements or holy places there. He also argued that the larger the area under his control, the more promising his ability to clamp down on troublemakers. Arafat placed great importance on establishing himself in the territories in order to deal, so he said, with Hamas. During the PLO's troubled sojourn in Lebanon, he told the Norwegians, he had been able to fragment the opposition by his authority, and so he would again in the West Bank and Gaza. Divide and rule was the man's second nature.

Terje and Mona shared their own impression that Arafat was keen on reaching an agreement with us. They described him with a mixture of awe and irreverence that enhanced our understanding of the man behind the symbol—the PLO leader who alone made all the meaningful decisions.

The next day, at a private lunch for Terje and Mona in Jerusalem's Laromme Hotel, Peres explained his belief that an agreement with the Palestinians would usher in a new era for the entire Middle East. He also asked them to tell Arafat, unequivocally, that three things were out of the question: "extending the autonomy arrangement to Jerusalem, in any way; ballooning the area of the Jericho enclave; and granting the Palestinians any form of exterritorial passage between the West Bank and the Gaza Strip. If he insists on these things, there won't be an agreement," he pronounced.

Suddenly we became aware that Peres was speaking quite openly, although our waiter (a Palestinian), who was constantly in our vicinity, was a man whose fate was being discussed, in one way or another, around that table. Yossi Beilin caught my eye as he jerked his head in the young man's direction, but Peres was oblivious to his distress. I had a panicked vision of weeks of subterfuge coming to grief right there. Fortunately, however, the waiter showed not the least interest in what Peres was saying.

Afterward, Mona and Terje told us how impressed they were by Peres's vision and determination. I came away from that meal feeling equally impressed by them. These two Norwegian "peace fighters" had been cast into an odd limbo between their humanitarian vision and the wily tactics being used to attain it. Just before they left, Terje took me aside and said, "I understand you better now—you and the Palestinians. You both deserve to live here in peace. Mona and I won't rest for a moment. I promise you that."

They kept that promise, having become as committed to the peace process as we were. Returning to Tunis to continue their busman's holiday, they brought Holst a letter from Peres repeating the "red lines" he had drawn at our luncheon meeting and asking him to try to speed up the talks. On July 20, Holst showed the letter to Arafat (in each of these sessions, the connection between the Israeli and Palestinian leaders became a little more concrete), and Arafat repeated the issues most vital to him. He hammered away at the importance of the passages between Gaza and Jericho and between Jericho and Jordan. The only imperative he pressed more fervently was his own presence in the territories. He tried to promote himself as a catalyst in the creation of common interests and accepted the need to accelerate the talks and grasp the opportunity at hand. "The PLO is ready to conclude and sign," Holst wrote, quoting Arafat, in a subsequent letter to Peres. "If we delay now, we will lose control, all of us. Both of us need peace. We have to compromise. Israelis and Palestinians must learn to live together."

Holst's contribution in clarifying the positions, followed by "the team's" deliberations with Peres and consultations between Peres and Rabin, laid the groundwork for the next round of talks on July 24–26. Oslo had now reached a moment of truth, and if we arrived expecting swifter progress and a readiness for compromise, we were promptly disabused of those notions—for this time the Palestinians reiterated their positions, in full and in an entirely new document. Despite their promise to step up the process, they seemed to be retreating from the positions we thought we had already established. Their document ignored the one we had presented on July 4 (and to which their objections had been added). They now demanded ten thousand Palestinian policemen in Gaza and Jericho, Palestinian control of the border crossings, Israel's withdrawal from Gaza within three months, and that the scope of every further redeployment be determined by negotiation. For the first time, their new document specifically cited the PLO as our partner in implementing the agreement. My response to all this was categorical.

"Abu Ala, you have reneged on all our understandings," I said. "If we show your document to Rabin and Peres, it will mean the end of this track. Either we return to negotiating the July 6 document or the talks will come to a halt."

I then stood up and walked out of the room. Following me into the hall, Abu Ala asked that we talk in private (which we did a number of times a day).

"We haven't ignored the July 6 document, and these positions are open to discussion," he said. "But if you completely ignore our document, we won't be able to go home!"

I suggested we return to the July 6 draft and incorporate their latest demands. Thus in that late July round in Halvasbölle, we worked for over two days trying to reconcile the July 6 text with the points in the Palestinian document, a tense process. We sat for fifty-five hours almost without letup. Even the calls from Jerusalem about renewed fighting in south Lebanon (Operation Accountability) failed to distract us. The Palestinians showed not the least interest in the events in Lebanon. They were focused exclusively on the text.

They had been joined, in the meantime, by Mohammed Abu Koush, who replaced Maher al-Kurd. One of the PLO's envoys to the UN headquarters in Geneva, he was a thin, shy man of about fifty. Abu Ala had introduced him jokingly during the previous round by standing in the doorway and ceremoniously announcing: "The infamous and deadly terrorist Mohammed Abu Koush!" When I later wondered aloud what had befallen al-Kurd, Abu Ala replied curtly: "Don't ask questions." We worried about the amiable economist until the mystery was cleared up. Al-Kurd had apparently been insufficiently discreet in talking with Arafat's associates and was banished to Canada as a result. (He later returned to Tunis and was reinstated as one of the chairman's advisers.)

Abu Koush added a measure of courtesy and modesty to the group in Oslo. But during these three days, I concentrated on one of our veterans, Hassan Asfour. I was struck by the relationship he had developed with Yoel, a foil, in a sense, to the one I had with Abu Ala. Yoel Singer and Asfour were both deeply rooted in their respective societies. At first they clashed hotly. But soon Yoel came to appreciate Asfour as an honest, highly intelligent man who was undergoing a profound change in his attitude toward Israel. He didn't express himself well in English, but his eyes betrayed an intensity of feeling that slowly changed from contempt for the people sitting opposite him to mounting curiosity and even a surprising degree of empathy.

One day when we chatted near the hotel, he told me that as a militant Communist and disciple of George Habash, he had quarreled more than once with Arafat. But after settling in Tunis and coming under Abu Mazen's sway, he began to adopt a more moderate stance toward Israel.

"You know," he told me as we sat imagining a new relationship between Israelis and Palestinians, "there are people among you who think like before and people among you who think like after. All the Israelis I've met here look toward the future. That encourages me to believe in a peace based on equality between us."

He said that at a time when the negotiations—the tenuous link between past and future—were facing a difficult test. By now, the Palestinians had dropped a number of demands, including the negotiation of each further redeployment. But on sixteen other points we remained far apart. The air in the negotiating room grew increasingly close as the Palestinians chain-smoked. The mood at mealtimes was no longer mellow, and the Norwegians seemed unhappy. On the afternoon of July 26, we decided to make a last-ditch effort. The Palestinians were irritated by our refusal to yield on responsibility for our citizens' security in the Palestinian autonomous territory. We were now shouting and exchanging harsh recriminations.

"You want full responsibility for security, but you won't grant us full civil jurisdiction. You won't recognize our national rights. The settlements are to remain intact. And you call this self-rule?" cried Abu Ala. "It's nothing but the continuation of the occupation by other means! We prefer to wait another decade for a fair agreement."

"All you do is refuse and reject. Extremism won't get you anywhere," I said. "Why won't you recognize what we can set in motion? Why won't you see that once we sign and begin transferring powers, the five-year countdown to the permanent settlement begins? Unless we start that clock ticking, you can wait—we can all wait—for the Messiah to come, while the suffering of our peoples goes on."

The Palestinians remained unmoved. I began speaking slowly, enunciating each word deliberately.

"We will not yield on security for Israelis. We will not make you responsible for it. Why should you be? We have been fighting for a century. We're just now beginning to build mutual trust. We will not recognize your national rights because that means assenting to a state. We must distinguish between these talks on autonomy and subsequent negotiations on a permanent settlement."

The quarreling continued. Asfour accused us of planning to maintain the occupation forever. Ron bemoaned the squandering of a great opportunity. Yoel, who disdained any discussion that did not relate to the text, sat slouched in his chair with his eyes closed, pretending he wasn't listening. I decided we had had enough.

"Abu Ala," I said in a formal tone, "it seems to me that we are no longer making progress. I suggest we each inform our principals that a crisis has developed."

For a moment or so, Abu Ala stared mutely at the papers in front of him. Then he arranged them in a pile and began moving as though he were about to leave. I too made gestures of finality; then suddenly he turned to me, saying: "Just a moment. I would like to make a personal statement." Straightening himself in his chair, he began in a low, somewhat shaky voice:

"My colleagues and I have invested a great effort in trying to reach an agreement with you. We were prepared to make significant compromises. But I don't see the point in going on any longer. We have reached an impasse. I don't blame anyone, but I have nothing more to contribute. This is a difficult moment for me, as I am forced to tell you that I have decided to resign from the talks. Abu Ammar [Arafat] will decide who my replacement will be. I hope he is more successful than I, because I believe in an agreement. I will remain at his disposal to advise and help him, if he so wishes. I thank you for your cooperation. Making your acquaintance has been a valuable experience. I wish you all success and hope we meet again in the future."

The room was silent. I could see Abu Ala had tears in his eyes, and I knew that I had to respond. But I wasn't quite sure whether he meant what he'd said or was adroitly bluffing. Perhaps he no longer knew himself. My instincts were to remain firm.

"We came here to pursue a dialogue toward reconciliation," I began. "We had begun to believe that the PLO is our partner in that endeavor. But apparently it's true that when the chips are down, the

PLO always retreats from a clear decision. I respect you all, but I don't understand you. Do you really believe any one of your followers, anyone living in a refugee camp, will condone the fact that because of a difference over a few words, you have postponed accepting responsibility for a large part of your people? Perhaps the PLO is more important to you than the Palestinian people. Perhaps those who say that you never miss an opportunity to miss an opportunity are right!

"We, too, have made mistakes. In 1971 President Sadat offered us a temporary settlement on the Suez Canal. We rejected it, and in 1973 a war broke out. Nineteen-ninety-three is your 1971. Instead of reaching a settlement in Oslo, we may find ourselves two years from now in violent conflict. In the hundreds of hours we have talked, I have come to admire and respect you. I regret your decision, Abu Ala. In my view, it is a mistaken one. But I will honor it. On behalf of my colleagues and myself, let me wish you the best. We will certainly continue to work with your replacement."

Abu Ala's expression remained blank, but I knew he wasn't pleased. Then Yair asked to speak and did so from the heart.

"Ron and I have known you for many months now. We were convinced that we could reach an agreement, not least because of you, Abu Ala. This is a black day, and history will not forgive us. I have fought for this peace all my life; now I see it slipping away from us. No one knows if this track will continue. Perhaps others will succeed, and perhaps we will have to wait many years. We are not here for ourselves. We are here for the sake of two peoples who deserve peace and a better life. It is them we are failing! This is the darkest day I have ever known."

These words moved us all. He had set before us, as only Yair could, exactly what lay in the balance. The tension was almost unbearable as all eyes turned to Abu Ala. His face was set in a scowl of futility as he stood up, ordered his colleagues to pack their bags, and strode out of the room. Without a word or a glance, the Palestinians filed out behind him, the rest of us following in silence. Seated in the lobby were Terje, Mona, and the six Norwegian security men. Our faces spoke volumes, but as I walked past Terje I mumbled, "This time it's really all over."

.   .   .

And yet, I wasn't sure. I herded our delegation into the room housing the FAFO computer, on which Ron had typed the successive drafts of the agreement. Yoel, schooled in crises, seemed remarkably relaxed. He and I had a solid understanding about tactics and shared the conviction that the most important thing to achieve—perhaps even more than a program for a settlement—was a change in the PLO's doctrine. In that hour of crisis on July 26, I sensed the time had come to address the source of the conflict. I asked to have a look at his draft proposal on mutual recognition between Israel and the PLO. I copied down its seven key points in diplomatic shorthand. We then compared the remaining sixteen points of disagreement on the declaration of principles with the concessions we were saving for last, and I jotted down the eight issues on which we could not afford to yield. When I had finished, Terje entered the room.

"Go see Abu Ala," he urged me. "He's sitting alone in the library."

"Has he asked or agreed to see me?"

"The truth is, I suggested a meeting, and he threw me out of the room."

I walked over to the library and found Abu Ala seated by a window. He was clutching the cane he'd been using since he sprained his ankle on one of our walks. Never had I seen him look so grim.

"How are you?" I said, for lack of something better.

"The situation is very bad," he said. "Both sides are now stubborn and don't understand the importance of this juncture. I can't go on like this."

His distress sounded genuine.

"If you're unable to deal with the symptoms, perhaps you can deal with the cause," I said. "What do you think about holding parallel talks on mutual recognition between Israel and the PLO?"

"What do you mean?" he asked in surprise.

"I'd like you to take down the following seven points," I continued and proceeded to read them from the paper I was holding.

NUMBER ONE,   recognition of Israel's right to exist in security and peace.

NUMBER TWO,	acceptance of Security Council Resolutions 242 and 338.
NUMBER THREE,	resolution of the conflict by peaceful means.
NUMBER FOUR,	resolution of differences through negotiation.
NUMBER FIVE,	renunciation of terrorism.
NUMBER SIX,	a halt to the intifada.
NUMBER SEVEN,	rescinding the clauses of the Palestinian Covenant that call for the destruction of Israel or otherwise contradict the peace process.

"If you can persuade Arafat to accept these conditions, I'll try to persuade Rabin and Peres to recognize and negotiate openly with the PLO and with Arafat—but as the chairman of the PLO," I stressed, "*not* as the president of Palestine."

Abu Ala looked interested. "I'll pass it on," he said.

"Please make it clear that I am doing this on my own initiative and must receive the approval of Rabin and Peres. I would also suggest, likewise on my own, that you ask Arafat to reverse his position on the following eight points in the declaration of principles. If he agrees, we'll try to persuade our leaders to be flexible on the eight remaining points."

I then listed the issues most important to Israel, including overall responsibility for the security of Israelis, the retention of certain civil powers, and control of the border passages.

"I'm willing to try," said Abu Ala. "But it will be difficult."

"It will be hard for us, too," I said. "But this may be our last chance to reach an agreement. All I ask is that, through Larsen, you send me an answer, positive or negative, on the two lists of points. We don't have time for bargaining now. In the next few days, Warren Christopher will be coming to the area, and the Syrian track may get moving, which is what the Americans prefer."

Abu Ala read me quite clearly. He knew I was exerting pressure but was taking a certain risk, as well, by giving him to understand that Israel was prepared to be flexible on the eight points I had *not* cited (recognition of Palestinian political rights, for example, and the transfer of the PLO leadership to the territories). We both appreciated that a conversation of this kind could take place only because of the trust we placed in each other. It derived from our belief that beneath all the cunning and manipulation lay a strong desire for peace. We also knew that this trust would have to serve us again in the future, so the time was as good as any to put it to the test.

I asked Yoel to join us so that we could go over all sixteen points in dispute. He dwelled on the issues that would require Palestinian concessions. He had a knack for doing this in a polished, dispassionate way that all but convinced his interlocutors that yielding was in their own best interest. Moreover, the Palestinians trusted him. They regarded him as a tough but absolutely fair-minded negotiator. At the end of Yoel's brief, Abu Ala stood up, sighed, and warned us sternly: "Explain to your people that if they're not forthcoming, it will be impossible to come to an agreement." He was back in the game.

Abu Ala remained in Oslo after we left. He sent Asfour to report to Arafat, and catch the opening round of fire, while he himself briefed the Norwegians. After his meeting with them, Holst wrote to Peres that he had found Abu Ala fairly optimistic. But by the time we reached Jerusalem and presented our report, Peres sounded troubled.

"I'm not sure you didn't go too far in proposing mutual recognition," he said. "This is more than extending feelers. As to the eight points of the declaration, I suggest we wait for their answer. Meanwhile, I think I should speak to Rabin immediately."

He took Yoel and Yossi Beilin along, and, given that anxious prelude, they expected to meet resistance. But Rabin surprised them. "If they accept the seven points, we'll recognize the PLO," he said matter-of-factly. The prime minister had a logical and pragmatic mind. For the PLO to accept our conditions would necessarily open the way to mutual recognition. On the declaration of principles, he doubted the Palestinians would accept our demands on security and jurisdiction. So he too counseled that we wait for their response.

It came sooner than we expected. That night, or rather at three the next morning, Terje rang me at home.

"Hi, this is Larsen the terrorist," he chirped, his ritual opening. "Hope I didn't wake you."

By then we were accustomed to these nocturnal phone calls. We were all on "Arafat time" and primed to perform during odd hours.

"Number One called," Terje continued, "and said that Grandfather and the Holy Ghost accept the seven points in principle and are prepared to discuss the eighth."

We read the message as only a partial response and decided to send a partial answer. We also postponed our next trip to Oslo until August 13, after Secretary Christopher's visit later that day. I contacted Terje and asked for a more definitive answer from Tunis. Abu Ala replied that he believed it would be possible to close a deal at the next session—an assessment he repeated to Yair when they met in Paris on August 6.

Meanwhile, there was indeed progress on the Syrian track while Warren Christopher and Dennis Ross were in Damascus and Jerusalem. It came on August 3 and 4 in an exchange of messages between Rabin and Syrian President Hafez el-Assad (through the Americans) that set the parameters of a possible deal on peace as Israel's full withdrawal from the Golan Heights in return for the full normalization of relations, satisfactory security arrangements, and an extended timetable for implementation.

But none of us knew this when we again convened in Norway on August 13, this time in a villa in Borregaard. The setting was more luxurious than before, though still reassuringly isolated. The owners of the house impressed us as being Norwegian aristocrats: naturally poised and slightly aloof with the wisdom of life etched on their faces. Upon our arrival they served champagne, which the Palestinians declined. Our hosts had been told that we were businessmen from the Middle East, and it wouldn't surprise me if some of our nervous mannerisms confirmed their worst suspicions about Levantine merchants.

We soon settled into a large, elegant room, and the talks moved along more smoothly than before. A taste of failure can shake the confidence of even the most seasoned negotiators, and we were now ready for the endgame. The obstacles began to fall. The Palestinians, we discovered, had not changed their stand on all eight points in the proposed declaration of principles, but they had eased up on a number of critical ones (such as not insisting that Palestinians living in Jerusalem could run for seats on the autonomy council). We reciprocated by agreeing to speed up the withdrawal from Gaza and Jericho and to recognize their political (though not national) rights. The size of the Jericho enclave was left open to later negotiation.

On August 14 we walked to a cabin a few miles away and sat by the fireplace planning our work once the agreement was signed: transferring authority, cooperating on security, soliciting economic aid. The future was suddenly becoming real to us: a signal would go forth to the Middle East from that cabin tucked away at the edge of Europe and profoundly change people's lives. The thought filled us with excitement and anxiety.

On the issue of mutual recognition, however, the Palestinians had agreed to our seven points but expressed them in their own way and wanted to create some symmetry by making parallel demands of their own (such as a halt to terrorism on their part against a cessation of violence on ours). Sensing that the two sides would not agree quickly, we decided to postpone the question of recognition until after the declaration was completed (but before it was officially signed). Completing the declaration was the paramount objective now.

Constructing a peace agreement means striking a balance in which each side can preserve its vital interests. Nothing is more important to the creation of a viable future. In Oslo, perhaps because we were working under intense pressure of shared and clashing basic interests, we were now structuring such a balance. The partnership we forged was destined to face almost impossible tests.

By the evening of August 14, only five points remained on the agenda. Abu Ala was in particularly good spirits. "I'll call Abu Mazen, suggest a number of bridging proposals, and I hope we can wrap up the talks tomorrow," he said. On that note we returned to the villa, where he phoned Tunis while Yoel and I sought out Mona for a chat (Terje was in Oslo at an official dinner).

"What will you do with yourself once you're rid of us?" I teased her.

She flashed one of her inscrutable smiles. Mona's delicacy was off-set by a fierce intensity and almost dogged singleness of purpose. "What makes Mona run?" was a question we asked ourselves more than once. She was not at all like her husband, who had built a bridge to our world and drew us into the atmosphere he was working to create. Mona operated differently, in a way appropriate to her Norwegian style of understatement. Her presence imposed an air of civility on the club, and as the only woman among fourteen men, she was also the object of considerable attention. Who sat next to Mona at meals was a source of tense but good-humored competition between Israelis and Palestinians. But she never once let on that she favored any of us. On the contrary, she moved as though escorting us, on tiptoe, through a marathon obstacle course. Abu Ala used to call her "my daughter," after his twenty-year-old of the same name, and he enjoyed teasing Terje by periodically announcing: "Larsen is nothing without Mona!"

On that evening, while Yoel and I were relaxing with her, relishing the sensation that we had reached our goal, Abu Ala suddenly descended the stairs, shaking his head in frustration. Arafat and Abu Mazen, he told us, had rejected his recommendations on the last remaining points. We immediately convened in the negotiating room, where the Palestinians explained the difficulties as control of the border passage to Jordan and the IDF's movements in Gaza. I directed our delegation not to respond, and we retired for the night.

At breakfast the next morning, Abu Ala asked us to stay another day to resolve the problems, but I refused. I sensed that if we relaxed the pressure, the talks would go on endlessly. Our departure had the desired effect. That night, even before we'd had a chance to report to Peres, Terje phoned to relay Abu Ala's message that, in talks with Grandfather, he had found a way to bridge the gaps.

The next day, August 16, was Peres's seventieth birthday. We managed to surprise him with a party in his office for a small group of staff and close friends. Four people spoke on that occasion, the last being Peres himself. He was embarrassed by events of this sort, as by any public show of emotion. But he was also aware that this birthday fell at an auspicious hour in our history, and he even allowed himself to say so. "Soon, perhaps even very soon, we will witness a historic breakthrough with the Palestinians," he predicted. Most of the people in the room, who knew nothing of the Oslo track, credited those words to his usual optimism. In a country so steeped in skepticism and haunted by its troubled past, it's easy to dismiss a positive view of the future as unrealistic. But Peres's unique gifts enabled him to see that Israel had to build on its strength in order to forge a different future. He closed by saying: "I have devoted most of my life to security. What's left to me, now that Israel is strong, is to bring our young people peace."

Directly from that party Peres went to a meeting with Rabin at which it was decided that during an official visit he was scheduled to make to Scandinavia, he would try to resolve the outstanding questions in the declaration of principles and have the agreement initialed in Oslo on August 19. The next day he left for Stockholm, accompanied by Avi Gil. Yoel met them there. Holst was asked to join them secretly, together with Terje and Mona. I stayed in Israel, ready to fly to Oslo. I used the break to steal away with Aliza for a much-needed rest. The three months of secret talks, added to my duties as the director-general of the Foreign Ministry, had me going up to twenty hours a day—and the toll was showing. We hid out in a seaside hotel and pretended to be on vacation. The game lasted barely a day. At 6:00 A.M. on August 18, Avi Gil called.

"Listen," he barked on hearing my groggy response, "we've just finished seven hours of phone calls between Stockholm and Tunis. Holst did the talking here, with Shimon, Yoel, and me beside him. Abu Ala was on the other end, next to Arafat. All the issues were settled except one. That'll be your job." Avi listed the points that had been resolved (such as coordination on the international passages) while I took mental notes. "I'm going to bed now," he ended. "You've rested enough! Take the first plane and get yourself to Oslo. And, Uri," he added almost as an afterthought, "mazel tov!"

A few hours later I was on my way to Oslo with Yair and Ron. From the airport we were taken to the penthouse of the Oslo Plaza

Hotel, where the Palestinians awaited us in a suite that had obviously been designed for sybaritic tycoons, not lowly negotiators like ourselves. We toyed with all the buttons, dimming the lights and blasting the sound system, until someone remembered there was still work to do. In one of the smaller rooms, I spotted a new face: Taher el-Shash, an Egyptian legal adviser whom the Palestinians had brought to go over the declaration. Yoel knew him from the early 1980s, and the two of them sat poring over the text while Abu Ala and I resolved the last outstanding issue by agreeing that the final-status talks would conclude no later than five years after Israel's withdrawal from Gaza and Jericho. Thus the clock toward a difficult reconciliation was set in motion. Then both delegations went over the Economic Protocol (which had been vetted for us by Prof. Emanuel Sharon, the chairman of Bank Hapoalim, without my telling him where it came from). Unfortunately, economic cooperation, which had been so prominent in our thinking at the start of the talks, would be overshadowed by security concerns and political considerations for the Palestinians and for us, a pattern that would recur in later agreements as well.

While in the Oslo Plaza Hotel, Abu Ala and I were writing the speeches we would give at that evening's secret ceremony, Peres was talking to his Norwegian hosts. Holst gave a dinner for Peres at the government's guesthouse, to which the leaders of Norwegian society were invited. The guests left at 10:30. Peres and his entourage retired to their rooms. To all appearances the day—a rather routine one, as state visits go—was over.

Close to midnight Terje walked into our suite, formally attired and visibly nervous, to brief us on the initialing ceremony. When he had finished, Ron produced his camera, and the secret Oslo Club was photographed together for the first time. The picture shows us dressed in dark suits (except for Abu Koush, who stands out in light blue), ready to play our parts on history's stage—without an audience. As the shutter clicked, the phone rang. It was Avi calling to ask whether he should reveal to Peres's Israeli bodyguards, who knew that some event was planned for that night but not its precise nature, the identities of all its participants.

"You'd better tell them," I advised him. "Imagine what will happen if they find someone they have listed as a PLO terrorist in Peres's lodgings at two in the morning!"

Soon after, we were driven to the government guesthouse. Entering through the back door, we walked through the scullery and up one flight to a large room with parquet floors, heavy orange draperies, and an oak table the Norwegians had borrowed from a museum (it was the one on which the 1905 agreement separating Norway from Sweden had been signed). Geir Pedersen of the Norwegian Foreign Ministry, who was one of the people responsible for organization during the talks, had prepared the documents for signature in red-leather folders. Each of the delegations was shown into a smaller side room. Awaiting us in ours were Peres and Avi Gil. Peres was tense. Earlier that day Israel had lost seven soldiers in Lebanon. Rabin had just described the tragedy to him on the phone. It often seemed that every step forward in this process was marred by violence, every triumph tempered by pain. Peres explained that the agreement would be initialed by the heads of the delegations (it had been agreed that Yoel Singer and Hassan Asfour would join us). The foreign minister himself would not be able to sign, or speak at the ceremony, since the Israeli government had not yet approved the declaration. Except for Rabin and Peres, our government still wasn't aware of its existence.

At 2:45 A.M., August 20, while the rest of his entourage slept unawares, Peres took his place in the receiving line beside Johan Jørgen Holst, Marianne Heiberg, Terje Larsen, Mona Juul, and Geir Pedersen. At Avi's suggestion, agents of the Norwegian secret service, who were used to filming events of a rather different nature, immortalized the ceremony on videotape. After the two delegations had walked down the reception line, Abu Ala and I sat at the table with Holst between us. All the others were lined up behind us except for Marianne Heiberg and Peres, who retired to the side of the room as though he were a mere witness. After initialing each page of the agreement, Abu Ala and I stood up, shook hands, and embraced. We were replaced in the chairs by Yoel Singer and Hassan Asfour. The two men who had displayed such bristling animosity toward each other when they first met now signed the agreement they had created together. Though we were only a small group, four speeches followed to mark the historic occasion. Gnawing at us all was the paradox of the agreement's momentous importance—for our peoples, the Middle East, and perhaps the whole world—and the clandestine way in which it had been sealed.

Holst was the first to speak, praising the national leaders and their negotiators and promising Norway's continued help. "We are always here if you need our services," he said. "But the task is yours, and the work has to be yours." Abu Ala followed, with tears glistening in his eyes as he described how the PLO leadership had wept for joy after the long phone conversation with Holst and Peres two nights earlier. Turning to Peres (who was struggling to conceal his emotions), he said: "Welcome. I have keenly followed your declarations, statements, and writings, which confirmed to us your desire to achieve a just, permanent, and comprehensive peace. In the name of the Palestinian delegation and its leader, Yasser Arafat, I would like to welcome you and to congratulate you on your seventieth birthday, hoping you all success for the great battle of peace.

"We start today a new journey toward a new future, in a world whose final form has not yet been shaped and which is open to all sorts of change. The future that we look for will not materialize unless we together overcome the fears of the past and learn from the past lessons for our future."

When my turn came, I had to check my powerful emotions. I too spoke of the future. "Today, indeed, is the beginning of the future. A future in which legitimate Palestinian desires to be in charge of their lives through self-government are compatible with the Israeli desire to be in charge of our fate, through security. It is the beginning of a transitional period, bridging the anarchy of past conflict with the order of future permanent coexistence."

Last to speak was Terje Larsen. He addressed the negotiators, mentioning each of us by name. "One thing has united you here: the concept of friendship," he said, "a friendship that will stand as the foundation of your relations in the future." For Terje, the process we had experienced was of universal significance. He strove to bring out the good in man, and the "peace laboratory" he had helped create for us had given him a glimpse of what he'd been searching for all his life.

Then Peres and Abu Ala met for a half-hour tête-à-tête, the first meeting at such a high level between the two sides. They expressed their commitment to the agreement just initialed, and Peres impressed Abu Ala with his willingness to encourage international economic assistance to the new Palestinian endeavor. Peres also discussed the economic assistance with Norwegian Foreign Minister Holst, suggesting the creation of an international mechanism for that purpose.

It was after four when we returned to the hotel, feeling slightly giddy and drained. Each of us autographed copies of the Declaration of Principles as mementos for the others, and for a while I sat pensively flipping through its pages.

The "Declaration of Principles on Interim Self-Government Arrangements" was a step-by-step approach toward a settlement according to certain clear-cut principles. "Gradual" was the key word describing the transition from occupation to self-rule, from violence to peaceful coexistence, from a political road map to true reconciliation.

- Israel was to withdraw its troops from the Gaza Strip and Jericho within six months of the declaration taking effect (on October 13, 1993).

- The redeployment of Israeli troops in other areas of the West Bank, along with elections to the Palestinian Council, was to take place within nine months of the agreement going into effect.

- Negotiations on the permanent status of the West Bank and Gaza Strip were to begin no later than two years after Israel's withdrawal from Gaza and Jericho and conclude no later than five years after it. (The withdrawal began on May 4, 1994, and the permanent-status negotiations started two years later, on May 5, 1996, so that the permanent settlement is scheduled to be concluded by May 5, 1999.)

- Civil authority and powers (though not *all* the powers held by Israel's military government) would be transferred to the Palestinians first in Gaza and Jericho and gradually in the West Bank. The Palestinian

Council would have jurisdiction over "West Bank and Gaza Strip territory," except for those areas (Jerusalem, the settlements, and security locations) to be negotiated in the permanent-status talks.

- Security powers would gradually be transferred to a strong Palestinian police force, to be created by recruiting policemen locally and abroad, while Israel would retain responsibility for the overall security of Israelis, for the settlements, and for defense against external threats.

- The two sides would coordinate on the border passages between Gaza and Egypt and between Jericho and Jordan (which, from a security standpoint, would be under Israel's exclusive control as part of its responsibility for external security).

- The authority of the Palestinian Council would be extended in stages. Israel would withdraw first from parts of the Gaza Strip and the Jericho enclave. Its forces would then gradually redeploy in the rest of the West Bank, leaving first the populated areas (before the elections for the Palestinian Council) and then, in stages, the nonpopulated ones, not including the Israeli settlements and other "specified locations" to be defined by Israel.

- The elections for the Palestinian Council would be held under international supervision. The council's powers, together with the exact mode and conditions of the elections (including in Jerusalem), would be decided in the Interim Agreement.

The Declaration of Principles also foreshadowed the permanent settlement in establishing that the aim of the negotiating process was to "strive to live in peaceful coexistence and mutual dignity and security" and to achieve a "historic reconciliation" between the Israeli and Palestinian peoples. The negotiations on the permanent settlement would "lead to the implementation of Security Council Resolutions 242 and 338" and would cover the issues of "Jerusalem, refugees, settlements, security arrangements, borders, relations and cooperation with other neighbors, and other issues of mutual interest."

As cooperation was deemed an essential condition at every stage, the declaration stipulated the establishment of a number of joint committees on security, economics, the refugees from the 1967 war, and the implementation of the agreement.

The map that was to lead two peoples from confrontation to reconciliation had been drawn in the clear, crisp air of the fjords near Oslo. The road itself ran through the dusty Middle East, past obstacles of resentment, insecurity, and mistrust. Our initial effort had produced a fair compromise between two visions of freedom: one from foreign domination, the other from hostility. The partners to the agreement were two national movements that, after being locked for a century in existential conflict, were ready to coexist. There was almost no precedent for such a consummate turnabout.

But on the night of August 19–20, all this was still a deep secret. Sitting in the Oslo Plaza, overwhelmed by the event and for the first time free from the tension of the negotiations, we passed the time by impersonating one another to prove we had seen through our adversaries' ploys and stratagems. I phoned Yossi Beilin, who, as the initiator of the Oslo track, was sorely missed that night. As we were about to leave, Abu Ala beckoned me to his room and removed a document from his briefcase.

"You noted in your speech that even when the negotiations got rough, we always agreed about one thing: that we must secure a better future for our children. That's why you suggested dedicating the agreement to them and all their peers in the Middle East. Let's set an example. I'll dedicate my speech to your daughter, and you dedicate your speech to mine. They're both twenty years old; they both can have hope now."

Sitting on opposite sides of the room, we each wrote a few words on our speeches. When we compared the texts, they were almost identical.

Abu Ala wrote:

Dear Maya,
    May I congratulate you on two things:
    —The first is your great father

—The second is the great achievement he made for you and for my daughters Mona and Manal, whom I hope that you will be friends with in the very near future, in peace. Good luck. The new history has begun.

Abu Ala, August 19, 1993

The next day, after landing in Tel Aviv, I drove to the restaurant where Maya was waitressing during the summer break from her studies. When I'd left for Oslo two days before, I'd told Aliza and Maya that I might be coming back with the agreement. Seeing me through the window, Maya came running toward me, fell on me with a hug, and leaned back to eye me quizzically. I pulled Abu Ala's speech out of my briefcase. She looked at the text first, then read the dedication, and then, standing there on the sidewalk, amid the curious pedestrians and grating noise of traffic, she wept.

19th Aug. 1993

Exc. Mr Holst
Exc. Mr Perez
Mr Uri
Ladies and Gentlemen

Dear Maya
May I congratulate you
for two things:
- The first of your great father
for the great achievement
he made for you and for my daughters
Mona and Manal too, and I hope
- The Second that you will be friends in the
very near future, in peace
good luck
the new history
opened

Mr Holst.
I would like to confirm that we are indebted to Norway, to you
personally and to all the women and men who contributed to this
great historical breakthrough. Indeed it is our obligation towards
your friendly country and towards you personally to recognize here
your courage, wisdom and persistence and outstanding role in this
back channel.

Mr Perez. *Welcome,*
I have keenly followed up your declarations, statements and
writings which confirmed to us your care to achieve a just,
permanent and comprehensive peace. In the name of the Palestinian
delegation and its leader Yassir Arafat I would like to welcome you
and to congratulate you on your 70th birthday, *hoping you all*
success for the great battle of Peace

We start today a new journey towards a new future, in a world whose
final form has not yet been shaped and which is open to all sorts
of change. The future which we look for will not materialize unless
we both together overcome the fears of the past and learn from the
past lessons for our future.

1

Dedication by Abu Ala to Maya Savir on his copy of the speech made at the
initialing of the Declaration of Principles, August 19, 1993.

3

MUTUAL RECOGNITION

Our success in keeping the agreement secret was almost miraculous, considering that at least a hundred people—seventy-five Israelis, Palestinians, and Norwegians and also about twenty-five Americans, Egyptians, Moroccans, Tunisians, and Russians—eventually knew about the talks. The secret was kept because of the sense of responsibility of all those involved, the skepticism of outside parties that we would reach a breakthrough, and much luck.

While we were engaged in the talks in Oslo, our lives ostensibly went on as usual. After taking over as director of Israel's Foreign Ministry on May 1, 1993, I announced a thoroughgoing reform of the foreign service, which consumed a great amount of my time and attention.

I strongly believed that we had to structure a new Foreign Ministry, which would rid itself of traditional defensiveness toward a strongly perceived international hostility and be open to the world, in order to create a network of concrete economic, scientific, and cultural international relationships. The world was changing. The role of our diplomacy was to help Israel link up to the new sources of strength in the world, and where possible contribute to them. For there was a clear line between Oslo and the ministry's reform—building a bridge between Israel and the nations.

Yoel Singer faced a difficult challenge because, unless he had a double, it's hard to fathom how he weathered his biweekly jaunts among three continents without raising suspicions. And we all lived under the strain of silence. In none of our public statements did we even hint at what was going on, though our growing optimism must have been apparent. Those who listened to us, even closely, ascribed it to wishful thinking. On August 2, I almost slipped in a television debate taped in Jerusalem with Hanan Ashrawi, the articulate Palestinian spokeswoman, when I said: "Let us wait for tomorrow and the days to come and see what we are proposing, moving toward full and free Palestinian democratic elections while seeking our own security. I think the surprise will not come by an Israeli document, but by working together on the ground." As usual, Ashrawi was sharply polemical, and when we left the studio she asked me why I was so upbeat.

"You'll see that I'm right," I told her.

Her skepticism was certainly not exceptional. For most people, including the "experts," any change in the status quo was inconceivable, even when it was practically spelled out for them. The press as usual was obsessed with tomorrow's headlines and treated Peres's forward-looking doctrines as futuristic fantasies. It also believed itself to be the sole source of fact, to the point of self-delusion. A few months before the breakthrough, while Peres was working out the initiative of "Gaza first," Amnon Barzilai, one of Israel's more gifted journalists, wrote in the daily *Hadashot:* "Peres will pass the years ahead until retirement comfortably. The thin slice [of responsibility] that the prime minister has accorded his foreign minister leaves Peres an abundance of time to build the perfect Foreign Ministry. From time to time there are outbursts of vision, but they will certainly never be realized." Fortunately, this approach was characteristic of the Israeli press as a whole.

Almost a week passed from the day of the initialing ceremony before the first hints began to appear in the media—and even then the details were wrong. On the day Peres returned from Scandinavia (August 24), Shimon Schiffer of the mass-circulation daily *Yediot Aharonot,* who is renowned for his record at obtaining scoops, called me to boast: "I know from an impeccable source that Peres met a senior PLO man in Stockholm. There's no point in denying it. I just wanted to spare you the surprise when you open the paper tomorrow." Our position then was not to lie to the press, but neither would we help it learn the truth, especially not until the American government had been updated and the Israeli government had approved the declaration. I therefore told Schiffer he was wrong, and, technically at least, he was. The next day the paper nonetheless ran the headline PERES HELD SECRET MEETING IN SWEDEN WITH SENIOR MEMBER OF THE PLO. On the day after that, Ze'ev Schiff, Israel's leading analyst of defense and security affairs, wrote in *Ha'aretz* that Peres had met with a PLO official in Norway, in the presence of Uri Savir, but "that no agreement had been signed."

Meanwhile, we were busy with other matters. Immediately upon Peres's return to Israel, it was decided that he should personally inform Warren Christopher of the breakthrough. Christopher was then in California on vacation, and Itamar Rabinovich, Israel's ambassador in Washington, was told to set up the meeting. Peres left on August 28, accompanied by Yoel and Avi Gil. His plane landed in Geneva to pick up Johan Holst, Terje Larsen, and Mona Juul. Yossi Beilin and I remained in Israel to deal with the media exposure, which was now inevitable. On Friday afternoon, August 29—more than seven months after the start of the Oslo track and ten days after the secret initialing of the agreement—the Voice of Israel broke the story of Peres's trip to see Christopher, carrying the draft of an agreement with the PLO reached through secret negotiations in Oslo. The secret was out.

At Point Mugu Naval Air Station in California, the Israelis and their Norwegian colleagues met with Christopher and Dennis Ross, head of the United States' Middle East peace team. The session was a critical test, both of the basic trust between Israel and the United States and of American foreign policy. Throughout the Oslo negotiations, the Clinton administration had been aware of the secret track but doubted it would yield concrete results. Neither was the State Department particularly interested in the details of the Oslo talks. The Americans strove to build a peace strategy with Syria first. And then, out of the blue, Shimon Peres turned up in California carrying not only an initialed declaration of principles but a proposal for mutual recognition between Israel and the PLO. Peres feared that the

Americans, piqued at being left out, would react coolly toward opportunity being laid at their doorstep. The Norwegians were concerned that the United States might be too proud to accept the declaration as it stood. In the simulation games that Terje and Avi played on the way to California, Avi (in the role of the Americans) joked: "Norwegians? Who needs Norwegians?"

Thus, in presenting the document to Christopher, Peres spoke of a historic breakthrough that must now be exploited with vigor. He also intimated that from then on, the process should be led by the U.S. administration. Christopher and Ross asked to see the document. When they had finished reading it, the secretary of state asked Ross, the administration's top expert on the peace process, "Dennis, what do you think?"

"A great historic achievement," said Ross.

"Absolutely!" said Christopher with atypical verve.

Our American friends indeed showed themselves to be true peace seekers who were above petty considerations. It was a grand moment for a wise and generous superpower. Every American administration since Lyndon Johnson's had declared that it was the role of the parties in conflict to reach a solution, not the job of the United States to impose one. The Clinton administration really meant it. The Americans agreed to host a signing ceremony at the White House and implied that if the PLO accepted the seven points, the United States would recognize them too. This would require the consent of Congress. It was decided to sharpen the clause in which Arafat would disassociate his movement from terrorist groups outside the PLO.

Peres returned to Israel to find a country in shock. The headlines announced A HISTORIC BREAKTHROUGH BETWEEN ISRAEL AND THE PLO as the press began to spin out the story of the talks—still with only partial accuracy. On August 30 the Israeli government approved the Declaration of Principles after Yoel presented it as a major improvement over the Camp David Accords primarily because of the gradual redeployment in the West Bank in three stages, which was absent from the Camp David agreement.

At the same time Abu Ala and I were in Oslo discussing the terms of mutual recognition. The Palestinians had accepted most of our demands, which were similar to the seven points I had outlined on July

25, now meticulously worded by Yoel Singer. But the few remaining gaps were significant.

These talks reached their decisive moment in Paris on September 9 and 10. On September 3 Peres and Holst made another attempt to negotiate with Tunis by phone when Peres was in Paris to brief his close friend President François Mitterrand. Other calls were made from Cairo to Jerusalem when Arafat and Holst visited President Mubarak on September 6. The next day, Holst called me from Cairo to say that both he and the Egyptians were convinced that without a meeting of the two Oslo teams, mutual recognition would have, at best, to be delayed. He asked me to come with Yoel to Paris on September 8 for another round of talks aimed at clinching an agreement before the signing of the Declaration of Principles in Washington on September 13.

I was asked to recommend a "discreet" hotel, so that the press wouldn't find us. Sensing that the reporters would probably have every dark cranny in Paris covered, I suggested taking the opposite tack and meeting in the Bristol in the Faubourg St.-Honoré. It proved to be the right decision. On September 9, Orly Azoulai filed to *Yediot Aharonot:* "Talks are going on in a mysterious hotel outside Paris placed at the disposal of the negotiators by the French government." We were all registered at the Bristol under the name of Larsen, each using a first name beginning with his own initial. I was Ulaf Larsen, Abu Ala was Alf Larsen, and so on.

Seated around a low table in the lounge of a second-floor suite were Abu Ala, Mohammed Abu Koush, Holst, Marianne Heiberg, the real Larsen, Mona, Yoel, and myself. Each of the delegations had a phone in an adjoining room to stay in contact with the decision makers in Tunis and Jerusalem. During the most critical hours of the talks, Rabin and Peres were together in the Knesset and the prime minister's residence. Alongside Arafat were, among others, Abu Mazen and Hassan Asfour. We began the negotiations at 4:00 P.M. on September 8 and continued until 2:00 the next afternoon, with Marianne typing each successive draft. Of all the three years of trying and fascinating negotiations, those twenty-two hours were perhaps the most significant, because we were attempting to eradicate the doctrines that had sustained the prolonged struggle between our two national movements. The challenge was a matter not of words but of making decisions that would become new international commitments and set our relationship in a new direction. In Oslo we had drawn a pragmatic guideline for gradually ending Israel's rule over the Palestinians while preserving its security. Now we were dealing with the ideological roots of the conflict. Without a mutual change in attitude by the representatives of the Palestinian people and the State of Israel, the principles of the Declaration of Principles would never be realized.

We were thus at the point of declaring an end to the Israeli-Palestinian conflict and transforming our ties into permanent political relations. They might be good or bad, but they would no longer be all or nothing. We therefore demanded that the PLO recognize the State of Israel, accept Security Council Resolutions 242 and 338, renounce and combat terrorism, end the intifada, and rescind the clauses of the Palestinian Covenant that denied Israel's legitimate right to exist. Only then would Israel recognize the PLO as the representative of the Palestinian people.

The talks so far had revealed key differences about the degree of responsibility that the PLO should assume in combating terrorism and calling on the Palestinians to refrain from violence.

"How can we commit ourselves to prevent terrorism in the areas that are not under our control?" Abu Ala argued. "If we call upon our people to renounce terrorism, we will effectively be saying that they support it, and that isn't so."

"Terrorism has been the chief instrument of your struggle against us," said Yoel. "You must fight it in every way and emphasize to your people that it is not a legitimate means of struggle. Without a commitment of that sort, we won't be able to come to an agreement."

Most of the debate, however, centered on a broader issue: whether mutual recognition would be absolute or conditional upon the terms of the permanent solution of the conflict. In two places in the text, we demanded that the Palestinians recognize Israel's right to exist in peace and security. Abu Ala consulted with Tunis and came back saying that this was acceptable, with one small change: "The PLO will recognize Israel's right to exist within secure and recognized boundaries."

Yoel responded angrily: "That's taken from 242 and means that your recognition will take effect only if the resolution is implemented! And besides, who will define the borders within which the PLO will recognize Israel?"

"You want us to recognize Israel within its *present* borders?" Abu Ala growled. "That would mean we recognize the occupation! Never!"

"You must recognize the State of Israel unconditionally," I said. "That is not open to negotiation. We can discuss points of disagreement in the future. But recognition must be a matter of principle."

A similar issue arose when we discussed which clauses of the Palestinian Covenant would have to be repealed. Israel demanded that the PLO revoke the clauses denying Israel's right to exist by declaring them no longer in effect or operative. The PLO wanted to say only that they were no longer in effect.

"It's the same thing!" Abu Ala argued. "The covenant hasn't been operative for years, and it certainly isn't in effect. We decided to recognize Israel's existence back in 1988."

But that kind of passive dissociation wasn't good enough. We demanded that the Palestinians accept Israel not just as a fact of life but as a legitimate political construct. "We must be convinced not only that your ideology has changed but that your operative policy has too," I told him. "Therefore it must say that the relevant clauses are not in effect and not operative."

Abu Ala said: "I will have to call Arafat and ask him."

We had the impression that the Palestinians were agonizing over every word in the text. The significance of recognition was quite clear to them, but articulating the change seemed more difficult for them than accepting the new policy itself. The Palestinians claimed they couldn't find an English version of the covenant. I showed them the problematic clauses in the text, which we had brought along from Jerusalem. (The basement of the Foreign Ministry was brimming with dusty copies of the covenant, held in reserve to expose our enemies when necessary.) They called, inter alia, for "the liberation of Palestine, as a national duty, to purify the land of the Zionist presence." Statements like that had to be erased from the new ethos. Golda Meir had once said that there was no such thing as the Palestinian people, and that too had to be corrected. Mutual recognition meant, first of all, acknowledging reality.

There was an especially heavy feeling in the room when Abu Ala returned and reported that the PLO Executive Committee was busy deliberating the Declaration of Principles, so he couldn't talk to Arafat about amendments to the covenant. We decided to take a break. Around midnight Terje checked out the hotel dining room and found it empty. We took the risk of going down to console ourselves on good French food while the gentlemen in Tunis were making up their minds. As we were eating, the dining-room phone rang, and the maître d' called from the other side of the room: *"Monsieur Larsen, téléphone, s'il vous plaît."* Almost everyone stood up, because that was the name we had left for people trying to reach us from Oslo, Tunis, and Jerusalem. An explosion of laughter finally broke the tension. The call was for Terje, of course.

When we had returned to the suite and Abu Ala was again trying to get Arafat on the phone, four unexpected visitors arrived. First Maya, who was on a visit to Paris, turned up with a friend. Then came Abu Ala's wife and one of his sons, who had checked into another hotel and were worried when they hadn't heard from him. Returning to the lounge, Abu Ala introduced Um Ala and Issam. When I introduced him to Maya, he embraced the young woman to whom he had written his dedication. For a moment or two we stood mutely in a circle, unsure of our behavior in this completely new situation. Then, falling naturally into the role of icebreaker, Terje ended the silence by suggesting that Maya and Issam continue the talks.

"No problem." Issam laughed. "We'll go off to a discotheque and have this thing wrapped up in no time!"

The younger generation probably wouldn't have understood the argument, which to them would have seemed like nit-picking. When our guests had gone, however, we returned to the nits. Maya stayed behind as our "night operator" and took calls from Jerusalem (mostly from Avi Gil, who was updating Peres).

Finally Abu Ala reached Arafat. When he returned to the lounge, it was 2:00 A.M.

"I've had a long talk with Abu Ammar," he reported. "He can't make such an important decision on his own, so he's reconvening the Executive Committee and will get back to us."

While waiting for the call, we continued to rake over the same issues. At 3:00 I woke Peres and told him of the difficulties. He asked me to call him again at 7:00, before he went to see Rabin. As the discussion dragged on, three additional points were raised: Jerusalem, the intifada, and the settlements. The PLO wanted a commitment from Peres not to close Palestinian institutions in East Jerusalem. We agreed, provided they were clearly not organs of the PLO or bodies associated with the future Palestinian Authority but social, cultural, and religious institutions, which we had an interest in seeing develop. Peres asked that his commitment to this effect not be made public. Even though it wasn't actually an Israeli concession, anything having to do with Jerusalem hit a nerve and could do nothing to promote the ratification of the agreement by the Knesset or its acceptance by Israeli public opinion. Abu Ala insisted on a letter (from Peres to Holst) but agreed not to publish it.

Then Abu Ala demanded a freeze on all settlement activity in the territories, which drew an enraged response from Jerusalem.

"What is this, at the last minute!" Peres shouted. "Tell him we will not agree to freeze construction as a result of Palestinian pressure. And explain to him that in 1992 the government took a decision to halt new building."

"Look, it's not important how you freeze the settlements," Abu Ala responded when I passed on Peres's message. "Just bear in mind that if the building of settlements goes on, the peace process will collapse."

When we raised the matter of the intifada, which had greatly abated but not altogether ended, Abu Ala was equally indignant. "You're not ending the occupation, which is the reason for the intifada. So how can we stop it? That's not within our control!"

"Look, you have to decide between violence and a meaningful peace process that will enable you to build your society and economy," said Yoel. "It's best that you tell us your choice now, because it will affect our whole attitude toward the agreement."

Abu Ala said he would recommend that Arafat call upon his people to return to their normal lives and concentrate on developing their economy—in other words, stop the violence. Holst proposed that this commitment be put in a letter addressed to him. We agreed on that at five in the morning.

Arafat still hadn't called back about the covenant. At six we decided to watch the news on CNN. The bulletin opened with an item on our talks in Paris and moved on to shots from Israel and the territories, where demonstrations of support and protest were going on.

"Look what we have done," Yoel murmured.

Reality had broken in on our closed little circle. The next item reported that Israel's interior minister, Aryeh Deri, had left the government and taken the ultra-Orthodox Shas Party (one of the three coalition partners) along with him. Abu Ala served as our commentator and assured us that the government would not fall. The Palestinians were compulsive students of Israeli politics. Their intelligence-gathering organs may have been weak, but they learned an amazing amount about our political life from the media.

Meanwhile the media still hadn't found us. The "Bristol maneuver" was an almost total success. The one exception was Jane Corbin of the BBC, who had managed to get a note through to me saying that if I agreed to give her an interview, she wouldn't divulge where we were meeting and would run her piece on the day of the signing in Washington. I could hardly refuse. While the others continued to watch the news, I returned to my room. At 6:30 A.M. the Norwegian security guard was surprised when I reemerged combed, shaven, and neatly dressed, so unlike my usual look during the marathon negotiations.

"I'll be in room 534," I told him.

Waiting for me there were Corbin and her film crew. (She later interviewed all the members of the Oslo Club at length and wrote an excellent book about the talks.) I took my place in front of the camera.

"What are you doing down there on the second floor?" she began.

"We're burying the conflict."

"Tell me, is Abu Ala your friend?"

"He's enough of that for me not to say."

Suddenly there was a timid knock on the door. Alarmed by my mysterious departure, the security guard had awakened Terje and been ordered to find out what had become of me. The poor man seemed enormously relieved to see me being filmed.

At seven, as ordered, I called Peres, who responded to my update with impatience.

"If Arafat is stalling over basic issues, we can do without mutual recognition. We'll leave it for a later stage and sign the Declaration of Principles," he said, as Rabin's deep bass echoed in the background.

At 7:30 Maya made sure I got some sleep. At 9:00 I woke to hear Abu Ala report that the PLO Executive Committee was still deliberating.

"It seems to me there's not going to be an agreement," I said.

"Then there won't be an agreement," he replied, turned, and stalked off to his room.

Terje took off after him and suggested that Holst talk to Arafat. By then Holst was looking very tense. He phoned the French Foreign Ministry to report that he would be leaving Paris at three that day— either for Tunis and Israel with an agreement, or to return to Oslo without one. Then he called Arafat, speaking politely but firmly.

"Abu Ammar, *you* must decide," he said. "You cannot convene your colleagues now."

Arafat promised to consult with his advisers and call back soon. Meanwhile Peres, on the other line, told us that the cabinet would be meeting at 5:00 to ratify the agreement—if there was one. Jerusalem was adding to the pressure of a deadline. The PLO had sat for three days and three nights of stormy debate over the declaration. Now there were only hours left to arrive at a decision on mutual recognition. The Palestinians had no problem recognizing Israel in the context of the peace process. But here we were speaking of recognizing it unconditionally, or at least without reference to its borders. We were prepared to recognize the PLO as the representative of the Palestinian people but not the PLO's version as leaders of a Palestinian state. Thus we insisted, on orders from Jerusalem, that Arafat would sign his letter to Rabin as the chairman of the PLO and not, as he had been accustomed to signing his correspondence since 1988, as the president of Palestine.

By midday of September 7, a conversation took place between Abu Ala and Abu Mazen, who finally conveyed the PLO's consent, after fierce deliberations, to the form of recognition we required. They also agreed to amend the Palestinian Covenant, renounce terrorism, and call an end to the intifada. We reciprocated with our readiness to recognize the PLO and by promising that Peres would write a letter to Holst pledging that the non-PLO institutions in Jerusalem would remain open; on settlements we would send the Palestinians the 1992 government decision to freeze them. Without such a policy there clearly would have been no agreement.

After we polished a few more words, the two letters of recognition were ready for final typing so that the Norwegians could take off for Tunis and Jerusalem. Incidentally, Rabin had given us strict instructions that the first letter from the prime minister of Israel to the chairman of the PLO should under no circumstances begin "Dear Mr. Chairman" but only "Mr. Chairman." The same rule was applied to Arafat's letter to Rabin. Marianne had almost finished typing the final copies when Maya entered the room, her cheeks flushed, and whispered in my ear that the prime minister wanted to talk to Yoel and me. Taking the call in my room, I heard Rabin request that we change one word in the last sentence of Arafat's letter to him. The original sentence read: "Accordingly, the PLO undertakes to submit to the Palestinian National Council for formal approval the necessary changes in regard to the Palestinian Covenant." Rabin wanted "accordingly" changed to "consequently." I winced at Yoel, who covered the handset with his palm and said that he couldn't see any difference in meaning. But knowing Abu Ala, I was sure he would suspect that the simple lexical amendment had some deeper political implication. We returned to the lounge to find the Norwegians anxious, even before I asked Abu Ala to join me in the adjacent room.

Seated on the bed, I raised my arms in exasperation and told him the simple truth.

"Rabin wants to change 'accordingly' to 'consequently.' For the life of me, I don't understand the difference. Decide what you will."

His lips formed a peculiar smile. "I understand," he said. "You people are obsessed with words. There is no difference. I will prove it to you, and it will give me a little satisfaction with the group out there. It'll be all right." Then he stood up, clasped my hand, and added, "We have an agreement!"

Back in the lounge the Norwegians were thoroughly puzzled. Putting on his best scowl, Abu Ala proceeded to explain: "I told Uri that in order to arrive at mutual recognition, all I am asking is to change one word—a word that will make things easier for us—and Uri has turned me down."

"Which word?" Holst snapped. "The letters are typed, and I must leave in half an hour. You can't add something new every minute."

Abu Ala asked for the copy of Arafat's letter and pointed to the word "Accordingly." "Here I am asking for 'Consequently,' " he said.

Yoel kept a poker face. The Norwegians practically begged us to relent, and after a brief "consultation" in the next room, we agreed. Marianne made the correction, and the final copies were done.

In hand we now had four letters: the PLO's recognition of the State of Israel (given in a letter from Arafat to Rabin); Israel's recognition of the PLO (given in a letter from Rabin to Arafat); Arafat's call to his people to renounce violence (given in a letter to Holst); and Israel's commitment not to close non-PLO institutions in Jerusalem (given in a secret letter from Peres to Holst, and later revealed by Arafat in a speech in Johannesburg). We faxed all four to Jerusalem and packed up copies of the originals.

At 2:00 P.M., as the Voice of Israel reported difficulties in the talks, we sat back, relieved. Terje produced bottles of chilled champagne and orange juice, and I called Maya in to join us. Holst led the celebration by toasting the start of a new era in relations between Israel and the PLO. Then the Norwegians and Palestinians left for Tunis, and we flopped down on the couch. We had forgotten to arrange transportation to the airport, so I called our embassy for a car. As we were about to enter it, a photographer from Reuters came running up and took a shot of us. Just before that I had parted from Maya, who gave me a hug, trotted off a few steps, then turned and called back to me, "Daddy, remember: I was there!"

. . .

That night, the PLO Executive Committee approved the exchange of letters, and from the moment it did so the Palestinian Covenant was from a practical point of view null and void. From the standpoint of the PLO leadership, this was a significant step. Two and a half years later, in April 1996, the Palestinian National Council formally approved the amendment of the covenant at a special session held in Gaza. Nevertheless, the Israeli right insisted, on the basis of an arcane literary exegesis, that the original covenant was still in effect. What would they do, I wondered, without the familiar and comforting wall of hostility?

But the wall had fallen during the early hours of September 10, when Arafat signed the relevant letters in Tunis and Holst brought them before the Israeli and international media in an understated ceremony in the prime minister's office in Jerusalem. With Peres sitting on one side of him and Holst on the other, Rabin signed, with a modest Pilot pen, on behalf of the government of Israel, the letter recognizing the PLO. The historic missive was all of one sentence long:

Mr. Chairman,

In response to your letter of September 9, 1993, I wish to confirm to you that, in light of the PLO commitments included in your letter, the Government of Israel has decided to recognize the PLO as the representative of the Palestinian people and commence negotiations with the PLO within the Middle East peace process.

Three days later, on September 13, 1993, the mutual recognition received its most dramatic expression on the South Lawn of the White House, when, at 10:00 A.M., after Shimon Peres—for Israel—and Abu Mazen—for the PLO (as was added in handwriting minutes before the ceremony)—had signed the Declaration of Principles. Then President Clinton drew together two men no one expected ever to see standing together: Yitzhak Rabin and Yasser Arafat. They clasped hands in what surely must be the most photographed handshake in history. There had been other important ones in recent years: between Richard Nixon and Zhou Enlai, Ronald Reagan and Mikhail Gorbachev, Nelson Mandela and F. W. de Klerk. But the importance the world ascribed to the touch of those two hands was an expression of the magic embedded in the solution of one of the most complex and emotional conflicts of them all and the hope it planted in hearts the world over.

Sitting in the first row of a large audience on the lawn, next to Yossi Beilin, the man who had set the move in motion, I whispered, "Can you believe it?"

"If it were true," he said, "it would be magnificent." Indeed it seemed surrealistic.

On the stage, alongside Clinton, Christopher, and Russian Foreign Minister Andrei Kozyrev, stood the chief actors in the drama: Rabin, Peres, and Arafat. The atmosphere on that platform was more tense than jubilant. As I listened to their words and watched their faces, I could not imagine three men who were more unalike than the deeply ambivalent Rabin, the incorrigibly optimistic Peres, and the half-bemused Arafat. The friction among them stemmed from the facts of life and the vicissitudes of history. During the Oslo talks, Rabin and Peres had adopted a positive attitude of pragmatic cooperation, but their feelings toward each other had not yet changed. The proceedings of the ceremony had to be meticulously worked out between them in advance. Peres, the visionary who had come to Washington prepared, even glad, to represent Israel vis-à-vis Abu Mazen (he thought Arafat's and Rabin's presence premature), was deeply conscious of the challenges and opportunities that now faced his country. Rabin, the pragmatist, saw the agreement as a national imperative and regarded the Palestinians as partners in peace but still felt toward them, and especially toward their leader, revulsion that he had great difficulty concealing. He revealed his disdain even as he shook Arafat's hand, reflecting the feelings of many of his countrymen, perhaps, but not the spirit of reconciliation so coveted and needed by Israel. Just before Peres shook Arafat's hand, Rabin whispered in his ear, "Now it is your turn." Arafat looked as though he had just landed from another planet to find himself standing beside Clinton, Rabin, and Peres. His appearance hadn't changed, but the world saw him differently that day and applauded him as a harbinger of peace. He was able to rise to the occasion but apparently saw it as the vindication of his long struggle, not the celebration of a revolution in values.

Yet I thought these three different men had some things in common—they were strong and experienced leaders not easily shaken by the tremors of change. They were all lonely and driven, convinced of the justice of their cause, and bent on achieving their goals. All three were schooled in patience and would be more influenced by the process as it went on. But on that sunny morning in Washington, the stage they shared was a wobbly bridge to a still-obscure future. The tension between their commitment to partnership and their perceptions of reality was to affect the course of the peace process from that day forward.

After the ceremony, as the crowd began to disperse, I saw Abu Ala standing amid a group of Palestinian leaders. As I walked over to him, he gave me a distracted glance. No longer sheltered by the intimacy of Oslo but caught in the open in that surreal setting, we suddenly felt an estrangement. In that instant, it seemed, we had turned from secret partners into members of different camps about to embark on a common journey. In fact, on the White House lawn that day, one sensed the various camps preparing to respond to the new situation, each in its own way.

On the starting line stood the two new partners, Israel and the PLO, who now had to translate the Declaration of Principles into something tangible. Could they work together? Could they prepare for the intricate negotiations on bringing autonomy to Gaza and Jericho? How would they deal with the reactions of their constituencies? These questions required a whole new agenda.

The first working session between Israel and the PLO was held in the afternoon of September 13 in a fifth-floor suite of the Mayflower Hotel, where Peres was staying with his entourage. Present were Peres, Abu Mazen, Yossi Beilin, and the two Oslo teams. As though rolling up his sleeves to start work, Peres outlined the three priorities in this new agenda.

"First, it's important to immediately appoint negotiating teams to implement the agreement. Second, we must focus on the key issue of economic development in the territories. I have spoken with the Norwegians, and they have already laid down a Scandinavian basis for international aid. The Americans will support it, and during my visit to Brussels I secured the cooperation of the European Union. A special organization will be established to strengthen you economically. We want to see you succeed, as we have an interest in living alongside prosperous neighbors. We have no interest in running your lives, but we are certainly willing to help you. Finally, I think we should be in daily contact and suggest that Abu Ala and Uri Savir serve as our liaisons."

Abu Mazen responded by telling Peres that he had always admired his efforts on behalf of peace. He was less businesslike than Peres but agreed that it was important to cooperate. "Yes, we must work together on the economic situation," he stressed. "Our people must feel the difference." This was the first time we met the man who had been Yossi Beilin's counterpart on the Palestinian side as the initiator of the Oslo negotiations. He was a striking presence, with his dark complexion framed by silver hair, while his embarrassed smile and soft, steady tone conveyed warmth. Abu Mazen showed no hint of the staccato manner that marked so many of his colleagues.

We didn't understand at the time that his winsome reticence and the vagueness of his response reflected the Palestinians' unreadiness to begin implementing the agreement swiftly. Their problem lay in the absence of standard constructs of government, in the overconcentration of power in Arafat's hands, in the friction among his close advisers, and in an inherently indulgent approach to time. Paradoxically, the Palestinians tended to believe time was on their side, while we were dogged by the concern that it was running out. In those first days, it was also difficult to decide what each side would do independently and what we would do in collaboration. The internalization of the change in our relationship would be gradual, even erratic. We had entered into a kind of purgatory between conflict and cooperation.

After that meeting in the Mayflower, I accompanied the Palestinians down to the lobby. We parted at the entrance to the hotel as a group of Israeli journalists stood peering at the drama of Israeli and PLO officials exchanging addresses and phone numbers (information that not long before would have been a boon to intelligence officers). I listed Abu Ala somewhere between Abba Eban and Shlomo Avineiri: "Tunis number: 2161788708."

"You can dial Tunis directly," he said, "but we still can't dial Israel or the West Bank and Gaza. It's time we came home."

"Welcome. *Ahlan wa-sahlan*," I said, extending an invitation to do so.

"*Ahlan wa-sahlan*," he echoed, either to express his amusement at my Arabic or to hint that, in his eyes, *we* were not the hosts. Our lexicon was working on two levels: one literal, the other of implication. These codes would continue to develop throughout the peace process, virtually developing a new language between us.

We took leave that day not knowing that the separation would be for a relatively long time. Arafat broke off contact with us for a number of weeks, and I didn't hear from Abu Ala for much of this time. Instead, I suddenly received a call from Abu Koush, the PLO's third man in Oslo, who asked me to meet him in Frankfurt. When I arrived, he formally announced that he was now the PLO's liaison with Israel. I was taken aback. This was our first exposure to Arafat's technique of keeping his associates off balance. In Oslo he had strengthened Abu Ala's hand, and now he was pushing him aside. But this meeting was also to be the last time I saw Abu Koush. From time to time a new Palestinian turned up as the PLO's latest liaison—though for most of the period of serious talks, Abu Ala was again my interlocutor.

The jockeying for position within the PLO was the main reason that Arafat stalled on choosing a delegation to the talks on implementing the agreement. Neither did the Palestinians do any serious preparatory work. The situation on our side was precisely the opposite. Rabin chose a new team of negotiators that launched into detailed staff work. Led by Deputy Chief of Staff Gen. Amnon Shahak, it was composed mostly of military officers. When the military grumbled bitterly at having been shut out of the Oslo talks, Rabin explained that the issues discussed in Oslo had been mainly ideological and political. But he did not reject the criticism, led by Chief of Staff Ehud Barak, that, when it came to day-to-day security, the agreement was "riddled with holes." Rabin appreciated the frustration of the men who were being asked to execute a program from whose conception they had been excluded. Yoel Singer, who represented the Foreign Ministry, was blamed for the lapses in "his" agreement. The most minute details of the future autonomy plan were subjected to meticulous scrutiny as if it were imperative to arrive at a solid prescription for every possible contingency. We had developed an almost mystical faith in the power of the written word to control reality, not always sufficiently assessing the impact of the quality of relations between the two sides on the stability.

Thus an attempt was made to harness to the Declaration of Principles forces that, having been denied a voice in its composition, had become its sharpest critics. On the part of the Palestinians, this was done by playing for time and avoiding an examination of details. On the Israeli side it was done by exploiting time and becoming obsessed with minutiae. The contrast reflected not just different approaches to the new reality but differences in the two political cultures. As they stood together on the new starting line, the Oslo partners had the same road map in hand, but they were hobbled by a number of problems, from lack of experience with each other to dissension within their respective ranks. As a result, the leaders of the two sides soon began to portray the accord as a necessity rather than an achievement.

Standing alongside the two partners was an amazed international community, which marveled at the agreement that had prompted the handshake and wanted the new partnership to flourish. On October 1, foreign and finance ministers from around the world convened in Washington, at Shimon Peres's initiative, to create an aid package for the Palestinians. They agreed to $2.5 billion (which later grew to over $3 billion) in grants and loans, primarily from the United States, the European Union, and Japan. (Once again the wealthy Gulf states disappointed their Palestinian brothers.) Norway, the modest hero of the Oslo effort, was chosen to head the aid endeavor, under Johan Jørgen Holst and Terje Larsen. Terje asked me: "Did you think you'd ever see the day when Israeli ministers would be soliciting funds for the PLO?" Israel itself pledged to contribute $25 million to the new Palestinian Authority over a period of five years.

The Arab world was stunned by the agreement. Naturally, the "rejection states" piled abuse on it. Its greatest champions were countries that had been in on the Oslo secret, mainly Egypt, Morocco, and Tunisia. In between lay a group of moderate states that were taken totally by surprise. They had long shown the Palestinians moral support but had strong reservations about their political aspirations. Jordan feared for the interests of the kingdom. The Gulf states still resented Yasser Arafat for his embrace of Saddam Hussein during the Gulf War. Yet many of these states felt liberated by the Oslo breakthrough. While we were negotiating in Norway, Abu Ala had said to me: "You'll give the key to the United States to us, and we'll open the door to the Arab world for you." Those doors began opening immediately. The day after the signing ceremony in Washington, an agenda was set for talks between Jordan and Israel that was effectively the framework of their future peace treaty. On our way back from Washington to Israel, our plane landed in Rabat, where Israel's leaders were royally welcomed by Morocco's King Hassan, a pioneer in the Israeli-Arab peace efforts.

Israel's desire to end the occupation and its recognition of the PLO relieved many Arab states of the burden of rejecting Israel implied by support for the Palestinian cause. Because we had tended to believe those Arabs who belittled the Palestinians, we had failed to understand fully that as long as Israelis ruled Arabs, there would be no peace in the Middle East. On the White House lawn, Yossi and I found ourselves seated next to the ambassador of Saudi Arabia, the suave Prince Bandar, who had been something of a star in the United States since the early 1980s. Turning to us at the end of the ceremony, he said: "I've heard a lot about you, gentlemen. Congratulations to you." Afterward, at a lunch organized by Warren Christopher, Bandar had a conversation with Peres. A few years after our brief encounter, an American official told me that in permitting Bandar to attend these events, his government had instructed him to mute his admiration for Arafat. Yet had it not been for Yasser Arafat, our meeting with a Saudi leader would not have happened. Neither would Israel's meeting with much of the rest of the Arab world.

· · ·

Our plane landed in Israel at 4:00 A.M. on the eve of the Jewish New Year. The trip, from end to end, had been less than seventy-two hours. We arrived utterly exhausted. When the plane came to a stop, Avi leaned over and whispered to me, "You'll see: Rabin will come out and wish everyone a happy new year. Peres will come out and tell us to be in his office for a meeting at eight." Indeed, Peres told us to be in his office at seven.

With sagging shoulders and bloodshot eyes, Yossi, Avi, and I arrived to find Peres looking as if he had just returned from vacation. Nothing sparked him more than a feeling of accomplishment. Sitting down opposite us, he solemnly said: "It's time to storm Jordan!" The three of us burst out laughing, then explained the reasons for our doubts. They did nothing to alter his conviction. "The king won't lag behind," he said and asked Yossi to do the groundwork for a meeting while Avi organized a trip to Amman. On October 1, Peres met for the first time with Jordan's Crown Prince Hassan, hosted by President Clinton in the White House.

Four weeks later, Peres, disguised with a porkpie hat and mustache, Avi, and Efraim Halevy of the Mossad crossed the Allenby Bridge and made their way to the royal palace in Amman. Peres, indeed, "assaulted" his host with a vision of regional peace and prosperity and the role of the Hashemite kingdom in realizing it. By the end of their conversation, King Hussein and Peres had reached an understanding on the parameters of a future peace treaty and initialed a four-page document. Since economic development stood at the top of Peres's priorities, he then proposed a daring initiative: "What do you think, Your Majesty, of inviting four thousand businessmen to Amman to discuss investing in the New Middle East?" Peres spelled out the logistics of the plan, including flying the guests by helicopter to and from Israel. King Hussein agreed in principle, and the idea was added to the understanding that had been reached between the two old friends. The secret document bore the date November 2, 1993.

Peres came home euphoric. Rabin had of course approved the trip, but he was skeptical that King Hussein would be forthcoming so soon after the deal with the Palestinians, which had been cut behind his back. Neither did the Americans expect any progress, especially given Syria's disapproval of "separate deals" and its menacing position toward Jordan. I was in Paris at that time, and at dinner with Dennis Ross and American ambassador Martin Indyk, I read them the details of the conversation in Amman. Ross was surprised. "I've stopped doubting Peres's ability to do the impossible," he said. "Please congratulate him for me." I heard in those words a change of heart about Peres, whom the Americans had considered well meaning but a bit too unorthodox for their tastes. Thereafter our working contacts with the American peace team became almost daily.

On November 4, Peres met in Jerusalem with Klaus Schwab and Gregory Blatt, the heads of the Davos World Economic Forum. Detailing the initiative he had discussed with Hussein and the king's agreement in principle, he asked them to organize an economic summit. Schwab, blessed with great imagination and drive, consented to take on the task. We suggested he work with my good friend Leslie Gelb, one of America's best political minds and the president of the Council on Foreign Relations in New York. Not a single member of Peres's close circle believed that a gathering of such magnitude would materialize in the foreseeable future. Behind his back we called it the "Conference of the Forty," after the number of people who would probably show up. Yet a year after that meeting, the Middle East and North African Economic Conference opened in Casablanca with four thousand participants from the world of business and finance. The Jordanians chose not to host it after all, but they followed Morocco's lead a year later with a meeting in Amman. All of this happened as a result of the signing of the Declaration of Principles with the PLO.

Meanwhile, a very different process was under way. What Israel, the PLO, and the supporters of peace perceived as a new point of departure was treated like a line of scrimmage by a loose coalition of forces interested in foiling the peace. The Muslim fundamentalists regarded it as a liability because their movements thrived on social and economic instability. The standard-bearers of Arab nationalism opposed compromise out of a narrow view of their interests and an incorrigible mistrust of Israel. Quickly recovering from the shock of Oslo, these groups deployed against the "threat of peace."

On the Palestinian side were such Syrian-backed opponents as George Habash, who declared that "Arafat must be thrown into the garbage"; Ahmed Jebril, who predicted for Arafat a fate identical to Sadat's; and Naif Hawatmeh, who swore to destroy the agreement by brutally violent means. There were people within the PLO proper who also viewed Arafat's compromise as capitulation to Israel's dictates. Leading this faction was Farouk Kadoumi, the equivalent of the PLO's foreign minister and formally its number-two man.

The Syrian government was not pleased by the accord, born just days after a significant (discreet) development in its own negotiations with Israel. President Assad suspected a plot to neutralize his opposition to the declaration. Nevertheless, encouraged by the American government (which had promised to continue working toward a Syrian-Israeli accord), he allowed his spokesmen to grudgingly bestow their blessings on the agreement.

The "rogue states" in the Muslim world—Iraq, Libya, Sudan, and the patron of fundamentalism, Iran—flayed Arafat for his ignominious surrender to the Zionist enemy and pledged to keep fighting on. Hamas, Iran's ally among the Palestinians, geared up for a campaign of terror meant to turn Israeli public opinion against the agreement and destroy all hope of reconciliation. These forces accompanied their shrill declarations with effective work on the ground. For the next three years, while national leaders took difficult decisions, negotiators continued talking, and new agreements were signed, death squads all over the Middle East were busy building bombs. On that line of scrimmage, two clocks began ticking: one to move the peace process toward a permanent settlement, the other to set off bombs designed to provoke fear and despair. As diplomats set out with briefcases of documents, terrorists set out in the Middle East carrying suitcases of explosives.

In Israel, too, elements began planning to foil the peace by word and deed. The radical right-wing opposition—led by settlers from the occupied territories who regarded the Oslo agreement as a threat to their ideology even more than to their personal security—was wild with rage. Hanan Porat, of the settler-supported National Religious Party, called "the relinquishment of Gaza and Jericho an act of treachery." Such inflammatory statements sowed the seeds of violence. The settlers were joined by members of the political opposition, about half of the Knesset, led by the chairman of the Likud Party, Binyamin Netanyahu. On the day that Rabin stood before the world in Washington and declared, "Enough of blood and tears," Netanyahu railed that "Israel faces an unprecedented threat to its security. The government is allowing the PLO to carry out its plan to destroy Israel." What a majority of Israelis seemed to embrace at the time as a hope for peace, others in Israel saw as an "existential threat."

The Declaration of Principles compelled those for and against Oslo to take a stand, because as soon as the agreement was signed, movement toward concrete changes on the ground was inescapable. The whole region was about to be transformed, and every faction was forced to define its core interests and how it meant to protect them. On September 13, 1993, the kaleidoscope of colliding interests and new symmetries had begun to turn. The Oslo agreement was wedged between faith in an evolving new reality and ingrained suspicions and prejudices; between common pragmatic economic interests and traditional religious and cultural convictions. But the sharpest clash over Oslo was between the supporters of a delicate, intricately crafted peace process and its ideological and physical opponents; between two partners who had decided upon a division of assets as a strategic objective and forces that wanted to have it all; between those who wished to see the walls of hate crumble and those who saw in them a necessary protection of traditional values. Thus, on the day of the famous handshake, the fate of the Middle East was no longer in Oslo but in the laboratory of real life.

Some three months after the signing ceremony, Abu Ala and I were invited to Oslo to receive a medal from King Harald of Norway. It was there that our families met for the first time. Abu Ala came with his wife, Um Ala; their daughter, Mona; their son Ala; their daughter-in-law, Delilah; and their granddaughter, Zeinah. Aliza, Maya, and I were joined by Maya's friend Avital. The younger generation hit it off quickly, especially Maya and Mona, fulfilling the hope that Abu Ala and I had expressed in our dedications to them. We toured in the Norwegian snow and listened to Oriental music, with Terje and Mona constantly at our side. It was a three-family vacation. When we visited the place where we had first met only half a year earlier, I realized how much my "Enemy Number One" had become a friend.

The king received the two of us alone. "Your Majesty," Abu Ala told him, "we have come here today as one delegation to thank you for Norway's role in the peace talks and the wonderful work of Terje Larsen and Mona Juul, but especially, today, for the part played by Foreign Minister Holst."

At that hour Holst was lying in the hospital, having suffered a stroke earlier in December. The doctors believed that his condition had been caused by overwork during the negotiations. After our audience with the king, we asked to see our ailing friend. His wife, Marianne, told us that the doctors would not permit it; his speech had been severely impaired, and he was in a deep depression. Nevertheless, later that evening Terje came to the Oslo Plaza to report that Holst wanted to see us. A Norwegian security agent drove us to the hospital, where Holst's daughter Gretchen met us in the corridor.

"He's waiting for you, and he's feeling better. He may be transferred to a sanatorium soon, for physiotherapy, because half his body is paralyzed. Don't be shocked when you see him," she warned.

But we were shocked, terribly. The Holst we knew was difficult to imagine as being ill. A tall, blond Norwegian in his fifties, he had held us in thrall with his penetrating blue eyes. The Holst we saw now propped up in bed in a dim, narrow room had tears in his eyes. His hair looked gray, and his robust body had shrunk. Yet he made a great effort to smile when he saw us.

"I'm sorry I couldn't be at the ceremony honoring you," he said in a garbled whisper.

"You were with us," I told him. "How are you feeling?"

"Better. I'll get through this. I promise I will. I'm so happy to see you, my friends," he said as he motioned us to come closer, one on each side of the bed, and held our hands.

"Promise me that you'll continue what you started here," he whispered. "Promise that you'll never give up."

We gave him our word, and Abu Ala added: "Together with you, of course." But both of us feared that these would be his last words to us.

We left the room silently and didn't speak again until we had reached the hotel, where we called Marianne to tell her, with some relief, that Holst had spoken far more fluently than we had expected and had impressed us as fighting valiantly.

"Yes," she said softly. "The doctors are optimistic."

Two weeks later, on January 18, 1994, Johan Jørgen Holst died. The postmortem showed that during the months of negotiations, he had suffered a series of mild strokes. We all flew to Oslo for the funeral. On the evening before, the tape of the August 19 secret ceremony was taken out of his safe, and we sat watching it together—Israelis, Palestinians, and Norwegians, committed to implement the agreement that our late Norwegian friend had labored to bring about.

II

Change

4

CONTRASTS AND
CONTRADICTIONS

AFTER A CENTURY OF BRUTAL COMBAT, ISRAEL AND THE PALESTINIANS now found themselves partners in what promised to be a long process of reconciliation. For thirty years Yasser Arafat had pursued a strategy of terrorism and the delegitimization of Israel. Yitzhak Rabin and Shimon Peres, who had each served as prime minister and defense minister of Israel during the worst of the PLO atrocities, had practiced a policy of harsh retaliation and fought rigidly against the intifada in the occupied territories. They had habitually portrayed the other side as savages, and their peoples adopted such language. Hardly an Israeli or Palestinian family had been spared the wounds of the seemingly endless struggle, and both peoples bore scars—physical and psychological—that remained forever fresh. And then, literally overnight, their leaders presented them with an agreement that turned mortal enemies into hopeful confederates so that neither side felt defeated. Past, present, and future merged into a swirl of new doctrines and emotions as well as a multitude of internal contradictions.

Each side hailed the agreement as a historic step. Each spoke of the great hopes it inspired for its people. But neither expressed a true change of feeling toward its erstwhile enemy. This fusion of long habit with the anticipation of revolutionary change led to an often ambivalent process, one that alternated between retreat into the familiar and bursts of constructive creativity.

Immediately after the Declaration of Principles was signed, each side had to deal with elements in its own ranks that, having been shut out of the negotiating process, were sharply critical of its results. Arafat experienced considerable difficulty (to which he was not accustomed) in getting the agreement approved by the PLO's Executive Committee, six of whose eighteen members resigned in protest over what they called capitulation. For the most part, however, he was able to neutralize the opposition by deft political maneuvers. (The Houdini of Arab politics is, among his many other talents, a master of the art of mollification.) When charm failed, he was not above resorting to the ultimate pressure by pointedly noting the lack of any alternative to his leadership. He misrepresented the agreement to his associates as a guarantee of a Palestinian state according to a fixed timetable. He also ignored its details, whenever possible, and was in no rush to start negotiating its implementation. After hearing how Arafat described the declaration to the media, Peres remarked dryly that he related to the declaration the way most travelers treat the agreement printed on the back side of their airline ticket. "It's the destination that counts, not the small print."

After the signing ceremony in Washington, Arafat distanced Abu Mazen and Abu Ala from the center of decision making. They had received far too much international attention for his taste. Abu Mazen's response was, in effect, to seclude himself in his Tunis home for over a year. Abu Ala, who was interested in strengthening the Palestinians' ties with their immediate Arab neighbors, plunged into negotiations on an economic treaty with Jordan. He even arrived at a draft that would have ensured the Jordanians a preferred status in the emerging Palestinian economy (including the adoption of the Jordanian dinar alongside the Israeli shekel). But Arafat stopped him from signing this agreement, effectively scuttling it (though he later asked Farouk Kadoumi, an opponent of the declaration, to conclude a similar agreement).

The Palestinians in the West Bank and Gaza received the declaration with a mixture of satisfaction and skepticism, for while they would finally achieve self-rule, they doubted, after twenty-six years of Israeli occupation, that much would really change. To the media, most Palestinians said that they hoped their lives "will be better, God willing"—a statement that paralleled the equally vague Israeli response, "It'll be all right." Suffering peoples tend to be fatalistic.

Yet the colors of the Palestinian streets changed immediately. Overnight Palestinian flags appeared on balconies and rooftops all over the territories. Israel dropped its foolish policy of sending soldiers to tear them down, having learned, the hard way, that you can't defeat a flag. And pictures of Arafat began to appear on houses, storefronts, and public buildings, though there was a certain ambivalence among his fellow Palestinians about the role he was about to assume. Now that the symbol of their national struggle was to become a flesh-and-blood ruler, many Palestinians worried about the arrival of the Tunis leadership, sensing that it would deny their locally grown leaders a share in power. The Palestinian intelligentsia was also concerned about taking immediate steps to start building a "civil society" in the soon-to-be autonomous areas. Dr. Haidar Abdel-Shafi, the distinguished Gazan physician who had headed the Palestinian delegation to the Madrid Peace Conference and negotiations in Washington, flew to Tunis hoping to extract a commitment to a democratic regime. He came away empty-handed; Arafat had no desire for a competing power base.

Sensitive to the public mood, however, he did take pains to sell the new agreement to his somewhat wary constituents. He spoke proudly of the declaration as the first step on the road to victory and emphasized its real significance for Palestinians by telling them: "It has put us on the geographical and political map." The sharp contrast between the PLO's routine hostility to Israel and its sudden entry into an agreement with it confused the Palestinians and slowed their preparations to carry out the agreement.

In Israel, meanwhile, preparations were intensive, almost frenetic. A new team was planning the upcoming negotiations: Deputy Chief of Staff Gen. Amnon Shahak, the head of the Israeli delegation; Gen. Uzi Dayan, chief of the General Staff's Planning Branch, the head of the committee on security issues; Gen. Danny Rothschild, the coordinator of activities in the territories and head of the committee on civilian affairs; and Yoel Singer, the sole remnant of the original Oslo Club, prepared their homework thoroughly.

Unlike Arafat, Rabin faced no difficulties getting the agreement approved by his own government, which by then was the most homogeneous one Israel had ever had (being composed of the Labor and left-leaning Meretz parties). Rabin's ministers welcomed the declaration as a historic achievement and treated his own predominance as unquestioned. Thus throughout the period following the Oslo Agreement, Israel's peace policy was decided and conducted by two men only: Rabin and Peres. Even Yossi Beilin was kept out of the loop, especially after he had irritated Peres by portraying himself, Yair Hirschfeld, and Ron Pundak as the unconventional pioneers and "heroes" of the Oslo channel, rather than supporters of the security and policy structure that was being established by Rabin and Peres. At the same time, Yossi felt the need to distance himself from his formidable mentor and strike out on his own—a decision that contributed to his impressive advance in Israeli politics but not to his future involvement in the official peace process.

The Israeli public responded to the agreement along predictable political lines. Rabin described it to his countrymen as a positive but above all necessary development that would move Israel closer to its primary goal of security. But he too ignored the need for reconciliation, and stressed the creation of a new instrument for reaching traditional objectives.

"If the Palestinians do not pass the test of reality, we can instantly control any diversion by them from the path we have agreed on. . . . We have made peace with Egypt and we will do the same with the Palestinians, even though with them it will be more difficult. . . . It is my responsibility as prime minister to put an end to the cycle of bloodshed."

Israelis and Palestinians were both caught in the contradiction between their awareness of a historic breakthrough and their efforts to implement it without jettisoning their habitual prejudices.

While each side struggled to fix its point of departure for the negotiations, it was also necessary to create the framework of the joint endeavor. On October 6, three weeks after the declaration was signed in

Washington, Rabin and Arafat met in Cairo for their first working session. It was a businesslike meeting, held in the kind of broad forum that usually permits only a formal exchange of views, not a candid dialogue. Conspicuous by their inclusion in the Palestinian retinue were three "local," as opposed to Tunis, leaders: Faisal Husseini, Hanan Ashrawi, and Ziyad Abu-Zayyed, a Jerusalemite known for his ties with the Israeli left. The Israeli delegation included Rabin's three closest aides: Eitan Haber, his chief of staff; Shimon Sheves, director of the Prime Minister's Office; and Jacques Neria, his foreign policy adviser.

The chief accomplishment of this meeting was the creation of the framework for conducting the negotiations on the exact nature of the autonomy arrangement in Gaza and Jericho, which were to be held in the Egyptian resort of Taba, just over the border from Eilat on the Red Sea. The Palestinians wanted Egypt to host these talks, since President Mubarak had long been among the most fervent supporters of their cause. Taba also had symbolic importance to them as a patch of Sinai that Egypt had won back from Israel as a result of international arbitration in 1986. Israel chose Taba primarily as a convenient location from which its negotiators could cross back into Israeli territory each night and hold their own discussions with less circumspection. Economic issues were to be negotiated in Europe (Paris) under the direction of Israel's finance minister, Avraham Shohat, and Abu Ala.

For the rest of the session Rabin, typically, lectured Arafat about security as the key test for the Palestinians, and Arafat, just as typically, presented Rabin with a number of requests. Rabin brusquely told him: "Everything must now be discussed in the new frameworks." He did, however, grant Arafat's request on one matter of symbolic significance: that the Palestinians being held under detention in Gaza would no longer be transferred to Israel.

On October 13 the initial, purely ceremonial, meeting of the Senior Joint Liaison Committee took place in Cairo between Peres and Abu Mazen and the negotiations on Gaza and Jericho opened in Taba. Heading the respective delegations were Amnon Shahak and Nabil Shaath. As they posed for the obligatory photo, the Israeli general—tall, silver haired, the very picture of aplomb—looked like a

Hollywood version of a war hero. Though a stickler for Israel's security interests, Shahak quickly earned the trust and esteem of the Palestinians, perhaps more than any other Israeli negotiator, for his humanity and ability to consider their claims and sensitivities without prejudice or presumption. Shaath, an economist who won over the press with his impeccable English, came across as a kind of Palestinian Abba Eban. He too quickly won his partners' admiration for his polished arguments and keen understanding of Israeli society, probably more than for his efficiency as a negotiator. After the formal opening remarks, the two men stole away for a private walk along the Red Sea shore. As soon as they were sighted, a herd of photographers swooped down on them for the first shots of a PLO leader in conversation with an Israeli general against the backdrop of pink mountains and an azure blue sea—photos that indeed captured the charmed mood of their talk.

But the honeymoon in Taba was short-lived. For upon setting forth their opening positions, both sides grasped that there was a huge gap between their interpretations of the Declaration of Principles. The Israeli reading stressed the civil and military powers that Israel was to retain after withdrawing its troops from Gaza and Jericho. Following a literal and legalistic interpretation of the declaration, this implied that Israel, as the official "source of authority," would grant the Palestinians limited powers and, most important, retain direct control of the crossings in and out of Gaza to Israel and Egypt, including the right to decide who was entitled to enter and leave the Strip. Israel would also continue its direct administration of the three sectors of the Strip containing Israeli settlements, their infrastructure, their agricultural lands, the roads to and between them, and the main routes affecting their security.

The Palestinian position demanded just the opposite. Israel had to withdraw completely from the Gaza Strip and Jericho, transfer control of the border crossings to the Palestinians, and patrol the international borders jointly with them. According to this approach, the Israeli settlements in the Gaza Strip would receive minimal military protection—and that only from inside their perimeters. The security of the settlements should not detract from Palestinian rights, the Palestinians claimed.

What's more, they demanded that civil powers be transferred to them wholesale, not piecemeal. As their demands were a function of their strategic goal in the peace process, one of the papers they presented in Taba explicitly stated: "Our aim is the establishment of a Palestinian state in accordance with the 1967 borders."

These were opening positions, of course, but they were reiterated ad nauseam in the course of the talks that followed. Reporting to Peres and me after the early rounds of the talks, Yoel Singer, who had no problem providing a legal basis for the Israeli position, felt that there was little chance of making headway at Taba. What was going on there, he said, was not negotiations but endless soapboxing, press briefings, and news conferences. Having gained access to bona fide PLO officials, the Israeli media relished the chance to penetrate the political process. But its involvement brought a price: pragmatic positions turned into public postures.

Each side's basic position remained essentially fixed even as the gap between them incrementally narrowed, mostly to the benefit of the stronger side. That Israel's approach was dictated by the army invariably made immediate security considerations the dominant ones, so that the fundamentally political process had been subordinated to short-term military needs. An example was an internal discussion held in Tel Aviv about how Israel should respond to the Palestinians' demand for their own state television and radio network. Eight of the ten participants in that meeting were IDF or Shabak officers, and the discussion focused on security problems—such as the possible use of these media to incite against Israel—rather than on the political benefits for the new Palestinian self-rule.

The Foreign Ministry had strong misgivings about this military emphasis but did not express them publicly. Peres did send Rabin an analysis by the Foreign Ministry Political Planning Unit that pointed out the weaknesses of the Israeli approach. Harry Kney-Tal, who headed the unit, noted that the Palestinians enjoyed the advantage of having a clear strategic goal, while Israel's attention was focused on the conduct of everyday affairs. "Israel's approach necessarily limits Palestinian freedom of movement, which undermines its own interest in cultivating ties [with them]," he argued. "This model is a prescription for hostile relations." He was right.

. . .

The Taba talks highlighted a paradox that would grow more irksome as time went on. While committed to achieving a division of powers with the Palestinians, Israel tried to impose on them a security doctrine requiring everything Israel considered important to remain in its control. The Palestinians were likewise asking for the impossible. They wanted to separate themselves completely from Israel without taking into consideration Israel's most vital interest: combating violent opposition to the peace process as the foundation of a joint strategy. Thus, contrary to the guiding principle of the Oslo negotiations, each side wanted to extract the maximum from the other, rather than exploit the advantages of a partnership.

Basic differences also emerged in the economic talks in Paris. The objective set by Israel's finance minister, without any real opposition from Rabin or Peres, was to create the economic partnership prescribed by the declaration at minimal cost to the Israeli economy. Thus Shohat proposed that the Palestinian autonomous areas remain in a single customs union with Israel; that their trade with Jordan and the rest of the Arab world be limited to a list of products determined in advance; and that the quality of their agricultural produce and environment be held to the same standards as Israel's. Above all, however, Israel wanted it understood that the free movement of Palestinian goods and citizens be subject to security considerations. In short, the Palestinians would be wholly dependent on Israel's economy and security—or, to be more precise, on Israel's *sense* of security.

The Palestinians, of course, aspired to a far broader trade with Jordan and Egypt, and they wanted lower rates of customs and value-added tax than those of their economically powerful neighbor. Most important of all, they wanted to be assured of the free movement of their workers and goods to and from Israel and beyond.

The only Israeli who warned of the negative effects of our policy was the Foreign Ministry's representative to the economic talks, Oded Eran. The independent-minded Eran (who was the Israeli diplomat most deeply involved in this peace process after Yoel and myself) rightly if unsuccessfully argued for granting the Palestinians far greater economic independence.

When I met Abu Ala in Paris, during the economic negotiations, he told me that he was impressed with Shohat as a down-to-earth, open-minded man with whom he could build a relationship of trust. He spoke of his efforts to improve the terms of the economic agreement, so that the Palestinian economy would have a real chance of getting on its feet. But he was realistic about his prospects of increasing its independence and could only hope that Israel, as the strong partner, would be wise enough to appreciate the advantages of enabling the Palestinian economy to flourish.

"Remember, without prosperity there can be no security," he said, repeating his Oslo dictum. "We must move along more quickly. Amnon Shahak is a fine man, and he'll reach an agreement with Shaath. But we must start thinking beyond the Gaza-Jericho treaty."

"It took you people a while to get organized," I chided.

"Our leaders are abroad now. Abu Mazen is in the Gulf, Arafat is in Europe, and they're being well received. They are trying to obtain as much aid as possible for the Palestinian Authority.

"But moving ahead is the key thing," he repeated. "I suggest we enter into parallel secret talks to lay the groundwork for the Interim Agreement, which is the *really* important one. This is our baby. The others see the trees but not the forest: the partnership we agreed to in Oslo. In Taba, only Yoel Singer and Hassan Asfour understand that."

I promised to talk to Peres about holding parallel secret talks. But I reminded Abu Ala that the key thing was to reach an agreement on Gaza-Jericho and quickly bring about a concrete change on the ground. He agreed, and reminded me that the sides were obliged to complete the agreement by December 13.

"You're the ones wasting time on details," I said. "What about preparing Palestinian society for autonomy by building the institutions of self-rule? That's much more important than haggling with us."

"Uri, I agree with you, absolutely," he said. "But I'm alo-o-o-one!"

We laughed and promised to stay in closer touch by phone. Neither of us expected that we would soon be seeing much, much more of each other.

Alongside the special relationship I had formed with Abu Ala in Oslo, an even more surprising chemistry was developing between Israelis and Palestinians at secret meetings in Rome and Geneva.

Amnon Shahak revealed this to me when we traveled to Cairo together in mid-December. Over the previous weeks, he and Ya'akov Perry, the chief of the Shabak, had met with Mohammed Dahlan and Jibril Rajoub, the men appointed to head Palestinian internal security ("Preventive Security") in Gaza and Jericho. The two Israelis presided over large, veteran, and highly experienced security organs. The two Palestinians were former street fighters who had pitted themselves against our "army of occupation" and consequently spent a good part of their adult lives in Israeli jails. Dahlan had been imprisoned for five years and, after being released, moved on to Tunis to become one of the heads of Arafat's security unit. As such he was a member of the chairman's inner circle and was able to build a relatively independent force composed mostly of exiles from the territories. The most striking feature of the tall, portly Rajoub, as Shahak described him, was a gravelly voice uncannily like Marlon Brando's in *The Godfather.* Both men spoke fluent Hebrew, peppered with coarse Israeli slang, and were intimately acquainted with almost every aspect of Israeli life, from politics to soccer. While in prison (Rajoub for fifteen years) they had tried to learn as much as possible about their enemy. Rajoub was particularly impressed by Menachem Begin's memoir *The Revolt,* which he liked to say was a model for his own persistent struggle against the occupation.

In their talks these four men discussed how the PLO's security forces would operate in the territories and how to coordinate their efforts to thwart terrorism. But perhaps the most remarkable (and ultimately profitable) outcome of their conversations was a backslapping relationship marked by gruff humor. They were erstwhile enemies of a special kind: oppressors and oppressed in the eyes of one side; terrorists and soldiers in the eyes of the other. Yet the Palestinians were able to curb their residual resentment, and the Israelis were careful to avoid any hint of condescension. Oddly, it was the Palestinians who felt confident that they could exert considerable influence over their own people, while the Israelis limited themselves to security issues. In any event, it was their common mastery of a language of force, tempered by human sympathy, that made their relationship so special and was to prove valuable at critical moments in the process.

Such visceral understanding was, however, not the rule. The broader matrix of the Gaza-Jericho talks was fraught with contradictions: between the commitment to a new partnership and a lingering zero-sum mentality.

Given the opening positions, the talks at Taba quickly stalled. Yoel did his best to prod the participants past a repetition of claims and counterclaims to the preparation of position papers as the basis for joint drafts. But the gulf was too wide. It would take the intervention of their leaders to get the negotiations moving. Peres and Arafat had an opportunity to meet on December 11, during a meeting of UNESCO's Committee for Cultural Exchange in Grenada, Spain. Two days later, on December 13 (the date on which the declaration timetable called for the negotiations on the Gaza-Jericho agreement to be completed), a more formal meeting took place in Cairo between Rabin and Arafat. These sessions were unpleasant but necessary, just as a crisis is sometimes needed to set negotiators on the path to progress.

In Grenada, Peres had painstakingly explained to Arafat Israel's stand on security, especially external security and the border passages. "Mr. Chairman, I'm going to give you the truth straight, without embellishment," he said. "Rabin and I are aware of your difficulties, and we're interested in seeing you succeed. But you must appreciate that violence by Hamas, which we can foresee as part of their antipeace strategy, will be met by our sharp response. We will not compromise on the operational side of controlling the border passages [to Jordan and Egypt]. We're concerned about the smuggling of weapons. Ten pistols can make for many victims," he stressed. "This is absolutely vital to our security."

Arafat, who translated this straight talk into a vision of Palestinians caged in on all sides, replied: "I cannot go for a Bantustan. Please look for another formula. You don't trust me!"

"We don't trust Hamas!" Peres replied.

"I cannot agree to this, given the opposition I face and the criticism of my associates. It's a matter of our honor. We will not permit security violations. We'll be tougher about this than you. And we can coordinate with you."

But Peres's voice turned harder. "On this we *cannot compromise*."

"Look, you have the upper hand. But don't push me into a corner," Arafat warned. "My back is up against the wall. I can't tell my people that you will control every point of entry and the border in every direction."

"The very nature of an interim arrangement is that it leaves external security in Israel's hands."

"But I rule today not on the basis of a majority but by virtue of my personal credit."

"And it's in our interest that you keep that credit. We'll go a long way to help you do so."

"But what you're offering is a Bantustan. How can I live that way?"

"We're talking about the start of a process, an interim agreement. You can explain that to your people."

The points stressed in this talk—Israel's insistence on controlling the borders, assurances of its desire to support Arafat, and the explanation that these were the terms of an *interim* agreement—were to be rehashed again and again in the negotiations. In the end, Israel's security doctrine generally prevailed. Would compliance with Arafat's demand for more power and responsibility have improved Israel's security? The truth is, we will never know.

The clash over these same issues was even more pronounced in the meeting between Rabin and Arafat in Cairo two days later. After a joint discussion with President Mubarak, the two men were left alone—for the first time. Their talk lasted about three hours, during which Mubarak waited outside the room. "Let's see which of them is stronger," he joked to Abu Ala. On the other side of the door, Rabin sat aghast as Arafat set forth his reading of the Declaration of Principles, especially of clauses on responsibility for external security. Arafat apparently felt after his earlier talk with Peres (as well as a preparatory session in Tunis with Rabin's adviser Jacques Neria) that he should take a more aggressive stance with Rabin himself. He told the prime minister that the Palestinians' relationship with Egypt and Jordan—including how they managed the borders with them—was none of Israel's business. Israel, he allowed, was entitled to defend itself against strategic threats. But the control of the borders and points of entry was strictly a Palestinian affair. That, at least, was how he understood the declaration.

Rabin, who realized that Arafat hadn't the foggiest notion of what Israel meant by "external security," treated him to a detailed explanation of the concept, which included border passages under Israel's control. From Israel's standpoint, this provision had far-reaching implications, on two counts. First, anyone entering the Palestinian autonomous area from Jordan or Egypt was effectively entering Israel as well, since there was no frontier between Israel and the West Bank or Gaza Strip. Thus, yielding to Arafat on the border crossings would strip Israel of its sovereign right to decide who could enter (and leave) its territory. Second, the autonomous entity was to be endowed with only "a strong police force" to "guarantee public order and internal security," which would fall far short of an army capable of defending national borders. So the logical conclusion, as Rabin saw it, was that Israel alone would bear responsibility for defending the borders, as well as the international crossings, against armed threat. If Arafat stood firm on this issue, the peace process would be dead. But Rabin was also determined not to let that happen. So the press was informed that the two leaders had failed to break the deadlock but would continue their discussion in another ten days.

Rabin came home appalled by Arafat's take on the declaration. Loath to hash the matter out with Arafat again, he decided that the Joint Liaison Committee—headed by Peres on the Israeli side—should be convened for a thorough clarification of the dispute. Bringing Peres back into the negotiating picture meant that the "Oslo track" was about to be revived.

At that time a few members of the old Oslo Club gathered in the InterContinental Hotel in Paris. We began by meeting for dinner in Terje Larsen's suite. Abu Ala brought his son Amer along. Yoel came with me, and the British journalist Jane Corbin, who had just completed her book on the Oslo negotiations, was invited to join us. At dinner we reminisced about Oslo and groused about the present state

of the talks. For the past few months the tables had been turned, and
we were the ones who had been kept "out of the picture." Abu Ala
was of course involved only in the economic talks in Paris. Amer
complained that he never saw his father anymore. "I'm fatherless,
penniless, and countryless," he said.

Our relaxed reunion was interrupted by a call from Mona telling
us that in a series of phone calls with Tunis, Jerusalem, and Oslo, the
Norwegians had been asked to host a meeting of the Joint Liaison
Committee, cochaired by Peres and Abu Mazen. It was to take place
in Oslo within forty-eight hours, and it was our task to contact Abu
Mazen.

Taking the phone, Abu Ala tried to locate Abu Mazen in Tunis.
Protocol and a sudden attack of mischievousness prevented me from
telling him that I knew Abu Mazen was in Morocco—courtesy of my
friend André Azulay, a Moroccan-Jewish businessman, one of King
Hassan's most trusted advisers, a friend of Abu Mazen, and an ardent
peace advocate. After a string of fruitless calls, Abu Ala finally gave up.

"Let *me* find him for you," I said, and I soon had Abu Mazen on
the line from the Hyatt Hotel in Rabat. I could see from Abu Ala's
face that his esteem for Israel's intelligence community had risen even
higher, and I did nothing to alter his impression.

At all events, it was Terje who got on the line and asked Abu Mazen
to fly to Oslo, only to hear him flatly refuse. Bewildered, he passed
the phone to Abu Ala, who plunged into a high-pitched conversation
in Arabic that likewise ended in failure. My own efforts to woo Abu
Mazen to the bargaining table suffered a similar fate. He was resolved
to have nothing to do with the peace process, whose tenor was no
longer to his taste (neither, apparently, were his relations with
Arafat). So, while waiting for Mona to call for her report on the
preparation of the talks (it was on that night that Holst collapsed in a
plane carrying him from Madrid to Oslo), we returned to the dinner
table to discuss how to ease our way back into the negotiations.

"First we must isolate the main issues: the passages, the size of the
Jericho enclave, and the transfer of powers," Abu Ala began.

"I suggest we also translate the declaration into Arabic," I said,
"because I have the impression that some of your people have never
read it."

"Or it could be that your people did a slightly 'creative' translation into Hebrew," he replied.

The next night our delegation landed at a military airfield near Oslo and was taken to the Sarpsborg guesthouse, where we had held some of our secret talks the previous summer. This time the press knew we were there, but we were determined to keep at least the substance of our meeting secret. Even though an iron fence enclosing the guesthouse was firmly locked and guarded, reporters stood watch in the freezing December cold, hoping for something to leak. They waited in vain. We had returned to secret diplomacy.

Participating in the talks, alongside Peres, were Yossi Sarid (a minister from the Meretz Party), Amnon Shahak, Yoel Singer, and myself. The Palestinian delegation, headed by Yasser Abd Rabbo, included Nabil Shaath, Abu Ala, and Hassan Asfour. Abd Rabbo, a newcomer to the negotiations who had never been a Fatah man, had split with the Democratic Front and its militant leader, Naif Hawatmeh, to found the small Palestinian Democratic Union (FIDA). The issues on the table were external security (including the passages), the size of the Jericho enclave, and security arrangements for the Israeli settlements. We worked mostly at translating our conceptual differences into concrete alternatives, so as to lay the ground for compromise. Peres, however, was resentful about having to take part in these detailed negotiations. His way of trying to win the Palestinians over was to dismiss their objections as petty and portray our doctrine as unimpeachable. Essentially he had come to offer them a flat deal: security in exchange for history.

Now that we were in Norway again, I hoped we could shift back onto the right track. Every negotiation is colored by a certain atmosphere. In this case it was the "Oslo spirit." The setting was familiar to many of us. Terje and Mona were again in control of the environment. Yet the gaps remained formidable. The Palestinians had in no way altered their position on the borders and border passages, though they were prepared to consider the notion of joint control. For the Jericho enclave, they continued to demand an area ten times larger than what Israel was prepared to offer (the difference between a district and a city). Meanwhile, insisting on its doctrine of territorial defense, Israel demanded full control of 15 percent of the Gaza

Strip in order to protect the area's three thousand Jewish settlers (compared with its one million Palestinians).

Peres did his best to persuade the Palestinians that resistance was pointless when it came to any aspect of Israeli security; he was simply not in a position to yield. Sarid, who was the very emblem of the Israeli left, backed him with vigor. Shahak held his peace during most of this discussion, leaving the work to the politicians. He knew that Peres did not always agree with the army's demands about the arrangements with the Palestinians (which he sometimes considered exaggerated) but that Peres always deferred to them. Such discipline was vital to the relationship between Israel's government, which made the principled decisions in the peace process, and its military, which had to put them into practice.

Our differences were not settled in Oslo. The Liaison Committee went on to meet four more times in the next two months, in Paris, Cairo, Davos, and Cairo again. Our next session took place on December 16, at a hotel in Versailles placed at our disposal by the French government. The setting, plus the invitation to avail ourselves of the comforts of "regal" French hospitality, helped ease the atmosphere a bit more. The Palestinians, for example, accepted Peres's suggestion to divide the terminals at the border crossings into two sections: one for all travelers to Israel and the West Bank (except Jericho), to be run exclusively by Israel; the other specifically for travelers to the Palestinian area, first in Gaza and Jericho, to be under joint Israeli military and Palestinian civil control.

It was in Paris that a more casual relationship began to develop between the two delegations. One night at dinner Peres, who as the senior member of the group sat at the head of the large, elegantly appointed table, asked both delegations their opinions on whether Syria's President Assad would make peace. Most of the Palestinians expressed skepticism (probably born of self-interest, if not outright hostility toward the Syrian leader) and ventured that Assad would try to gain time by remaining inflexible. Abd Rabbo, who was most familiar with Syria and its society, was positive that Assad would hold back out of concern for the stability of his regime. In those early days of the peace process, hearing Arabs talk freely about other Arabs— like being given a peek into your neighbors' family life—was an experience we savored. The Palestinians, like their Arab brothers, did not deprive us of it.

The negotiations themselves, however, barely inched forward. A week later, when we again convened in Cairo, Peres was totally fed up with the pace of the talks and decided to jolt them forward by mounting an attack on our counterparts, this time strengthened by the one-time presence of Abu Mazen.

"I'm going to give this one more chance. I haven't come here to play around," he bellowed, to the astonishment of both the Palestinians and his Israeli colleagues. "You're wasting precious time, and you can do that without me! As far as I'm concerned, you can sit here all month. You're bickering over details and don't see what's really important!"

The scolding was in part tactical but mostly an expression of his genuine exasperation. Usually a man of great forbearance, Peres has little patience for anything he considers trivial. Not only did he read the Palestinians' stand as pigheadedness but the Palestinians were the only object at which he could vent his frustration, since he could hardly direct it at our negotiators without causing turmoil in his own house. When we got down to the bargaining itself, Shahak cut the Palestinians some slack on Jericho by offering to increase the size of the enclave to twenty-one square miles. The focal issue then became the border passages—and justly so, since they were a microcosm of the autonomy concept as a whole.

For almost twenty-seven years since the Six-Day War, the Allenby Bridge connecting Jordan with the occupied West Bank had been kept open to the passage of people and goods even though Israel and Jordan were formally at war. Tens of thousands of Palestinians crossed it every month. But the search procedure at the bridge, which was also a potential entry for terrorists and weapons, was humiliating in its thoroughness. For hours, sometimes an entire day, Palestinians would wait to undergo a body search, after every item in their luggage had been scrupulously examined. Those endless waits became one of the most hated symbols of the occupation.

Eradicating this symbol, and creating a foothold at the Jordan River, was more important to the Palestinians than almost anything else. Our partners stressed the need to put a stop to the humiliation—a word voiced repeatedly in the talks, out of genuine pain and anger. It was imperative, they argued, that the Palestinians sense a radical change when they entered their home territory. They therefore demanded the "Palestinization" of the border crossings, by the introduction of Palestinian symbols, the presence of Palestinian officials, and a thorough revision of the search and administrative procedures. We continued to insist, however, that a security check of every Palestinian entering the autonomous area, thereby becoming a potential visitor to Israel, remain Israel's exclusive prerogative.

"We'll have our security and you'll have your dignity" was how Peres put it to the Palestinians.

The problem was that the two needs clashed at every point of the border passage—as they essentially did everywhere else—and the solution would have to be creative. Since security is an absolute value to Israelis, our room for maneuver was limited. The Palestinian claim that relieving the humiliation would improve security held little weight with our generals. The territories, they countered, were already rife with terrorists, to whom the values of human dignity and respect for others were irrelevant. Hence our first dialogue in Cairo soon deteriorated into an argument in which both sides had valid but irreconcilable claims.

"Amnon, you see everything only in terms of immediate need and never consider the long-term ramifications," Shaath complained.

"Nabil, if there is terrorism, there won't be any long term to worry about," Shahak shot back.

Peres, who was now bored with the bickering, decided to intervene in almost every detail of the crossing procedure in order to find a creative solution. Calling for a large sheet of paper, he ordered it placed on the floor and, as almost everyone else got down on all fours, described his conception of the border terminals while Shaath and Shahak translated it into a sketch. It was at this point that the door suddenly opened and in walked Abu Mazen, who had finally agreed to rejoin the talks. At first he stood rooted in the doorway, startled by the sight of grown men in suits and ties sprawled on the floor of the negotiating room. Then he joined us there.

Each terminal was to have two entrances: one for Israelis and other travelers destined for Israel, the other for Palestinians. We were able to agree on the general structure of the building, and it was understood that Israel could do as it pleased in its half of the terminal. The debate was over the procedure on the Palestinian side.

It began as a sharp disagreement over whether the Palestinians would fly their flag and station one of their policemen at their entrance. Actually, the Palestinians wanted these two symbols of sovereignty to be featured on the Allenby Bridge itself. They also demanded that the electronic metal detector, through which travelers would have to pass inside the terminal, be flanked by two security men: one Israeli, the other Palestinian. The search of any Palestinian who "beeped" while walking through the detector would be conducted in a special closed cell by a Palestinian policeman (or policewoman) in the presence of an Israeli counterpart. Luggage would be channeled to a closed Israeli facility for an electronic scan. Suspicious suitcases would be opened and checked by an Israeli policeman, in front of their owner, with a Palestinian policeman present.

Following the security check, Palestinian travelers would move on to Passport Control and present their documents at a Palestinian counter, after which, we insisted, they would repeat the procedure at an Israeli counter. If our officials had reason to suspect a Palestinian entering the area, they could interrogate him, or her, without a Palestinian policeman present. But the Palestinians howled at the idea of a separate Israeli passport check. They reiterated that every Palestinian entering the autonomous area must savor the feeling of coming home. They were even more opposed to the conduct of interrogation without a Palestinian policeman in the room. It was outrageous, they cried, that a citizen returning to his native soil should be forced to answer to outsiders. We countered, yet again, that anyone entering the Palestinian area could later make his way into Israel, so we refused to yield.

At that point Peres, who had been nursing his anger since the session began eight hours earlier, lost his patience altogether and decided simply to try to impose the terms of a compromise. Summoning Avi Gil's assistant, Yoni Peled, a young cadet in the foreign service, he stood in the middle of the room and began dictating—at an impossible rate—his version of the understanding ostensibly reached in that session. To prevent the Palestinians from getting a word in edgewise, he barked at the terrified cadet, "Write faster!" When Shaath nevertheless tried to amend the wording at one point, Peres bluntly told him not to interrupt. He accepted the first part of the Palestinians' claims about the flag, policeman, and metal detectors while stressing Israel's passport control and security check.

So went the genesis of the "Yoni Document." The Palestinians were handed a photocopy of it, in Peled's shaky scrawl, and they took it to Cairo Airport, where they were to meet Arafat as he passed through for an update on the talks. Once again the PLO chairman proved to his negotiators, and ours, that one and only one man makes the decisions for the Palestinians. He summarily rejected the document.

When the Palestinians returned to our hotel and reported Arafat's reaction, Peres became even angrier. Springing out of his chair, he announced that we were leaving Cairo and told them to relay their objections to Jerusalem as soon as possible. Two days later, on December 30, Peres and Shahak each received a fax from Nabil Shaath that included an integrated summary, as the Palestinians understood it, of the points settled in Oslo, Paris, and Cairo (the Yoni Document). Following it was a list of more serious amendments requested by Arafat, including the posting of a Palestinian policeman on the Allenby Bridge, the deletion of an Israeli passport check for Palestinian travelers, and a significant extension of the Jericho enclave eastward to the Jordan River and southward toward the Dead Sea. Ever since the days of the Oslo track, the Palestinians had been fighting for a foothold on the border with Jordan.

Peres sent back a sharp reply that Israel would abide no changes in the understanding reached in Cairo other than stylistic ones. Shaath agreed to the resumption of the Taba talks, but they were nevertheless postponed. By then I was in Oslo with Abu Ala on our joint family vacation, and we began to explore ways to reach a more solid understanding. He was convinced that given the disarray within the Palestinian delegation, caused by the friction among Abu Mazen, Abd Rabbo, and Shaath, it was necessary to bring Arafat directly into the negotiations. Three weeks later that's exactly what happened.

On January 20, Arafat and Peres were both in Oslo for Johan Jørgen Holst's funeral. It may well have been this "return to the source" that brought us back to more productive negotiations. Peres and Arafat met twice during their stay in Oslo and agreed to let Yoel Singer and Abu Ala prepare a legal draft of an agreement, leaving the disputed points open. They also pledged to continue meeting until all the issues were resolved, and they appointed new teams to work under them.

The decisive meetings on the border passages were held on January 28–29 in Davos (where the Conference of the World Economic Forum was being held) and on February 7–9 in Cairo. The Palestinian delegation, headed by Abu Ala, included Akram Haniye and Gen. Abdel Razak Yihye. With the approval of Rabin and Shahak, Peres appointed working groups that later became the core of the Israeli delegation to the talks on the Interim Agreement. I was named head of the working groups, along with Uzi Dayan and Yoel Singer. Uzi, Moshe Dayan's nephew, had inherited much of his uncle's intelligence, originality, charm, and cheek. A bold and forthright man, a war hero, a veteran commando officer, he has a knack for captivating interlocutors, regardless of their origins or station, though one never knows whether the arrows he is aiming at their hearts are tipped with honey or vinegar. He was responsible for forging much of the Israeli security doctrine that would prevail in the future. At first the Palestinians found Uzi arrogant and hostile, but in time they appreciated his qualities as a hard but wise and sensitive man. Uzi and I are very different men, who came to the negotiating table from almost polar opposite backgrounds, yet we soon became close colleagues and friends. Our ability to complement each other contributed to the conceptual foundations of the two future agreements. In time, Rabin and Peres encouraged full cooperation between us.

So we sat nights in Davos, and afterward in Cairo, raking over the issue at the heart of the autonomy concept: the border passages to Jordan and Egypt. After the earlier work done in Oslo, Paris, and Cairo, four problems remained. The Palestinians insisted on flying their flag and stationing a policeman on the Allenby Bridge. They also wanted to manage the Palestinian wing of the border terminals, were adamantly against a separate Israeli interrogation of suspect Palestinians, and wanted to issue entry visas to their area for up to nine months, without Israel's approval. We opposed them on almost every point. We vetoed the possibility of placing a Palestinian policeman and flag on the bridge because we were determined to avoid any sign of a Palestinian presence on the actual border with Jordan. We also insisted that suspect Palestinians be interrogated by Israel, without a Palestinian policeman present. We agreed, however, to extend the length of Palestinian visas, but only to a maximum of six months.

The negotiations were brutal. Once again we came up against the great gap in our perceptions of what was important. For Israel the critical issue was security; for the Palestinians it was political and national pride. Yet we made some progress in the long, nocturnal talks in Davos, particularly on the wording of details. The negotiations on these sticking points peaked in Cairo on February 7. It was 1:00 A.M. by the time Peres and Arafat sat down for a chat in the Egyptian Foreign Ministry while the two delegations waited outside, fearful that once the tête-à-tête had ended, our leaders would promptly send us to work while they themselves went to sleep. If that was what they had in mind, we vowed solemnly, we would refuse. At 2:00 A.M. Arafat and Peres emerged from the room and strode toward us smiling. Then Peres, while clapping his hands, announced: "We've agreed, the chairman and I, that our delegations will work around the clock, in order to arrive at an agreement swiftly. If there's a problem you can't solve, feel free to wake us at any hour."

We looked at one another gingerly, and someone dared to say: "Fine. We'll start out fresh tomorrow morning."

"My dear friend," Peres replied with a grin, "by morning you'll have finished the job."

We surrendered, of course, and as our "common enemies" went to sleep, we arranged ourselves in the Palestinian wing of the official guesthouse in the Andlous Palace, three on each side of the table. Abu Ala began, as usual, on an optimistic note.

"If we're prepared to accomplish many things together, we'll reach an agreement quickly. The chairman told me today that we must be forthcoming on everything related to security but must insist on one main condition: giving our people the sense that things have changed as a result of this agreement. It is necessary that when they enter, they will feel pride in having come to their home—without Israeli humiliation along the way. If you share our goodwill, we too can go to sleep before morning."

"Abu Ala, you know that we've made every effort to change the situation," I replied. "The dignity of the Palestinian citizen is important to us too. And his sense that the agreement has changed things for him is critical. But I can promise you, with certainty, that we won't compromise on anything related to security. You're still inexperienced and don't understand our own problems with our own people. The passages lead not only to the autonomous area but to the State of Israel. If a bomb is smuggled in, no amount of pride and self-respect will salvage the agreement." I then suggested that Uzi Dayan present our demands. As he spoke I noticed that his tone was more placating than usual.

"We have no interest, Abu Ala, in embittering the lives of 99.9 percent of your people, who are undoubtedly peace-loving citizens," Uzi began. "For their sake, as well as ours, we must block the entry of weapons and of terrorists bent on destroying our agreement. We have many years' experience doing this. We want to check their luggage on our own. Above all, we must insist on defining who is a suspect and interrogating him, if necessary, alone."

"And recruit him to the Shabak." Akram Haniye laughed bitterly.

"Akram, you can make jokes," Uzi said, his tone growing harsher. "But on this point there will be no compromise."

"Uri, you know that even back in Oslo we wanted to share responsibility for the passages," said Abu Ala. "We're prepared to move closer to your position, which essentially gives you control over security. But I will not agree to the degradation of my people! You, here,

I trust. But tomorrow some officer or border policeman may come along with a yen to torment Palestinians. They can do that, if you like, but not with our consent. You're already doing that without our consent. If that's what you want, fine—keep on doing it."

One could almost hear the teeth gritting in the room. Yoel, who had been silent up to that point, tried to ease the tension by suggesting that we systematically review the stages of the passage that had yet to be agreed upon and try to find solutions. "If we fail, we'll wake the leaders. They deserve it," he said.

Our laughter cleared the air a bit, and Abu Ala picked up saying, "I agree that you can check the belongings on your side of the terminal. But the luggage must be opened together."

"That's fine," Uzi conceded.

"If a Palestinian is spotted as a suspect, you will not check him alone," Abu Ala continued.

"Abu Ala, a suspect is a suspect," Uzi countered, "and you've yet to prove that you appreciate the extent of the danger."

Abu Ala did not take well to preaching. "We understand what our people feel, and if you don't, there won't be peace."

"I'm aware of both your feelings and your obligations," Uzi replied. "So you will be able to question the residents of Gaza and Jericho at your passport control counter. But afterward, Israel will have to check their passports and ask the relevant questions."

"If the Israeli isn't visible, we're prepared to agree to that."

"The Israeli can stand behind a one-way mirror," I added. "But after checking the passports, which will be handed to him by a Palestinian policeman, he must be able to ask questions."

Abu Ala emitted a shriek of laughter. "Do you know what will happen to my grandmother if a mirror suddenly starts talking to her? She'll have a stroke. On the spot! And it'll be your fault." We laughed.

"Perhaps we can arrive at a solution whereby the Israeli will not be seen or heard but will be able to check the documents and interrogate suspects in a closed place," Uzi said.

"Uzi, we've heard you speak of that closed space as a 'sterile area,' " Abu Ala charged. "You relate to our people like animals!"

At that point, I too raised my voice. "If you want to conduct a polemic, we can join you. Remember, we're talking about averting terrorism. We have no intention of humiliating your people; we want to prevent the destruction of the process. Now, to the point, what do you think of the idea?"

"I must consult with the chairman." Abu Ala retreated. "It's almost morning, so let's take a break. We'll talk with Arafat and continue tomorrow."

At breakfast the next morning in the hotel's large dining room, we were able to report a measure of progress. Yoel had summed it up in a new draft. Peres told us to keep going on the basis of the previous night's proposal. But at the same time he discovered, in discussing some issues with Uzi, that every word of our talks was being relayed to the General Staff by one of Uzi's assistants, to be scrutinized by an IDF Planning Branch team that had been appointed by Rabin and Ehud Barak. Peres was infuriated. He felt that Rabin was not giving him sufficient backing, even though he was putting himself on the line in defending the security establishment's doctrine.

"This is no way to conduct negotiations!" he growled as he left the table angrily. He returned to his room, with only Avi Gil at his side. Our whole delegation—and perhaps others as well—could hear him shouting into the phone at Rabin: "If someone in Tel Aviv wants to censor me, I'm prepared to come back home. What was agreed between us, Yitzhak, is the only thing that's binding. We're fighting a tough battle here, and I won't work this way. The team sitting in Tel Aviv is negotiating with itself! How about sending them here? Let *them* persuade the Palestinians!"

Rabin apparently tried to calm him, and the "watch committee" in Tel Aviv stopped relaying its picayune comments to Cairo. From Peres's standpoint, this was also a signal, to everyone involved, that what he decided together with Rabin was all that counted for everyone, including the defense establishment. But he continued to boil all that morning. He wanted to make progress, and when he is driven, he's better—more forceful—at negotiating than anyone else. He then invited in Egyptian Foreign Minister Amr Moussa and gave him a piece of his mind.

"The Palestinians are toying with words," he groused. "They're trying to play for time. Tell them that I don't have time. Tell them they must move forward, not stick to their guns over nonsense. Otherwise there's no point in my being here."

Moussa tried to soothe him by promising to speak with Arafat. Then I had a private talk with Abu Ala and warned him that Peres's patience was running out.

"I understand him," Abu Ala said, "but his demands are unreasonable. You want to continue the humiliation by calling it 'security.' We can speed up the pace of the negotiations. But we can't bypass the issues."

It was midday by the time the two delegations reconvened. Meanwhile Uzi had refined the original compromise. Palestinian residents of the autonomous area, it now read, would be met at Passport Control by a Palestinian official, who would check their official documents and ask the relevant questions. An Israeli policeman would sit behind a one-way mirror and be neither seen nor heard. The Palestinian passport would be passed to him in a box. If it aroused any suspicions, its bearer would be sent for a further check in a room manned only by an Israeli. Finally, Israel would have the right to detain any suspect, after informing the Palestinian police.

Abu Ala was still not satisfied. "I insist that the criteria for choosing suspects be defined in advance, in the agreement," he said. "For example, a person trying to smuggle weapons, or planning an attack, or carrying suspicious documents. That will ensure you can't detain whomever you please."

This made it clear that the Palestinians had finally grasped that Israel would not yield on its security concept, therefore they would have to accomplish as much as they could within its limitations. Yoel offered to formulate this clause in a way acceptable to both sides. Then Abu Ala went off to confer with Arafat. Upon returning, he announced that the compromise was a painful one for the Palestinians, but they accepted it. However, they continued to insist that the Palestinian wing of the terminal be managed by Palestinians, with an Israeli security officer stationed there.

Uzi objected vigorously. "The place is fundamentally a security area," he said, "and it must be managed by Israel."

So we plunged into yet another crisis and retired for more consultations. It was Peres who suggested that Abu Ala and I try to solve the problem between us, which we did. The terminals at both Rafah and the Allenby Bridge would be directed by an Israeli, responsible for both wings, with a Palestinian deputy, bearing the title "manager," responsible for the Palestinian wing. Abu Ala added that the Palestinian manager would be backed up by security and administrative aides. We had arrived at last at a compromise that satisfied both sides.

The agreement on the border passages was now ready. In both its problematic aspect and its style of problem solving, it stood as a paradigm for the network of relations that was being woven around Palestinian autonomy as a whole. The detailed annex on the border passages was ultimately 180 pages long. It allowed Israel to continue to control its security and the Palestinians to have their national symbols and maximum respect for their dignity. Most important, it fixed the parameters of an operational system that required close cooperation on the ground.

Having overcome that barrier, we immediately went on to tackle some of the broader security problems. The chief issue was control of the three lateral roads leading from Israel to the blocs of Israeli settlements in the Gaza Strip. This would have to be settled directly with Arafat. In the afternoon a map was spread out before a large group of Palestinians, Egyptians, and Israelis in the guesthouse dining room. It revealed, for the first time, Israel's proposal for handling security in the Gaza Strip.

"Without control of the lateral roads, we cannot reach any agreement," Peres said to Arafat. "They're integral to safeguarding the settlements, and we won't leave that task to you. Why would you want it, anyway?"

Arafat accepted in principle, but he balked at the notion that the roads themselves would be marked as Israeli territory, since that would effectively fracture his hegemony over Gaza. Instead, Arafat suggested that the Palestinians would build positions from which to protect Israeli traffic to and from the settlements.

Someone in the room whispered: "Did I *hear right*?"

In the end, Yoel came up with the formula that on the three lateral roads, including their adjacent sides, "the Israeli authorities will have

all necessary responsibilities and powers in order to conduct independent security activity." Peres insisted that these understandings be
initialed in order to cement the breakthrough and allow the negotiations on the other issues to proceed. Abu Ala complained bitterly that
we had presented the Palestinians with a fait accompli by showing
them the maps at the last minute. Seated beside me at the ceremony
that evening, he tried to avoid initialing the attached map. It took
Mubarak's intervention to have Arafat order him to do so. This con-
tretemps was merely a prelude to a drama to come.

President Mubarak was optimistic at the initialing ceremony and announced that the negotiations on the rest of the Gaza-Jericho agreement would be completed within a few weeks. Yoel took Peres aside
and made it clear that although a breakthrough had been achieved,
most of the work still lay ahead. Shahak and Shaath and their teams
would have to produce dozens of pages of detailed paragraphs on security arrangements, legal issues, the transfer of powers, and so on.

"Will you finish in another two weeks?" Peres asked.

"It will take at least two months," Yoel replied—and he was the
most experienced member of our team.

Yet once Amnon Shahak resumed command over the working
groups in Taba, the talks began to move along quickly. Yoel and Nabil
Shaath managed to turn out pages and pages. Within two weeks, the
agreement was in sight, if not actually in reach. The IDF had begun
to plan its withdrawal from Gaza.

And then the roof fell in.

5

FROM TUNIS TO GAZA

At about five in the morning on Friday, February 25—in the midst of the Jewish holiday of Purim and the Muslim holy month of Ramadan—Dr. Baruch Goldstein, a religious settler from Kiryat Arba, born and raised in Brooklyn, donned his IDF reserves uniform, picked up his Uzi submachine gun, hitched a ride to the Cave of the Patriarchs in Hebron, entered the hall where Muslims were at prayer, and opened fire on the worshipers. Thirty-one men were cut down in the massacre before he was killed by other worshipers. The news spread swiftly through the West Bank, the Gaza Strip, the Arab states, the Muslim world, and the entire globe. The response was shock, rage, and, among the Palestinians in the territories at least, chilling fear.

Goldstein, who was described by his neighbors as a quiet and kindhearted physician, had been the spokesman of Rabbi Meir Kahane's racist Kach movement in the United States and remained identified with its branch in Kiryat Arba. Although the leaders of Israel's political and religious establishments condemned the atrocity, Goldstein soon developed a following among religious settlers. Hundreds of people attended his funeral, and many of them lauded him as a "hero" and a "saint" who had acted on behalf of all Israelis. Rabbi Ariel, the former Rabbi of Yamit, compared Goldstein with Samson and Judah the Maccabee. The press reported threats against any resident of Kiryat Arba who dared denounce the massacre. Most outrageous of all, Baruch Goldstein's grave in Kiryat Arba became a shrine.

Perhaps even worse than the extremists were the people who spoke of the massacre in ambivalent terms. Judith Katzover, wife of the mayor of Kiryat Arba, commented that Dr. Goldstein had committed an act with important implications, though she didn't think she would educate her children to emulate it. Such equivocation reinforced the moral position on which Goldstein had been nurtured: that murder can be a constructive act if committed, at the discretion of the individual, for the sake of the common good. It's impossible to know, in statistical terms, the extent of support for this view in Israel. In any case, although few supported the atrocity itself, the ideology that inspired it held considerable sway over large segments of the extreme, mostly religious, right in Israel. The impression left by the massacre's aftermath was that the Israeli government would hereafter be forced to combat terrorism on two fronts. The peace process was now facing a threat from both Arab and Jewish fundamentalism.

Most of Israel was in shock when it heard the harrowing atrocity committed by one of its own citizens. In Jerusalem, I convened the Foreign Ministry's division heads. David Afek, director of the Center for Policy Research, explained the gravity of the incident by saying that the massacre would be perceived as an assault on Islam and would become fixed in Muslim history. He also made it plain that Arafat now found himself in a very difficult situation, with a slaughter in the midst of talks on implementing an agreement that at any rate far from satisfied the Palestinians' national aspirations. Rabin and Peres plunged into a round of consultations. We all sent Arafat our deepest condolences. When rioting immediately broke out in Hebron and another five Palestinians were killed, the army decided to quell the frenzy by imposing a curfew on the city. In the eyes of the world, this made matters worse, as the Palestinians charged that it was the victims of violence who were now being punished. At the same time, members of the radical Israeli right were placed in detention, and the government outlawed two racist groups: Kach (to which Goldstein had belonged) and Kahane Chai ("Kahane Lives").

A tumultuous debate was raging in Israel over how such a horror could happen and whether Baruch Goldstein was insane and an isolated phenomenon or his deed was a symptom of a full-blown epidemic of fanaticism. The answers to these questions came later, in the course of 1995.

But the most drastic decision was taken by Arafat. He announced a halt to the talks with Israel. In response, Rabin promptly sent his policy adviser, Jacques Neria, to see the chairman in Cairo. Upon returning to Jerusalem, Neria described Arafat's mood in very somber tones and relayed his conditions for resuming the talks as the removal of all Jewish settlers from Hebron to Kiryat Arba, the establishment of a Palestinian police force in the city, and the introduction of an international force in Hebron to help calm the fears of its residents. At the same time, Arafat had asked the UN Security Council to convene in order to condemn Israel and endorse his terms for renewing the talks. There were some in Israel who thought Arafat was exploiting the tragedy to strengthen his political hand. But Rabin and Peres took his plight seriously and felt that he must be helped at this time of anguish to his people. In the days following the massacre, Dennis Ross, the U.S. State Department's peace process coordinator, also entered the picture. He maintained ongoing contact with Arafat and every few hours called me in Jerusalem and Terje Larsen in Oslo to discuss how to navigate through the crisis.

I was unable during those frightful days to contact my partner Abu Ala. I could only begin to imagine how depressed he was. Terje told me that Abu Ala was holed up in his house. He felt responsible for the Oslo Agreement and believed that the criticism now being dumped on it was aimed directly at him. Terje advised me not to phone Abu Ala, and I knew that this was at his express request.

On March 14 Rabin and Peres decided to send Uzi Dayan, Jacques Neria, and me to Tunis. Ross was also on his way to Tunis; so was Terje Larsen. In his briefing before our departure, Rabin asked us to explain to Arafat our difficulty in accepting his conditions. He also told us to try to move forward and explore bridging formulas for resuming the Gaza-Jericho talks. Peres asked us to lay the groundwork for his own future meeting with Arafat.

After taking off at 11:00 P.M. in a small executive jet, we spent the flight planning our approach to Arafat. As we flew over Malta, the pilot received the message that Peres wanted us to land in Rome. We were given no explanation but assumed that someone would be awaiting us. At Fiumicino we taxied up to the terminal and climbed out into the chill night. Though it was only 1:00 A.M., the huge airport was deserted except for two armed Italian policemen fast asleep in the arrivals hall. We decided to take a cab into Rome, where we could clarify the fate of our mission. But there were no cabs either. The money-changing machine wasn't working, the airport administrative offices were empty, and the director on duty was sleeping in a small car parked on the sidewalk. Even Uzi's calls over the P.A. system—"Hello-o-o-o! Is anyone there?"—were to no avail.

"We've taken Fiumicino!" Uzi joked. Finally I called my chief aide, Rafi Barak, in Jerusalem. Rafi was wide awake and expecting our call.

"What are you doing in Rome? You're supposed to be in Sicily!" he wailed. "The Tunisians won't let you land because the plane has Israeli markings. So Ross agreed to send the State Department plane to an American air base in Sicily for you."

"How in the Lord's name do you get there?" I asked.

"You think *I* know?" Rafi said. "Let me put you through to Ross in Tunis, via the State Department switchboard."

Dennis sounded tired and petulant, which was not at all like him.

"Get to Sicily!" he snapped. "I've sent the plane for you, and half my team—Dan Kurtzer and Aaron Miller—are waiting for you there. We've got a lot of work to do here."

Then he connected our pilot to his security man, who explained how to locate the field. We took off again at about four, searched for the base from the air, and were met there by the irritable Kurtzer and Miller. This was the second night they had gone without sleep.

We hoped that in Tunis we would all be able to sleep, because Arafat begins his workday relatively late. An American embassy car took us to the Hilton. In the lobby I was approached by a bearded young man.

"Are you from Tel Aviv?" he asked.

Warily I told him, "Yes."

"Excellent. Welcome," he said. "President Arafat is expecting you. Please register at the desk and wait in your rooms until you hear from me."

The atmosphere was unnerving. Waiting for each of us was a reg-
istration card under the name of the PLO! It was 8:00 A.M. "At least
we can rest," I sighed. I was wrong. A few moments after I lay down,
the phone clanged at my ear and a voice announced: "Monsieur Uri,
the president's driver is waiting for you downstairs." We were driven
to the Mutuel Ville section. Tunis was beautiful and very colorful. My
wife, Aliza, who was born there, had described it to me exactly as I
found it: a Mediterranean city set against softly colored sand and an
azure sea.

Within the city was an "exterritorial" neighborhood under the control of the PLO. We were taken to a modest guesthouse and waited,
tense and exhausted, in the lounge. The room was decorated in classic
kitsch, with paintings and photos of Arafat on the walls. Suddenly we
heard the screech of tires and a cry that must have meant "Attention!"
Arafat entered in a military stride, embraced Jacques Neria, and shook
Uzi's hand and mine. Then he invited us to sit on the sofa to the left
of his slightly frayed armchair. Behind him came his entourage, of
Yasser Abd Rabbo, Nabil Shaath, Akram Haniye, and Abu Ala. They
shook our hands coldly. Abu Ala avoided my glance.

Arafat pressed a small button, and a uniformed man appeared.
Smartly saluting the chairman, he was asked to serve a spread of
cakes, baklava, fruit, coffee, and tea. Arafat insisted that we partake of
them. Uzi refused a honey-drenched piece of baklava that was offered
him by Arafat himself. To avoid a diplomatic incident, he smiled and
said charmingly, "Mr. Chairman, I honor you greatly, but I fear my
wife even more." We all smiled, for the first time at that meeting. It
also proved to be the last.

We extended condolences, after which I added: "The situation is
very bleak. Israel, too, is in deep shock. Both sides are losing faith in
the peace process. Our mission, Mr. Chairman, is to find a way to
renew that faith, because the process is the only way. The prime minister and foreign minister would like you to tell us how you envision
the coming weeks. Last night, for the first time in Israel's history, the
government outlawed political groups that hope to thwart the peace
process by violence. Mr. Rabin has asked me to assure you that we
will fight extremists uncompromisingly. Rabin and Peres believe that

the talks should be accelerated now—especially now—perhaps far from the cameras. They want us to enter into marathon talks and effect a concrete change on the ground."

Arafat responded, "First of all, allow me to welcome you, gentlemen. I was very worried about you last night. All my colleagues here went to sleep. The only one who stayed awake out of concern was the chairman of the PLO. I should explain that we have an upside-down pyramid here: I work and they rest."

He paused for a few seconds and then came to the point. "Yes, the situation is very grave," he replied. "When Prime Minister Rabin phoned me to say you were coming, I was on the other line with my people in Hebron. They told me that after an understandable outburst of anger there, your army shot at our citizens. I don't understand your logic. Thirty-nine Palestinians have been killed since February 25, four hundred have been wounded, and you place the West Bank under curfew? You punish the victims? You saw the demonstrations in Amman, Rabat, Cairo, Indonesia, Iran, Tashkent, Egypt, Tunisia—everywhere!"

Here Arafat's tone became sad and tired. "In Jordan, Lebanon, and Syria, I'm accused of being a traitor. A traitor, gentlemen. *A traitor.* My people are living in dread of yet another massacre. *You* must take steps to rebuild *our* trust, otherwise the peace process will die. But instead, your army fires on my people."

"Mr. Chairman," I said softly, "time is working against us all. Matters haven't improved over the last seventeen days. We've come to find a way out of this situation, not to offer a cosmetic touch-up."

"This is a sad meeting," Uzi said. "I hear the grief in your voice, Mr. Chairman, and you have ample reason for feeling it. I personally am grieved and ashamed that the murderer wore an IDF uniform. An inquiry commission has been appointed to investigate the army's measures. There's no question that we take responsibility. We didn't prevent the massacre. We'll do all we can to prevent such an atrocity from ever happening again. But there are rumors about Palestinian plans to take revenge. Your people are in rage, and our soldiers are very tense. That's why we had to impose a curfew. We intend to lift it gradually. Our people are in contact with your leaders in Hebron."

Arafat and Haniye asked about right-wing elements and settlers serving in the reserves in the West Bank. Arafat repeated his theories about a conspiracy of Israeli officers against the commanders of the army or in collaboration with Palestinian extremists. It's not clear whether he did this for tactical reasons. But since he lives in a conspiratorial atmosphere, he may truly have believed these theories. At any rate, Uzi reacted sharply.

"The IDF acts solely at the government's direction," he said. "It is responsible for maintaining security, but the decisions themselves are taken by the cabinet. We bear responsibility for Israelis and Palestinians. We must decide how to restore the people's hope. They're in desperate need of it now."

"I remain faithful to the Declaration of Principles," Arafat assured us. "The question is indeed how to restore mutual trust, how to regain the feeling we shared in Washington on September 13. Imagine if I had already been in Jericho when the massacre took place. We must ensure the security of the Palestinians."

Arafat seemed restless and more tired than ever. His foot kept tapping on the floor, and I noticed his hands were trembling.

"Who can ensure the security of the Hebronites now?" he asked. "Perhaps you will agree to an international force? Is it possible to move the settlers out of Hebron? Altogether there are forty-two Jewish families there and a hundred and forty yeshiva students. Why not transfer them to Kiryat Arba? For them, too, it will be safer there. Our population in Hebron is special, more religious, and we have extremists on our side too. Hebron is especially worrying. Perhaps we can send some of our policemen there, in cooperation with your army and perhaps with an international force?

"You must understand me," he said just above a whisper. "I am definitely interested in moving forward, but I need the trust of my people. You have an elected government, a parliament, clear laws. Trust is not the only bond between Israelis and their leaders. But it's all there is between my people and me."

Then Abd Rabbo interrupted in a rage. "You're weakening the president," he spat out. "For all intents and purposes, you're deceiving him! Absolutely nothing has changed."

We decided not to aggravate the debate and asked leave to return to our hotel. At the Hilton, the journalists were reporting that Arafat's associates were not interested in implementing the Declaration of Principles right now. Many of them didn't want to leave the comforts of Tunis for the hardship of Gaza—and under the circumstances of a phased agreement at that.

In the afternoon we met with Ross and his advisers. Neria and I updated Rabin, but it was obvious that we were getting nowhere and would have to return home for consultations. When I told Arafat of our decision, he asked us to return in a few days. Only then would we be able to discuss a possible meeting with Peres. At this meeting, I immediately noticed that Abu Ala was absent. Arafat sensed my concern and promptly explained, "I've sent Abu Ala to Jordan for talks with prominent Palestinian businessmen."

That evening Ross decided to pressure Arafat by intimating that the United States would veto the Security Council resolution condemning Israel for the massacre if the PLO did not return to the talks. The tacit threat left Arafat enraged. Our mission ended in failure.

Neria flew with the Americans to Washington, where Rabin was expected. Uzi and I were returned, by propeller plane, to the American base in Sicily. As we crossed the Mediterranean at twilight, we both sank into our own thoughts. I feared for the fate of the entire process. You can conduct negotiations under any circumstances, I mused, but at the end of the day, what counts is the determination to make peace by not allowing fanatics to undermine it.

Our plane awaited us in Sicily, and by morning we were home. The one person who remained in Tunis was Terje Larsen, determined to salvage what he could. He stayed in touch with me by phone during the coming week and held talks with Abu Mazen. He even composed a working paper of his own, in coordination with Abu Mazen. It suggested transferring the Jewish settlers from Hebron to nearby Kiryat Arba, as the Palestinians wanted. But I told him that this was politically unfeasible and then read him our formula for a limited international presence in Hebron, alongside unarmed Palestinian policemen. Terje now had two documents in hand: Larsen 1 (the Palestinian demands) and Larsen 2 (our position).

At the same time, back in Washington, Ross was planning a gambit to reengage Syria's President Assad. President Clinton had called Assad, and the two leaders had agreed that Syria would rejoin the peace talks if the United States did not veto the Security Council resolution. Thus Arafat got his condemnation but lost his ability to stall the peace process in the region until his demands were met.

Under these circumstances, on March 20 Rabin decided to dispatch another delegation to Tunis. This time it included Amnon Shahak, Yoel Singer, Jacques Neria, and me. At the predeparture briefing, Gen. Uri Saguy, the head of Israel's Military Intelligence, shared with us his assessment that Arafat had decided to postpone the resumption of the Gaza-Jericho talks for about three weeks, while he maximized his gains in the Hebron negotiations. Deputy Defense Minister Mordechai Gur and Chief of Staff Ehud Barak doubted whether we should be going at all. But Rabin and Peres were intent on preserving the contact with Arafat. Few around the table that night were aware that on the previous evening Rabin and Peres had decided to evacuate some of the Jewish settlers in Hebron, including the yeshiva students, in order to reduce the tension. The timing of the move was to be chosen in consultation with the IDF.

We returned to Tunis via Sicily, again on a State Department plane. Ross was back in Tunis, on the day of the presidential elections there. We entered the Hilton to find it absolutely crawling with journalists. A frazzled Terje immediately joined me in my room, and I invited him out for a walk. As we took in the election-day atmosphere, I asked him to refrain from any further attempts at mediation. From day one in Oslo, we had been firmly against any third-party intervention in the substantive side of the negotiations. We welcomed outside involvement in creating a conducive atmosphere, persuading the sides to be flexible, and tempering their highs or lows. But the two parties had to arrive at the actual formulas of the agreements on their own. Thus Terje, who always honored the wishes of the sides, abandoned his attempt to compose a "Larsen 3" document as a compromise.

When we met with Arafat in the afternoon, he opened the discussion aggressively. "We can't move forward without your first remov-

ing the settlers from Hebron," he said, "and allowing us to send in
Palestinian policemen alongside an international force. The key item
on the agenda now is not Gaza-Jericho but Hebron. We won't be able
to return to the negotiating table before dealing with it. I know Prime
Minister Rabin understands this, because he told me over the phone
that he's sending you here on the basis of the Larsen document," he
said, waving a paper in agitation.

I wondered whether Arafat knew about our reply to Terje's proposal for removing the settlers—the "Larsen 2" document—at all.
Meanwhile, Shahak was expressing, in his soft, steady tone, his personal regret for the massacre. He added that strong measures had
been taken in Israel against the extreme right. They went as far as administrative detentions (which are effectively imprisonment without
trial). I was troubled by the misunderstanding over the Larsen document, and immediately tried to undo it.

"When Rabin spoke to you about Larsen's proposal," I said, "he
had a different document in hand. You can ask Larsen. He's not very
far from here."

Arafat consulted in Arabic with Abd Rabbo, who then said: "I
suggest we leave the documents aside and discuss how to solve the
problem."

"What are you proposing?" Arafat asked. "Exactly what is your
mandate?"

While Arafat had been talking with Abd Rabbo, I had asked Shahak what international presence already existed in Hebron. "The Red
Cross is in the area," he whispered. So I said: "We can talk about
some kind of international presence and some kind of Palestinian police force in Hebron."

"But you must remember," Shahak told me, "that responsibility
for security remains in our hands."

"You're pushing me into a corner!" Arafat cried. "What about the
settlers in Hebron?"

"That is a political decision to be made by the prime minister,"
said Shahak. "Only he can make it, and there's no chance that the settlers will be transferred out as a result of negotiation with you.
Whether he can do so depends on his political situation. I, as a general, don't interfere in such things."

Arafat fell silent for a long moment, then asked us, "What kind of international presence are you considering?"

I clearly made a mistake when I told him I assumed that Rabin would agree to enlarging the presence of the Red Cross units.

Arafat looked at me quizzically, then hunched forward, opened his eyes wide, and asked: "*What* units?"

"The Red Cross," I repeated. "They can have a calming influence."

We were not prepared for what followed. Arafat's voice rose to a screech.

"Did you hear that?" he shouted to Abd Rabbo. "Maybe I didn't hear it right. Savir is suggesting the Red Cross!"

Within seconds his outburst had escalated into a tirade that continued for a number of minutes.

"The Red Cross! *The Red Cross!*" he ranted. "What do you want to do? Bring in nurses to give people injections? I *can't* be hearing this right. They're burning my portrait in the streets of Hebron, and the Israelis are talking about *injections*! Perhaps we should bring in my brother Fathi and the Red Crescent! *Unbelievable!*" he shrieked. "You want to humiliate me, *humiliate* me!"

It was difficult for us to respond. Arafat was nearly apoplectic. His rage seemed genuine, but we knew he had little ammunition in this fight, and he had to present *some* opening position.

Calmly Shahak decided there was no point in continuing the meeting. It was dark outside by the time we made our way back to our hotel. We didn't say a word to the reporters, who continued to assume that the peace process was in its death throes. "Arafat is staying put," they pronounced.

In the Hilton I met with the Russian envoy, Victor Pasivaliok, who sounded equally grim. "Arafat can't resume the talks now because his standing in the territories is at a nadir," he said. "I've just seen him, and I can tell you that he's depressed, pessimistic, and crushed by your position." Dennis Ross, with whom we had a late-night dinner, could see no hope. The Americans, too, had found Arafat brooding and insistent that we meet his demands.

That evening I took a walk with Shahak, who had received word that Rabin had postponed the evacuation of the Hebron settlers, for fear of creating an uproar due to the vehement reaction the extreme right was preparing. The measure was in fact never carried out, which I believe was a serious mistake in the struggle against the radical right. In any case, Amnon and I agreed that the peace process was in very grave danger. We decided to tell Arafat the plain truth: that Rabin could not accommodate all his demands, that the prime minister would find a way to relieve his distress but it would take time. Nevertheless, we could work out some formula for an international presence and municipal Palestinian police force in Hebron. The key lay in Arafat's own ability to lead his people, and he faced some agonizing decisions. I suggested that Shahak talk with him privately, one general (as Arafat liked to describe himself) to another.

At ten o'clock the next morning, we returned to the PLO guesthouse for another meeting. Before Arafat was seated, Shahak asked to speak to him alone. They withdrew to the kitchen, next to the lounge, and spoke for about twenty minutes. Shahak later related that as they sat at the kitchen table, he told Arafat not to expect the impossible. Rabin would have to make decisions that took his own political situation into account, and these were not open to negotiation with the PLO. It was Arafat's duty to give his people leadership and prepare them for a resumption of the talks.

Seated before Shahak that morning was a very different Arafat: somber but composed and soft-spoken. "Tell Rabin that I understand his difficulties," he said, "and that I expect he'll do what's necessary when the time is right."

"We can move forward on the other issues," Shahak urged him. "We can appoint a committee to handle the Hebron problem and simultaneously continue the talks on Gaza-Jericho."

Arafat heard what Shahak was saying but did not reply. Instead he asked Shahak to inform Rabin that he knew, from his own sources, that the prime minister was in danger from high-ranking officers. "They may be planning a coup," he confided. Arafat, as we already knew, tended sometimes to drift between reality and melodrama. "As to your proposal," he said, "please return to your colleagues in the other room. I'll join you there shortly."

Shahak sat down next to me on the sofa, and we all waited in tense silence. It was obvious to the Palestinians in the room that he'd made some kind of offer to Arafat, but they didn't know what kind—and they were bristling with suspicion toward us. We, for our part, didn't know what kind of Arafat to expect. He finally walked back into the room, still buttoning the tan jacket he always wore, and sat down stiffly in his chair.

"After talking with General Shahak, I have decided that we will return to the talks," he announced in a formal tone. "Prime Minister Rabin is also under pressure, and I trust him to make the right decision about the settlers. As to an international presence and Palestinian police force, a committee will be appointed to discuss the details. I propose Yasser Abd Rabbo and Nabil Shaath from our side."

Shahak instantly delegated Yoel Singer and me to sit opposite them.

"Tonight and in the coming days, they must arrive at an understanding on this matter," Arafat continued. "At the same time, we will resume the talks on implementing the Declaration of Principles on Gaza and Jericho. That is my duty at this difficult moment. Our people can return to Cairo to negotiate. I hope and expect that the prime minister will find a way to meet our needs. I'll brief the Americans, Egyptians, and Norwegians."

The Palestinians in the room were stunned. Arafat had just made a hard and unpopular decision. The Palestinians in the territories and elements throughout the Muslim world were demanding the removal of the settlers from Hebron as an absolute condition of resuming the talks. Otherwise it would look as though they had gone back to "business as usual" after a slaughter in one of Islam's most sacred mosques. Arafat had hoped that he would eventually achieve that demand. But after talking with Shahak, he realized that there was no point in suspending the Gaza-Jericho talks until he did. Within the space of twenty-four hours we had seen Arafat demonstrate weakness and despair, and then the strength to make a hard and unpopular decision.

The Hebron crisis was over. Arafat had shown himself to be a true partner in the quest for peace and—once more—the one man in the PLO capable of making difficult decisions. These qualities strengthened his ties with the only men on the Israeli side who were capable of doing the same, so it became possible once more to implement the declaration despite the serious problems that lay ahead.

That night we hammered out the better part of an understanding on stationing an international presence in Hebron. The final document, we agreed, would be worked on in Cairo, while the Gaza-Jericho talks continued. It was also decided that we would ask the Norwegians to field the international force. Yoel Singer and Nabil Shaath drew up a draft of the agreement. And on the same evening, when Dennis Ross went to see Arafat, he found a new man, determined to complete the Gaza-Jericho talks as quickly as possible.

After we had returned home and reported to Rabin and Peres, I asked Intelligence Chief Uri Saguy how he explained Arafat's change of heart. All Saguy (a brilliant man, who understood well the general trend of the peace process) would say was "He went against his initial decision." This was not, I must add, the first time that intelligence or other experts had difficulty reading the dynamic decision-making process of leaders in transit between conflict and peace. During my involvement in the peace process, I had become skeptical of analysts and their "antennae" that didn't pick up changes in a situation in flux. What's more, the presumably accurate but partial information that reaches senior officers and officials dulls their senses about the other side's true intentions, and their reading of their own public opinion.

Analyzing raw intelligence in a time of change is admittedly a difficult business. It wasn't by chance that most if not all intelligence agencies failed to foresee Sadat's visit to Israel, the evolution of the Oslo talks, King Hussein's readiness to make peace with Israel before Syria had, or the fall of the Soviet Union. One reason for this failure is that the leaders who initiate an era of swift or radical change themselves don't know exactly where they will find themselves at the end of the venture. That is what happened to Arafat during the Hebron crisis, and the same was essentially true of Rabin, Peres, Hussein, Arafat, and Assad during the peace process. Under such circumstances the negotiators, and the signals they pick up from the other side, become a far more valuable source of intelligence than information believed to be reliable because of the considerable investment made in obtaining it. With all the existing technology, there's still no way to read what's going on in the minds of leaders who are pledged to a process of significant change. This is not the fault of the intelligence services. But they, and especially their principals, must be aware of the limitations of "hard" intelligence and learn to read the full range of changes overtaking the society of an erstwhile enemy.

That same week, we were reminded again of how difficult the transition to peace can be. As we were putting together material for the Hebron negotiations and Shahak was briefing his teams for the final phase of the Gaza-Jericho talks, we suddenly learned that five armed Palestinians had been killed by our soldiers in Gaza. On the plane to Cairo the next day, Shahak told us how grave the incident was. The dead were members of Fatah, Arafat's dominant faction of the PLO, who had been briefed by the Palestinian security chief, Mohammed Dahlan, to "prepare the ground" for the Israeli withdrawal from Gaza. They were on their way back from a celebration and were shooting in the air, a traditional sign of jubilation—but a breach of the understanding with us that guns in Palestinian hands would not be fired under any circumstances. In the eyes of soldiers in the field, a gun is a weapon, not a firecracker. And how could they possibly know, just by looks, who was a friend and who was a killer? Dahlan and Shahak had begun a fruitful dialogue on future cooperation on security. But now Shahak was concerned that the Palestinians' response to the incident would be more bitterness and suspicion.

In Cairo we were taken to a secret meeting place. The Palestinians arrived, looking grim. When Dahlan, Shaath, and the rest of their delegation had filed into the hall, Shahak immediately asked to speak with Dahlan and Shaath alone. But Dahlan was feeling ill and returned to his hotel. It's hard to imagine a string of more drastic reversals than the switch from conflict to cooperation, then the horror of the Hebron massacre, Arafat's decision to resume the process, Dahlan's men being killed by Shahak's soldiers, and now the renewal of talks in which Dahlan and Shahak were to continue cooperating on security. I can only suppose that when Dahlan sighted Shahak that day, he wasn't sure whether he was seeing a new colleague, with whom it was possible to build a better future, or a bitter enemy responsible for the death of his friends. Probably he saw both in one. After Shahak explained to Shaath what had happened the previous night, the Palestinians left to tend to their ailing friend. We met again that evening in our Cairo hotel. Shahak spoke to Dahlan privately and quietly for a few minutes. Their talk ended with a firm handshake and the resumption of the negotiations.

The Palestinians decided they were not interested in having a municipal police force in Hebron that would be subordinate to Israel. So we agreed that Norway, Italy, and Sweden would create a temporary international presence to stabilize the situation in Hebron.

In the negotiations that followed, Shahak led his delegation boldly. Uzi Dayan dealt with the military details, and Israel got what it wanted in security arrangements. Many key powers remained in our hands: responsibility for external security; the security aspect of the border passages; control of three east-west roads, Gaza's air space, and the sectors containing the settlements. Yet most of the territory and most responsibilities of Gaza were to be transferred to the Palestinians, and the agreement laid down a framework for cooperation. There would be a Joint Security Coordination and Cooperation Committee, three District Coordination Offices (DCOs) that would operate twenty-four hours a day, and joint patrols and joint mobile units (to monitor the situation from stationary positions and go mobile only when necessary).

Thus less than a year after the first official meeting between Israel and the PLO, two former enemies had created a complex apparatus to cooperate on security matters. This agreement shattered the deep-rooted Israeli belief that we could depend only upon ourselves. It was vital to relinquish this belief if Israel was to free itself from the occupation. But internalizing this message was difficult, primarily for our military people but also for our society at large, which had always assumed that self-reliance was a sine qua non for the survival of the state. Our partners in the fight against terrorism were themselves the terrorists of yesterday: members of Fatah and Force 17 who had been involved in the murder of Israelis. We agreed to release five thousand security prisoners who had not murdered Israelis. For many the turnabout would prove too radical, and in time implementation was not an easy task.

The main issue we still had to tackle was the national symbols, or symbols of sovereignty, demanded by the Palestinians. Peres now believed there was no longer any point in battling such emblems. He appreciated, more than anyone else, the significance of granting the Palestinians and the PLO legitimacy. And he believed that if we were going to insist on such matters as security prerogatives, we would have to be more generous on other issues. For Peres the agreement was a means to a common goal, not a statement that stood on its own.

The Palestinians were demanding passports for the residents of the autonomous areas. At first our position was that they would be given only laissez-passers, since passports implied statehood. Peres persuaded Rabin to have both words printed on the Palestinian travel documents. But some of us had difficulty accepting this change in status and wanted LAISSEZ-PASSER printed in larger letters. It was finally agreed that both words would appear the same size. In the end, the passports were printed in Germany, and the word PASSPORT came out in larger type. For the first time in history, the Palestinians had their own passports. Neither Jordan nor Egypt had agreed to this concept when they ruled the West Bank and Gaza. But Peres recognized this point as the prerogative of a people who deserved recognition of their rights and identity.

Although Israel was prepared to recognize Palestinian symbols, including the flag of the Palestinian Authority, it stopped short at freedom of movement for Palestinian citizens and goods. The Gaza-Jericho agreement permitted us to control entry into Israel, in line with security considerations, as well as entry into the autonomous area itself. This position spawned a contradiction between people who were to be free to express their national identity but whose physical movements were mainly at Israel's discretion. Thus liberty and the restriction of movement were joined in the intricate construct of the new Palestinian autonomy.

Finally, it was also in this last stage of the negotiations that a critical change was made: the PLO and its chairman would relocate to the autonomous area, so as to lead their people at close hand. Yasser

Arafat, the very emblem of his people's struggle against Israel, would now move to Gaza or Jericho. But we insisted that he do so as the chairman of the PLO or chairman of the Palestinian Authority, *not* as the president of Palestine. The Palestinians were amenable to this demand. The agreement also provided for the appointment of a twenty-four-member Palestinian Council to help Arafat administer the autonomous area until democratic elections could be held (after the conclusion of the Interim Agreement, which would cover the West Bank). Israel approved the entry of the PLO leadership—including not only people it had previously deported but some who were on its wanted list—according to rosters given to the IDF by the Palestinian security organs. The upshot of this arrangement was essentially the birth of a Palestinian government (even if called by a different name), whose mandate was to manage the affairs of the Palestinians and continue negotiating with Israel.

This move was probably one of the clearest expressions of the revolutionary change summed up in the adjective "Oslo." It meant that Israel would be dealing with an authoritative Palestinian regime, and from that moment onward the day grew closer when two governments would sign a permanent settlement. What remained to be seen—or built—were the terms of that new relationship. At this time neither side could know how much violence would come between the signing of this initial agreement and the conclusion of the final one. The agreement fixed the date for reaching the permanent solution as five years after the signing of the Gaza-Jericho accord. As the latter was ultimately signed on May 4, 1994, the permanent peace treaty was to be concluded no later than May 4, 1999. The countdown to full peace had begun.

Before the finishing touches were put on the agreement, another decisive meeting took place between the leaders themselves. On May 3, in President Mubarak's office and presence, Arafat met with Rabin. Also at that meeting were Peres, Warren Christopher, Dennis Ross, and the heads of the respective delegations. It was a rough session that lasted five hours, well into the night. Mubarak (who was celebrating his birthday) pressed the sides to reach an understanding on the last outstanding issues. Arafat demanded three familiar things: a considerably larger area for the Jericho enclave, civil responsibility for the southern coast of Gaza (the Muwasi), and the stationing of a Palestinian policeman on the famous Allenby Bridge. Rabin demanded a list of the twenty-four members of the Palestinian Council, which was supposed to be an appendix to the agreement. When Arafat protested that he was hearing this demand for the first time (though it had been raised with him before), Shahak and I smiled.

"I'm a clown in your eyes, I know it," Arafat spat. "So go on, gentlemen, laugh."

"Mr. Chairman," Rabin growled, "we treat you with the utmost respect. But you're obliged to honor understandings."

"You promised me answers about the policeman on the bridge. You promised an answer about the size of the Jericho sector. Now you're humiliating me with offers of a kilometer here and a kilometer there. You have the upper hand. You decide."

Rabin finally consented to extend the Jericho area by six square kilometers and give Arafat limited civil control over another five kilometers of the southern Gaza coast, despite their proximity to Israeli settlements. But he wouldn't hear of having a Palestinian policeman stand on the Allenby Bridge—though it was agreed that talks on that issue would continue. The meeting ended at two in the morning. The two teams were working around the clock, hammering out the final wording.

At 11:00 A.M., the signing ceremony began in the main Cairo Auditorium. After a few obligatory speeches, Rabin and Arafat signed the requisite copies of the Gaza-Jericho Agreement. As they did so, Rabin discovered that Arafat had not signed the maps that were appended to the document. He stood up and approached Arafat, pointed the lapse out to him, and demonstratively demanded that he promptly sign them. Arafat refused. Apparently he believed that the previous night's understanding to reconsider the policeman on the Allenby Bridge would be reflected in the maps. He was wrong—and his negotiators knew it. So Shahak and Shaath joined the dignitaries on the stage, where an uproar had broken out in full view of the world's television cameras. Everyone on the stage pleaded with Arafat and all but physically assailed him. But the man would not be moved. Finally President Mubarak cornered Arafat and demanded, in extremely blunt language, that he not disgrace the occasion or embarrass Egypt as its host. Arafat ultimately signed the maps, but only after extracting from Rabin a promise to send him a letter listing the issues that had yet to be negotiated—particularly the policeman on the Allenby Bridge.

The outrageous scene on the stage left a bitter taste in our mouths. Here stood a man who had gained for his people an absolutely unprecedented achievement behaving in a way that flouted the norms of relations between national leaders, and of international relations as a whole. But Arafat had other considerations. He sensed that he was signing a document that many Palestinians would scorn because it allowed Israel to retain a decisive influence over their affairs. It confirmed Israel's control of the border passages, it gave us a veto over Palestinian legislation as well as the right to approve the name of every Palestinian policeman permitted to enter Gaza and Jericho. Arafat wanted to show his constituents that he was fighting for their interests, against a broadside of international pressure, and was prepared to embarrass his partners in order to protect their rights.

Three weeks after that unsettling ceremony, on May 25, 1994, the IDF withdrew from Gaza and the desert oasis of Jericho. Twenty-seven years of harsh, sometimes brutal, Israeli control and of staunch, sometimes cruel, Palestinian struggle were finally drawing to an end.

On July 1, 1994, Yasser Arafat entered the Gaza Strip, after being received by an Israeli officer at the border. In Gaza's central square a crowd of about 100,000 people awaited him. When he addressed them the entire world, the whole Palestinian people, and all of Israel were watching. Surprisingly, few of my countrymen were outraged by his arrival. In fact, our departure from Gaza was widely considered a blessing. The celebrations, the sea of flags in the square, and Arafat's relatively moderate speech were accepted by most Israelis with quiet understanding, though a few felt obliged to fulminate. The idea first broached by Shimon Peres in the winter of '92 had come to fruition

Map 2: Gaza-Jericho Agreement, May 4, 1994

© Tammy Soffer

in the spring of '94. Arafat was now a leader in place. He had to build a society and an economy. He had pledged to enhance security. And he was duty bound to cooperate and negotiate with his new neighbor, Israel.

After the May 4 signing ceremony, I stayed in touch with Abu Ala by phone. He had signed the economic agreement in Paris back on April 29. It became part of the whole Gaza-Jericho Agreement and was subordinated (according to Arafat's agreement with Rabin) to the security part of the agreement, in case of a contradiction between the two, which ultimately severely hampered Palestinian economic development, as it allowed for prolonged closures of the autonomous areas as a result of terrorist action against Israel.

A few months before that, in the midst of the negotiations, Abu Ala's father had died. I called him in Paris to console him and suggested that he attend the funeral, though he would have to come here secretly. He told me that he chose to mourn his father in Tunis. He didn't want to come back to Abu Dis (a Palestinian village on the immediate outskirts of Jerusalem and part of the West Bank, then still under Israeli control) until an agreement had been signed and he could return with the PLO leadership. In mid-July, the phone rang in our home.

"Abu Ala here," he announced. "I'm calling from Abu Dis. The whole family has come back to my late father's house—Um Ala and the children—and we want to share our happiness with you."

"Welcome home!" I cried into the receiver. "We're thrilled for you, Abu Ala, and thrilled for ourselves, as well. Now we are finally neighbors!"

I could hear the joy in his voice and appreciated the happiness of a family that had settled in a place of its own. Just a year earlier, throughout my whole life, in fact, I never imagined I would be so delighted to hear that a PLO leader was living a few kilometers from my house.

We immediately made a date for lunch in Tel Aviv, and invited Terje to join us. We talked for hours about cooperation, especially in economic affairs, and then strolled down the beachfront promenade in the direction of ancient Jaffa. Abu Ala seemed almost euphoric. "I can hardly believe the day has come when we can meet together in Tel Aviv!"

He marveled at the sight of the shore and the hotels (it had all looked very different twenty-seven years before). "It will take many years for us to accomplish this," he said, "but I am filled with hope. This is what the agreement means to me personally. Many difficulties will lie ahead, but one thing is certain: there's no turning back now."

Then my two friends got back into their car, and I continued walking down the promenade.

6

PLANNING SECURITY

YASSER ARAFAT AND HIS COLLEAGUES ENTERED GAZA IN ORDER TO govern, for the first time in Palestinian history, their people—or at least some of them. There was hardly a mistake that wasn't made at the start of this endeavor, mainly because of the PLO's lack of experience in managing an actual society. Twenty-seven years earlier, Israel had captured the Gaza Strip from the Egyptians in a defensive war. In departing it left behind a physical presence, in the form of settlers and troops to protect them, and economic influence. But Gaza had become Palestinian. After centuries of rule by Turkey, Britain, Egypt, and Israel, Palestinians themselves had now become responsible for the area.

The Gaza-Palestine that was turned over to Arafat was in very poor condition, though far better off than it had been when Israel took over in 1967. Still, it suffered from overpopulation, rising unemployment, and the absence of an economic infrastructure. The economic situation had further deteriorated about a year before Arafat arrived as a result of the "closure" intermittently imposed on the territories by Israel. During that year the gross product in Gaza had fallen by 25 percent and unemployment had risen to about 50 percent. The refugee camps were overflowing, and the birthrate was among the highest in the world. Added to all this was a shortage and often a total lack of sewage facilities, electricity, roads, even potable water. Despair in Gaza was made all the worse because a vibrant and thriving but domineering Israel was literally walking distance away.

This despair had proven fertile ground for the growth of the Hamas and Islamic Jihad movements, which recruited tens of thousands of Palestinians seeking a better world in a fundamentalist faith. These movements perceived the "vision of Oslo" as a nightmare of ignominious compromise with an eternal enemy and a threat to a religious and social code fortified against outside influence.

Arafat began his journey as the chairman of the Palestinian Authority by relying on the methods that had served him so well in Tunis: trying to centralize his power through divide and rule tactics. His first objective was to create an instrument for policing Gaza and Jericho, manned mostly by veteran loyalists and members of the Palestine Liberation Army who were brought in from abroad and integrated with local supporters into a cluster of roughly a dozen sometimes redundant, or at least overlapping, security organs. Arafat created this network mainly as a prop for his regime.

Meanwhile the world, which continued to rally to the chairman's aid, was asked primarily to fund the establishment of his administration, meaning both a strong police force and a civil bureaucracy to manage its new responsibilities. Allocating funds to finance a foreign government is contrary to the aid policies of most of the donor states. But they made an exception in this case, because the Palestinians had to build their authority from scratch. The Palestinian Authority lacked even the machinery to collect taxes.

Toward that end, Peres proposed the creation of a special international fund, to be named in honor of the late Norwegian foreign minister Johan Jørgen Holst, to be used only and strictly for the purposes laid down in its charter for recurrent costs of the Palestinian administration. The Norwegians, represented by Terje Larsen, presided over the deliberations of the Holst Fund, the World Bank acted as the secretariat for supervising individual projects, and the International Monetary Fund served as financial mentor.

At the helm of this multi-institutional effort was the United States, through the good offices of Dennis Ross and Toni Verstandig, its dynamic representative to the Donors' Conference, who had joined the peace team after many years of working for Congress. The United States pledged a donation of $500 million to the Palestinians, far more than any other country. The great disappointment were the

Arab states. They had championed the struggle against Israel and helped their Palestinian brothers in time of war but ignored them when it came to building their national home. Under pressure from the United States, the Saudis contributed $100 million a year. But even Washington failed to coax the other wealthy countries of the region, specifically Gulf states that had still not forgiven Arafat for his infamous embrace of Saddam Hussein during the Gulf War.

Arafat, for his part, had great difficulty acceding to the donors' demands for "transparency" and "accountability," concepts that were alien to him. He treated the foreign aid as compensation that was naturally due to his people for suffering so valiantly throughout their history, particularly under Israeli occupation.

The Palestinians were at this time looking for ways to develop strong political institutions, not economic ones. At the Donors' Conference in Paris on September 7–9, 1994, the Palestinian representatives demanded that monies from the donors be allocated to their institutions in Jerusalem. I told Terje that the Israeli delegation would not so much as enter the hall if the Palestinians did not drop this demand. In an all-night session with me, Nabil Shaath was prepared to remove the subject from the agenda until Arafat ordered him not to give in. So I decided to scuttle the conference. I was angry that the Palestinians were using an instrument *we* had helped to establish, for their benefit, to boost the Palestinian Authority's standing in Jerusalem. So we all went home after asking the Norwegians to invite the two sides on September 13 to Oslo, when the first anniversary of the Declaration of Principles was being marked, to work out a solution then.

In Oslo, Peres and Arafat agreed to remove all policy issues in dispute between Israel and the Palestinians from the agenda of the Donors' Conference. Together we signed a formal Oslo Declaration and then attended a moving performance by Palestinian and Israeli children's choirs before an audience of cheering Norwegians, as Arafat addressed Peres as "my cousin." Peres concluded from the meeting that the chairman was indeed more interested in establishing himself politically than in building his economy or other vital institutions of a civil society.

. . .

In the first weeks of Palestinian self-rule in Gaza, it became clear to us that Arafat and his men were not using their new power base to dismantle Hamas and other violent opposition groups. Meeting with Arafat on August 10, Rabin demanded that the Palestinians do a better job of countering them.

"This is your test," he told the chairman almost menacingly.

On hearing demands such as this, Arafat claimed that he had to build strong support among his constituents before he could act vigorously. Indeed, many of his close associates explained that his methods differed from ours.

"You fought against terror by force—and you failed," Hassan Asfour told me the first time we met in Gaza. "Arafat has a different strategy, and it will succeed. Trust him; strengthen him, and you'll see. We're negotiating with Hamas, and many of their people are coming over to our side."

Though our security people usually pressed Arafat, on every possible occasion, to send his policemen from house to house confiscating illegal arms, they understood that Hamas was a broad popular movement and that we had to give Arafat a chance to deal with it through a combination of force and dialogue. Abu Ala even told me in mid-1994 of an evolving agreement between Hamas and Fatah, Arafat's mainstream faction in the PLO, that included an end to the use of violence and the acceptance of a central authority that would legitimize political pluralism.

Arafat clearly hoped that his unprecedented achievement in taking over the Gaza Strip would draw Hamas's followers to his banner. And there were signs that he might have been right. Terje Larsen, who was appointed in June 1994 as UN undersecretary in charge of the Palestinian aid coordination effort while Mona Juul was the number two at the Norwegian embassy in Tel Aviv, told me that the greatest change in Gaza was the nightlife on the beach. After so many years, the evening curfew on Gaza was lifted and people could relax day and night at the beach, where new restaurants had opened to serve them. He also pointed out that a most noticeable change was the slow disappearance of the long head scarves worn by many of the women (which could instantly be converted into veils) and the "creeping withdrawal" of skirt lengths. Terje, naturally, welcomed these developments as signs of Western-style "normalcy." The Hamas leadership, however, feared that this subtle cultural shift toward Israel and the West, alongside Arafat's political cooperation with them, would result in the death of their movement. Hence, while negotiating with the Palestinian Authority, Hamas—with encouragement from elements in Iran, Syria, and Jordan—stepped up its activities in the refugee camps and prepared to mount terrorist actions to "expose the dangers" of the "so-called peace."

Fifteen Israelis were killed by terrorists during the first six months of Palestinian Authority rule, eight of them in or near the Gaza Strip, and Rabin's response was vehement. Although he was careful to play up the difference between Hamas and Fatah, explaining to the public that the latter was working against terrorism, he told Arafat that he had to do a better job of suppressing fundamentalist extremism. To make that point unmistakable, in October 1994 he closed the West Bank and Gaza, sealing them off from Israel. If the Palestinian Authority could not prevent terrorism, and if the IDF was forbidden to fight it in the areas under Palestinian control, then all the Palestinians in the West Bank and Gaza would have to be denied access to Israel and their jobs there.

One mistake led to another. First Arafat failed to establish his authority by quashing the forces of violence. Then we, by our closure policy, punished not the terrorists but the Palestinians as a whole. Meanwhile, the Israeli public perceived closure as a blockade against terrorism even though our military did not necessarily agree that it was an effective means to that end. It may in the longer run have reinforced the terrorist movements by enabling them to portray the Gaza-Jericho Agreement as a continuation of the occupation by other means. More to the point, as the Palestinian standard of living suffered, the conditions for violence flourished.

Thus in the fall of 1994, the peace process took some very punishing blows. "This is peace?" people grumbled on both sides. And their leaders focused on stinging criticism of each other. The situation declined steadily from one of great promise to economic difficulties, terrorist violence, hostile rhetoric, and, in time, a political stalemate.

October 14, 1994, will be remembered as the day the contrast between the promise of the historic Declaration of Principles and the anguish of turning it into reality was sharpest. Five days earlier a nineteen-year-old Israeli soldier had been kidnapped at a hitchhiking post in the heart of Israel. The whole country held its breath as the army searched for Cpl. Nachshon Wachsman. Rabin maintained ongoing contact with Arafat through Ahmed Tibi (the chairman's Israeli-Arab adviser), and there was even talk of releasing Sheikh Yasin (founder and head of Hamas, who was ailing in an Israeli prison) in return for the Israeli soldier.

Meanwhile, as Arab members of the Knesset mediated between Arafat and the Islamic movements in Gaza, the IDF discovered that Wachsman was being held by Hamas not in the autonomous Gaza Strip—as Rabin had initially assumed—but in the West Bank town of Bir Naballah, which was under Israeli control. As the feverish contacts continued with Gaza, Rabin and the army were weighing the possibility of a daring rescue operation. Rabin also briefed Peres on this possibility. But all this went on behind the scenes, and no one beyond the most inner circles of government was aware that Wachsman's whereabouts were known. After almost a week of waiting for some development, the tension in Israel was unbearable.

Then, in a truly cruel twist of fate, on the afternoon of Friday, October 14, the Nobel Prize committee announced in Oslo that Yitzhak Rabin, Shimon Peres, and Yasser Arafat were to be that year's peace laureates. Peres learned only an hour before the announcement that he would be sharing the honor with Rabin and Arafat. I was at his side all that day.

Peres expresses little emotion. Contrary to appearances, he's introverted. He was raised to view emotion as a private matter, not to be shared with anyone—sometimes, I thought, not even with himself.

But years of working beside him had taught me to discern his con-
cealed feelings. The news that he was to receive the Nobel Peace
Prize moved him deeply. Peres is truly devoid of any sense of his
place in history. But receiving an honor of that magnitude was important to him, even if he chose not to acknowledge it publicly. There
were cries of elation among his staff, which Peres tried to silence in
deference to the gravity of the hour.

"Congratulations, Shimon" was all I said as I pumped his hand
warmly.

He looked back at me in silence for a moment to show, I believe,
that he could feel my joy. I had feared during those weeks that an in-
justice would be done. The honor was due to all three men: Rabin
and Arafat for the many hard and courageous decisions they had
taken, but certainly no less to Peres, who was the driving force behind
the peace process, the man with the clearest vision of what peace
should be and mean, who pushed tirelessly in the direction best for
his country and the region, with the rare combination of a passion for
peace and the patience to nurture a complex process.

All afternoon efforts continued to save Nachshon Wachsman.
Once it was clear that mediation had failed, Rabin decided on a military rescue operation. I was at home early in the evening when the director of the Foreign Ministry's Situation Room, Ron Prossor, called
to say that the mission had succeeded. The word from the IDF Operations Branch was that a military unit had penetrated the house
where Wachsman was held and taken him out alive. I was flooded
with relief. Then Prossor called again.

"Unfortunately, Uri, the initial report was erroneous," he said.
"Wachsman was killed in the operation, along with an IDF officer,
Nir Poraz."

All of Israel sat at home that night in shock. To some degree
Hamas's terror accomplished its aim on the night of October 14,
when the horror of seeing a family receive the worst news possible,
and the anguished cries heard outside the victim's home, overwhelmed the awareness that the peace process was meant to save
whole generations from misery. That night was the test of Rabin's
leadership as prime minister. He appeared very grim at a televised
news conference and described the rescue attempt with great

courage. He was again careful to distinguish between the murderers from Hamas and our partners in combating terrorism.

The next day I said to Peres: "The moment we stress terrorism as the main issue, we'll reinforce the murderers and other opponents of the peace, at home and abroad, because they'll understand how potent a weapon they have against the process. While fighting, we must try to be a little more British, keep a stiff upper lip, and tell the public the simple truth: that terrorism will go on until we achieve a comprehensive peace, and therefore we must not surrender to it."

Peres agreed with my analysis but was skeptical about my prescription, given the daily competition between fear and hope. He was right. Five days after Wachsman was shot by his captors, a suicide bomber blew himself up on a No. 5 bus traveling down Dizengoff Street in Tel Aviv. Twenty-two people were killed in the blast.

Israel was now literally in the grip of terror. Amid the outburst of rage and grief, the opposition hammered away at the Oslo policy and directly blamed the government for the loss of Israeli lives. During a demonstration that took place on October 22—in which Binyamin Netanyahu (Likud), Rafael Eitan (Tsomet), and Zevulun Hammer (National Religious) participated—the crowd shouted, "This peace is killing us" and "Rabin is a murderer."

Despite this response, Arafat still failed to grasp the extent of the menace posed by terrorism and did not mobilize all his resources to prove himself a full partner in controlling violence against Israelis. His strategic design took cognizance of the state of Palestinian society and assumed the defeat of fundamentalism through a less aggressive and more gradual process. That this strategy clashed with his commitment to work with Israel eluded him. And so the peace process suffered. Yet it was clear to us that it would go on, propelled by sheer determination and the understanding that terror must be countered mainly by a political solution, parallel to concerted action on the ground and the pressure on Arafat to act more decisively.

A second paradox dominated the last half of 1994. Although the Israeli-Palestinian track was in disrepair, Israel began to enjoy the fruits of peace that grew directly out of the breakthrough with the

Palestinians. The Oslo strategy had started to yield the regional benefits that we had hoped for. In October and November 1994, doors opened all over the Middle East. After months of secret negotiations with the Hashemite Kingdom of Jordan—conducted mainly by Rabin's team of Eliyakim Rubinstein, Efraim Halevy of the Mossad, and Eitan Haber (Rabin's dedicated head of office)—on October 24, 1994, Israel and Jordan signed a formal peace treaty.

The United States played an important role in this achievement. Rabin and Peres had convinced President Clinton to forgive Jordan's debt of $6 billion and cooperate with the two countries in launching joint economic projects. Together with Rubinstein, I led the Israeli delegation to trilateral talks, initiated by Peres, that spawned promising plans, especially for the Jordan Valley. Israel now had its second formal border, the first being with Egypt. It even promised to help Jordan overcome its irksome water problem. To the Palestinians' great displeasure, Jordan was also granted a special status in the Muslim holy places in Jerusalem. A deep rapport existed between King Hussein and Prime Minister Rabin, which had grown out of personal chemistry and a shared strategic outlook on the need to ensure the stability of the Hashemite regime—if necessary by cooperation against external threats. The treaty with Jordan was a charmed peace, devoid of the problematic element of gradualness. It came straight from the hearts of both countries' leaders, who gave it frequent and lavish expression. Hussein was the Arab leader that Israelis loved to love: the sovereign of an orderly, Westernized country who was emotionally accessible to them. Israel, which so longed to leap directly from hostility to love, had found its ideal partner.

The signing ceremony on October 27, 1994, at the new crossing point between the Red Sea towns of Aqaba and Eilat, highlighted these feelings. Generals who had fought against each other shook hands and exchanged gifts. President Clinton and Russian Foreign Minister Kozyrev flew in to join the celebration of a wholehearted peace. Even the Israeli right eagerly embraced the treaty, because it did not threaten its territorial aims.

Rabin and Hussein praised each other with real mutual affection. Hussein spoke warmly of a genuine peace, not just clauses of a treaty on paper. Yasser Arafat had not been invited to attend the occasion because of Rabin's and Hussein's personal aversion to him, though it was absolutely clear that the peace being celebrated at the Aqaba crossing would not have been signed had it not been for the Oslo breakthrough.

Nor would other channels to the Arab world have been opened to Israel. On November 2, a year after Shimon Peres first broached the idea of an international economic conference, another historic event took place in Casablanca. Regional and international leaders, together with thousands of businessmen from all over the world, gathered for the Middle East and North African Economic Conference. For the first time Israelis and Arabs were able to meet in an open forum and simply discuss business. The Israeli delegates were practically euphoric. Walls of hostility crumbled. The Arab boycott was history.

In a special tent made available by our host, King Hassan II of Morocco, Shimon Peres met with leaders and foreign ministers of some fifteen Arab countries. Kaffiyehs, elegant robes, starched uniforms, and Bond Street suits merged almost surrealistically, because of the inclusion of Israel into a framework that had hitherto been exclusively Arab. After we were received by King Hassan, Peres and I began chatting with Arafat, while the others looked on in satisfaction. It was an instructive picture. Israeli-Palestinian collaboration had made far wider cooperation possible. As the leaders sat in a rectangle listening to a few short speeches, I sat in the second row with Dennis Ross, enjoying a feeling of great promise. Indeed, the Casablanca conference unleashed strong forces of economic change in the region—gradual reforms in Arab economies, the growth of new, educated economic elites, cooperation among Arab, Israeli, and international businesspeople, and the initial creation of regional institutions, primarily a regional bank for development. I had worked in coordination with the Palestinians, Egyptians, and Jordanians to promote the establishment of such a regional institution, and Peres convinced Clinton to support it. The new Middle East was under way.

Rabin came to the conference for only a few hours. His speech there, like Arafat's, touched jarringly on the subject of Jerusalem. Before we left the conference, Rabin, Peres, and the members of our negotiating delegation met Arafat and his negotiators at a luxurious villa in Casablanca.

"Mr. Chairman," Rabin said sharply, "we must continue to fight against terrorism. No other issue has such threatening ramifications, for both sides."

"Yes, we must fight the fanatics, who have a lot of money," Arafat replied. "But instead of punishing them, you're indirectly punishing us. An anti-Clinton leaflet is circulating in Gaza, and its source is Damascus. The terrorists are being encouraged from outside. *Please*," he implored Rabin, "stop the collective punishment. I know that after the tragedy in Tel Aviv, it was hard for you to announce that you're committed to the peace process. And I thank you for doing so. But I think it's worthwhile releasing Sheikh Yasin. He will have an influence on the extremists. I know him. He will call for an end to the violence."

"We've checked. He's not prepared to do that," Rabin retorted. "And in any case, it's vital that you yourself continue to combat terrorism. That's the key struggle. Public opinion is rebellious in Israel. There are calls among the Jews to kill me."

"Me too," Arafat said almost proudly.

"Then we're in the same boat."

In all the conversations I witnessed, that was the only time Rabin referred not just to the agitated public mood but to the calls to murder him. He said it exactly a year and two days before a fanatic young law student heeded them.

Meanwhile, the terror continued. During November, two attacks near Israeli settlements in the Gaza Strip took the lives of ten people, seven of them soldiers. Rabin and Peres faced a dilemma. Not for a moment did they question the justice of their cause or their belief that it would in the long run enhance our national security. Neither did they doubt that if they brought the Oslo process to a halt, all the attendant benefits would come to grief. Yet the public—and not just on the right—had grown increasingly skeptical about Arafat's ability, or even desire, to take the terrorists on. Thus the room for maneuver was rapidly shrinking.

It was against this background that Peres came up with a new idea. On November 28 he proposed to Arafat (in a meeting in Gaza) that the order of events given in the Declaration of Principles be reversed, so that the Palestinian elections be held before Israel's redeployment in the West Bank (except, of course, for the day of the election itself, when the IDF would make itself scarce in Palestinian areas). After the elections, Israel would gradually extend civil autonomy to a more legitimate and stronger Palestinian Authority, beginning in the northern West Bank town of Jenin. Peres raised this new plan with Arafat secretly, and Arafat didn't reject it out of hand. He asked to think about it and consult with his advisers.

Peres hoped that Arafat would ultimately accept this idea, because the elections were of extreme importance to him as a way to legitimize his regime. I disagreed and told Peres that the chances of Arafat accepting any change in the declaration or the Gaza-Jericho Agreement were nil. And this was all the more true of the suggestion to hold Palestinian elections in the shadow of the occupation. Beyond that, I said to Peres, we finally had the opportunity we had hoped for to relinquish control over another people. Unless the occupation ended, we could never defeat terrorism. Admittedly, the fundamentalist violence was a function of more than just our rule over the Palestinians. It also reflected a power struggle between the fundamentalist factions and Arafat. But it drew greater support from the Palestinian public because they were being denied freedom.

Peres agreed with these aims but wasn't sure they could be achieved, given the effect of the terrorist actions on Israeli opinion. I asked to be allowed to continue the peace talks with the Palestinians, toward an interim agreement on the West Bank, provided they worked with us to intensify their struggle against terrorism. After discussing the issues, Rabin and Peres decided to explore the subject with the Palestinians. The delegation to these talks, which were held in Cairo, included Uzi Dayan, Gen. Gadi Zohar (the head of the Civil Administration in the West Bank), Yoel Singer, and me. Rabin's instructions to us were first to map out the various issues with the Palestinians. We were to continue insisting upon more vigorous Palestinian Authority action against terrorism. As we gathered our papers to leave for the airport, Uzi Dayan asked: "Who's the head of this delegation?"

"Uri Savir," Rabin replied.

I knew Peres had proposed that I be appointed head of the negotiations on the Interim Agreement. I also knew that Rabin had at first hesitated. Some time later, Amnon Shahak (who had by then replaced Ehud Barak as chief of staff) told me that he, too, had recommended me. He had stressed the importance of having a civilian head the negotiations. But I didn't know that at the time. So I was surprised by Rabin's decision—especially because, given my closeness to Peres, I didn't know how much faith Rabin placed in me as chief negotiator. His trust in me, I think, developed over time.

The Cairo talks with Nabil Shaath and his people were a rambling and wearisome discussion around a long table, essentially a cycle of mutual recriminations about who was to blame for terror.

When we returned from Cairo, I joined the entourage to the Nobel Peace Prize ceremony on December 9, a formal and very dignified event. All three laureates made a supreme effort not to betray their elation. But the award, the speeches, and the festive atmosphere in Oslo sorely tested their resolve. The question everyone asked was Who would ever have believed that Yasser Arafat would one day accept the Nobel Peace Prize beside two Israeli leaders? Yet the world celebrated the award to this odd trio with a respect for them bordering on awe. The significance of the joint effort to solve one of the world's most enduring conflicts was felt far more strongly outside the Middle East than by the Israelis and Palestinians themselves, who lacked historical perspective.

When the two delegations closeted themselves for a talk, in the presence of our Norwegian hosts, Rabin preached to Arafat about security and offered him two choices. "I'm not altering my commitment to the Declaration of Principles," he said. "We can, if you like, negotiate all the components of the security map of the West Bank after Israel's redeployment and then implement them. But I fear this will take a long time, while the opposition will continue to mount violent actions.

"The second choice is to progress gradually, as Peres has proposed, beginning with elections, and then let the elected body pursue the negotiations on redeployment."

Neither Rabin nor Peres gave Arafat a chance to respond. Instead they tried, each in his turn, to persuade him that the second choice was preferable. Finally, Arafat said he would think it over and suggested that they continue talking. The Norwegians who participated in the meeting—Foreign Minister Bjørn Tore Godal, Terje Larsen, and Mona Juul—urged both sides not to focus only on problems but to move the process forward. The Nobel Prize, they stressed, was meant as a reminder of what they had achieved in the past sixteen months.

Late that night, most of the veterans of "Oslo I"—Abu Ala, Hassan Asfour, Yossi Beilin, Yair Hirschfeld, Ron Pundak, and I—sat in the bar of the Grand Hotel and reverted, for a brief moment, to the raucous humor of the "club." A crew from one of the Israeli television networks approached us and was treated to the requisite statements of optimism. These declarations of faith from the people who had been in on the process from the start, and were deeply committed to it, were probably in themselves a force for peace.

When we returned from Oslo, I knew that I had been charged with a grave responsibility and offered a great opportunity to help realize the policy I believed in with all my being. I was convinced the solution to the present predicament lay in relinquishing our control over the Palestinians. I also believed that we could overcome terrorism and become members of a regional coalition that would serve Israel's security and economic interests for generations to come. The key to achieving these aims lay in both sides fully honoring the Oslo agreements.

But at that time hardly anyone shared my faith that we could negotiate and implement the Interim Agreement on the West Bank. Yossi Beilin, for example, thought that this prospect was no longer realistic and that we were better off proceeding directly to talks on the permanent settlement. He held secret talks, partly in Stockholm, together with Yair and Ron, with Abu Mazen and some of his colleagues—and while they made some interesting progress, they did not reach any real agreement. When Yossi at a later stage informed Peres for the first time of the talks with Abu Mazen and his colleagues, Peres asked him not to continue and passed an immediate message to Arafat that these talks were not authorized. Neither he nor I believed in the possibility of conceptual or detailed shortcuts, given the enormous gap between the parties' positions and the decisive nature of permanent status; such explorations would be used only to test Israeli flexibility.

Meanwhile, the press had already chanted the last rites over Oslo.

By then many Palestinians believed that the agreements had been a tragic mistake. Israel, they held, would move no further because it had already attained its goal of handing Arafat what they called "the prison of Gaza." They no longer expected freedom of movement to and from the West Bank. So perhaps the time had come to admit that the Oslo venture was a failure and return to armed struggle.

Abu Ala, however, shared my view that only by patiently pursuing the Oslo process could both sides flourish in the future. I met him on our return from the Nobel ceremonies for a full day's talk at the King David Hotel in Jerusalem.

"Uri, we must save the process," he began. "I'm worried that the enemies of the agreement will win. And I'm concerned that the partnership between our peoples, the secret of our success, will collapse. Casablanca was a historic event for me. But it wouldn't have been possible if not for Oslo."

Then he offered some welcome news: after he had met with Arafat in Tunis, on their way back from Oslo, Abu Mazen suggested that he conduct the future negotiations.

"Arafat suspects that you're not serious about continuing the process," he went on. "He fears that 'Gaza first' will turn into 'Gaza last.' And let me tell you: Peres's proposal and Rabin's suggestion that he choose between full implementation, which will take time, and going to elections immediately has only heightened his suspicion."

Abu Ala spoke of drawing the proper conclusions from the experience in Gaza and defining a more effective and systematic fight against terrorism as a Palestinian interest, not something done for Israel's sake. He also stressed the need to keep moving forward and offering his people hope for a better economic and political future. And then he laid out a new concept for crafting the Interim Agreement. He spoke of establishing three security areas in the West Bank: one under Palestinian control, one under Israeli control, and the third to be patrolled by a joint force.

"Israel will draw its security map according to its needs and the Declaration of Principles," he added, "and it will be implemented in stages within these three areas. Abdel Razak Yihye backs this conception, and has discussed it with Arafat."

Finally, Abu Ala proposed that we reopen a secret channel to discuss the most sensitive issues, particularly regarding security. "You can't conduct negotiations like a press conference," he said.

I promised to report his proposals to my principals and give him an answer about opening a new secret channel. When I briefed Peres on our talk, he was taken with the idea of reviving the old Oslo format, parallel to the overt talks in Cairo between Yoel Singer and the local Palestinian leader Sa'eb Erekat, on the issue of Palestinian elections. Then he raised the matter with Rabin, who likewise consented and suggested that Peres close a deal on a secret channel in his next meeting with Arafat.

It was Terje Larsen, who continued to enjoy the trust of both sides, who laid the groundwork for that session. Peres and Arafat met in Gaza on December 21. Most of their talk was a tête-à-tête, after which they joined their delegations in a small conference room on the second floor of Arafat's modest offices. Peres announced that the two of them had decided to allow the talks on the elections to proceed but that all other issues would be settled between them, alone, in frequent future meetings. I shot Abu Ala a quizzical glance. Peres evidently noticed it because he reached for a piece of paper, emblazoned with the Palestinian eagle and the words "Office of the President" and "Palestinian National Authority," scribbled something on it, and passed it to me. "As you see," it read, "we've agreed on a secret channel; the high level is a cover."

That was the beginning of the most complex set of negotiations held between Israel and the Palestinians. We were about to create an agreement that would apply the Oslo Declaration of Principles to the

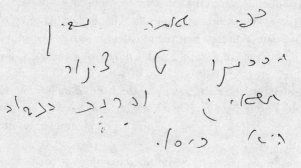

PALESTINE LIBERATION ORGANIZATION
Palestinian National Authority
Office of the President

منظمـة التحريـر الفلسطينيـة
السلطة الوطنية الفلسطينية
مكتب الرئيس

الرقم: _____
التاريخ: _____

Note from Shimon Peres to Uri Savir on PLO letterhead:
"As you see, we've agreed on a secret channel;
the high level is a cover."

West Bank, after having implemented the declaration in Gaza and
Jericho. The significance of this new Interim Agreement was obvious
to all: it would decide the fate of the area most disputed between Israel and the Palestinians, actually the heartland of the Arab-Israeli
conflict. It also pertained to the most bitter debate in Zionist history,
between right-wing Revisionist Zionism and left-wing Labor Zion-

ism—the former claiming the historical land of our ancestors, driven by a religious-national ideology, the latter arguing against Israel's domination of two million Palestinians and its corrupting effect on our society. Each camp felt the other was imperiling the very existence of the State of Israel and the lives of its people.

The negotiations were to decide the following issues concerning Palestinian autonomy:

1. Palestinian responsibilities for security (against the background of the Gaza-Jericho experience)

2. The cities and areas from which Israel would redeploy in the first stage in order to allow for free and democratic Palestinian elections

3. The modalities of the elections in the West Bank and Gaza for a Palestinian Council, together with the council's powers and responsibilities

4. The transfer of civilian powers to the Palestinian Council while certain powers would remain partially in Israeli hands, such as those pertaining to jointly used infrastructure like water, roads, and electricity

5. The legal status of the Palestinian Authority and its relationship to Israel

6. Future gradual redeployments of Israeli troops, resulting in the IDF's deployment in specified security areas, including the Israeli settlements (which were to remain intact)

7. The economic relations between the Palestinian Authority and Israel, as well as cooperation in other fields

In accordance with the Declaration of Principles, a new set of negotiations dealing with issues such as Jerusalem, the settlements, the refugees, and borders were to begin on May 4, 1996, and lead to a permanent settlement by May 4, 1999.

Given the magnitude of these challenges, the negotiations could easily have gone on for decades. Indeed, many astute and experienced people believed that even then it would be impossible to conclude an interim agreement. The iconoclastic Israeli scholar Meron Benvenisti,

Map 3: The West Bank

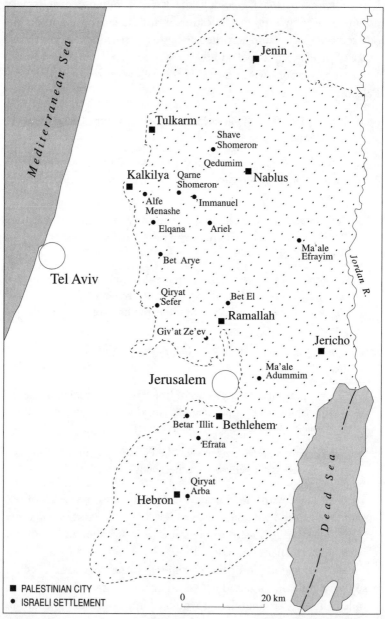

Mediterranean Sea

Jenin

Tulkarm

Shave Shomeron

Qedumim

Kalkilya   Qarne Shomeron   Nablus

Alfe Menashe   Immanuel

Elqana   Ariel

Ma'ale Efrayim

Bet Arye

Tel Aviv

Jordan R.

Qiryat Sefer   Bet El

Ramallah

Giv'at Ze'ev

Jericho

Jerusalem   Ma'ale Adummim

Betar 'Illit   Bethlehem

Efrata

Dead Sea

Qiryat Arba

Hebron

■ PALESTINIAN CITY
● ISRAELI SETTLEMENT

0   20 km

© Tammy Soffer

for example, argued that the Israeli settlements had created a political reality in the West Bank that was "irreversible." Others offered quick solutions, ranging from immediate "separation" (proposed by Police Minister Moshe Shahal) to scrapping an interim agreement and going immediately to talks on the permanent settlement.

Abu Ala and I understood that our preliminary talks would be critical, for only by agreeing on the lessons to be drawn from "Gaza-Jericho" and on a conceptual approach suitable for the West Bank would it be possible to reach an interim agreement within reasonable time. As in Oslo, we set out from the premise that only a commitment to true partnership would enable us to work profitably. Beyond that we realized that any attempt to attack, at the outset, such sensitive issues as redeployment or the control of water, land, and electricity would cripple us.

We agreed that any discussion of subjects related to the permanent solution—Jerusalem, the settlements, and so forth—was a recipe for disaster. We were painfully aware that the stakes were enormous. If we succeeded, we would free the Palestinian population from Israeli control and give Israel its only real chance of attaining security. If we failed, the peace process between Israel and the Palestinians—and, by extension, in the entire region—would also fail. Our profound common interest, burning motivation, and accumulated experience gave us hope that an agreement could be reached.

Another condition for progress was absolute secrecy, as the veterans of Oslo knew only too well. In order to protect our covert channel, we needed an overt one, as a diversion for the press. This, we decided, would be the Cairo talks between Yoel Singer and Sa'eb Erekat on the elections and between Gen. Gadi Zohar (and later Gen. Oren Shahor, the new West Bank and Gaza policy coordinator) and Jamil Tarifi on the transfer of civil powers. The emphasis of the secret talks would be on security matters. Once we had agreed on security, we would move to more open and integrated negotiations on all the other issues. Maintaining secrecy was far more difficult than it had been in Oslo, because this time the press knew the process was in train and relentlessly hunted us down to discover whether, behind the open talks in Cairo, secret talks were going on elsewhere. Also, this time many more people were involved in the preparations and the talks themselves.

My personal staff, in which my secretary Stella Shustak played an important role, found a site appropriate for our talks, the Yamit Hotel on the beachfront promenade in Tel Aviv (though some of our meetings would be diverted to the King David, Hyatt, and Moriah hotels in Jerusalem). Stella told the managers of the Yamit that from time to time we would be hosting a group of businessmen from Bahrain and that absolute secrecy was imperative. She would arrive there about two hours before the sessions began and, working with Uzi Dayan's aide-de-camp, Maj. Ivri Verbin, and his staff, transform the suite into a negotiation room.

As they approached the hotel, the Palestinians would call my driver, Oded Anavim, on his cell phone, to escort them to the Yamit's back entrance, which provided direct access to the rooms. There we awaited them, after having held a preliminary discussion on each occasion with the prime minister and foreign minister. We usually began by gazing longingly at the beach or into the busy yard of the nearby American embassy. Then the two delegations—Abu Ala, Gen. Abdel Razak Yihye, Hassan Asfour, and Hassan Abu Libdeh (a young and sharp-witted man who headed the Palestinian Office of Statistics) and Gen. Uzi Dayan, Gen. Gadi Zohar, Yoel Singer, and I—would settle in for a long discussion, often on weekends.

The secret channel began operating on January 4, 1995. For months the press failed to discover its existence. Immediately after each session, I would send Peres and Rabin a report that served as the basis for their next consultation with a group composed of Chief of Staff Amnon Shahak; the chief of Military Intelligence, Uri Saguy; the head of the Shabak, Carmi Gilon; Rabin's military secretary, Gen. Danny Yatom; and of course the negotiators themselves: Dayan, Singer, Zohar, and myself. At some stage the prime minister's media adviser, Aliza Goren, also joined this forum, which on Rabin's schedule was called "Savir's team." Neither the existence of this team nor the content of its discussions ever leaked.

At the same time, Uzi Dayan presided over a large team of security officers; Yoel Singer worked with a group of lawyers from the relevant ministries; and Zohar (followed by Shahor) held sessions to prepare the work of his team on the transfer of civil powers to the Palestinians. Twice a week the Steering Committee would meet in the Foreign Ministry or in Uzi's office. Yet only two people, Rabin and Peres, made all the critical decisions and, in the course of time, developed an extraordinary partnership. There was one, less discreet ministerial committee, composed of Moshe Shahal, Yossi Sarid, and later (after he became a minister) Ehud Barak. In our preliminary meetings with Rabin, he instructed us on the parameters of ministerial update.

The forum in which our Palestinian colleagues reported to Arafat consisted of the negotiators themselves. Every few weeks, Abu Ala also took the trouble to update Abu Mazen in Tunis.

THE SECURITY LESSONS OF THE GAZA-JERICHO AGREEMENT

The first sessions in the Yamit Hotel were devoted to the lessons of the Gaza-Jericho experience. Our conclusions were presented clearly and forcefully by Uzi Dayan.

"You lack a cogent security policy," he told the Palestinians. "You handle prevention on an individual basis, but you don't have the comprehensive policy called for in the agreement. If there's no change in this situation in Gaza, I, as the person handling security issues, cannot recommend to Rabin that we begin detailed negotiations on an interim agreement. There simply cannot be flawed security in the West Bank. You must demonstrate a considerable improvement in your policy, determination, and effectiveness in fighting terrorism. I'm not a politician; I am speaking from a military standpoint. But you must understand that our recommendation on security is very important to the decision makers. We have to deal with public opinion in Israel, and the public will ask the chief of staff a very simple question: 'Does the new arrangement assure us security or not?' "

"I agree with you about the importance of the security issue," Abu Ala replied. "It's crucial to us as well. We're making a great effort, and you've been no more successful than we. I'm also of the opinion that

we must develop a more comprehensive policy. But you must understand that you've turned our autonomy into a prison for us. You've
turned from occupiers into warders controlling our movements. This
weakens the Authority and its ability to fight those Palestinians who
benefit from the personal and economic distress of the population.
There's great disappointment in the agreement on our side as well.
Our population must be shown a ray of hope. We're not talking about
'give-and-take' here; we're talking about a new balance in relations.
You are the strong side."

"It's not our intention to make your lives miserable," Uzi replied.
"But you must take concrete steps if our relations are to change. First
of all, you must make it clear that the Palestinian Police is the only
body with military authority on the ground. Second, you must confiscate all unlicensed weapons. And third, you must halt the incitement to violence. The psychological and propaganda factor is also
important, and you must see to it that the murder of Israelis is delegitimized."

"We're doing that," Abu Ala protested. "Most of the Palestinian
population—according not just to my own view but to public opinion
polls—is opposed to violence. This is a major change. In the past
murdering Israelis was considered a legitimate act of heroism under
the occupation. But our people must also believe in the sincerity of
your intentions. If they see that the political process is deadlocked
and they find themselves unemployed, their motivation declines. The
two go hand in hand. And *you* haven't honored many clauses in the
Gaza-Jericho Agreement, such as opening 'safe passage' for Palestinians between Gaza and the West Bank!"

So the debate continued. The two sides had common as well as
conflicting interests. It was now time to analyze our errors, not an
easy matter. Yet the very effort to address these mistakes together
eventually brought back the "Oslo spirit" of a problem-solving partnership.

At another of these secret meetings, Uzi opened a map of the West
Bank city of Ramallah, just north of Jerusalem. He wanted to illus-
trate the complexity of the security situation in the West Bank, and
Ramallah was the most extreme example.

"Let's, for a moment, theoretically transpose the present situation in Gaza to Ramallah after redeployment," he began. "Given the measures you're taking against terrorism today, if we were to pull back from Ramallah, which is five minutes away from Jerusalem, there would be no hope of stemming the flood of terrorism that might come from that city. Gaza is surrounded by a fence; the West Bank is not. Rampant terrorism from a place like Ramallah would promptly destroy the agreement."

Then Uzi pointed to the Israeli settlements near Ramallah—one of which is perched immediately above it—and spoke of the tangled skein of life when two peoples inhabit such close quarters. To Israeli eyes, the notion of pulling our troops out of Ramallah seemed almost unthinkable.

At a separate session, Abdel Razak Yihye explained the Palestinian security doctrine.

"It's your conception of security that's failed, not ours," he began. "You want to impose your doctrine of security on us out of a narrow view of what security means. But you must understand that the answer lies in changing the psychological atmosphere. If you force something on us, Arafat will not be able to carry it out. If you appoint yourselves the arbiters of right and wrong, you will destroy the goodwill we have with our people. The way to bring about a radical change in atmosphere, which will ultimately serve the interest of both sides, is to create a security partnership."

At that point, the highly experienced and amiable Palestinian general surprised us. "We are proposing the establishment of a joint Israeli-Palestinian force to police broad areas of the West Bank," he said. "A concerted effort of this sort will contribute to a revolution in perceptions and bring calm to the area."

"Yes, cooperation is the key to success," Abu Ala added. "But you continue to behave like our masters. It seems to me that a good part of your army is not aware of the partnership implied by the agreements. Each time we must pass through a checkpoint—and there are many of them—your soldiers try to trample on our dignity by making us wait for hours or by throwing our identity cards on the ground so that we have to stoop before them in public view. I have no complaints about you; we sit here as equals. But out there, on the ground, your people behave as if nothing has changed. Most of us reach these meetings after having been shamed in one way or another. We are people of stature in our society, and even when we possess VIP identity cards we're deliberately humiliated in full view of other Palestinians. So imagine how the average Palestinian is treated!"

"I agree that we must educate our people to behave decently," I replied. "But I must point out again that this situation stems from the security problems. Our soldiers are very tense, for fear that someone will get past them with a bomb. The army is encouraging them to adopt a new attitude, but it will take time for it to sink in."

"I understand this takes time, and we may be able to endure the humiliation," Abu Ala conceded. "But how can we explain the deadlock in the peace process?"

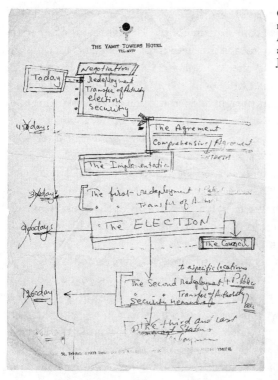

Chart by Abu Ala made during Interim Agreement negotiations at the Yamit Hotel, January 1995.

"To break it, you must prove to us that you've changed your approach to security in Gaza," Uzi said.

While the talks in the Yamit Hotel continued, Abu Ala and I held a number of meetings alone to hammer out a conception of the Interim Agreement. These discussions, which took place in Washington, Jerusalem, and Tel Aviv, centered on what would have to be done differently in order to make the Interim Agreement viable. The key word was "cooperation." Abu Ala held that this vital ingredient, which was so prominent in the Declaration of Principles, had been watered down in the Gaza-Jericho Agreement. So we tried to construct a more sweeping concept of cooperation, one that would embrace military and economic affairs, the transfer of power, consideration for public opinion, and our relations with Jordan. We also concluded that the full implementation of the Interim Agreement was imperative, so that we would have to create a whole gallery of instruments for working together, from joint civilian committees and a variety of security structures to a special annex to the agreement on cooperation in all spheres of life.

"Look, we'll agree to accommodate you on your security demands," Abu Ala told me at a long nocturnal meeting in Washington, "but you'll have to convince us that your concern is really security. What's important to us is leaving most jurisdiction to us, as we did in the Declaration of Principles, meaning that you'll transfer most of the powers in the West Bank to us. In that case, we won't object to security arrangements. Land is the main thing for us. Your expansion of the settlements is designed to close off options for the future, and there's no way we'll reconcile ourselves to that. The Oslo talks were based on your government's decision to freeze the settlements. Without an understanding on this, there wouldn't have been an agreement, and there won't be any agreement now."

I told him that if he wanted to know what was really going on in the settlements, he should listen to the complaints of the settlers, who regarded us as ideological foes. As to juxtaposing security and jurisdiction, I told him that was negotiable.

I used these private talks to explain to Abu Ala that Uzi Dayan and I agreed on the security issue, as did Rabin and Peres. The Palestini-

ans tended to suspect that the army had the final word on the negotiations. The truth is that we couldn't have made progress without the
army's involvement. Its influence was considerable. But its officers
never interfered in political decisions.

Meanwhile, the meetings in Cairo between Yoel Singer and Sa'eb
Erekat on the modalities of Palestinian elections were going
smoothly. At a certain point Yoel recommended that these talks, too,
should be held closer to home, namely, in Tel Aviv and Jericho.
Erekat was assisted in these talks by officials of the European Union,
which had agreed to help prepare the Palestinians for the elections.
Yoel understood the importance of a relatively pluralistic Palestinian
political culture, and Erekat supported him. By the end of March
they had an impressive joint draft, with a prominent gap on how to
conduct the voting in East Jerusalem.

Sa'eb Erekat, notorious in Israel as the Palestinian who had mili-
tantly sported a kaffiyeh at the 1991 Madrid Peace Conference, had
now blossomed—due in large measure to his dialogue with Yoel—into
a determined and productive negotiator. He meanwhile convinced
Yoel of the importance of how the vote would be conducted. Most of
us took a rather cynical view of the Palestinian elections, which was
also expressed around Rabin's conference table. The prime minister
felt that it wasn't our place to impose democracy on the Palestinians.
Yoel, however, convinced us to take the elections seriously by reporting on the disagreement within the Palestinian leadership about the
desirable degree of pluralism. Many Palestinians were looking at the
Israeli model; others wanted to keep the centralized system. No
democratic venture of this kind had ever been attempted in any Middle Eastern society outside of Israel. That Israel should contribute to
it, by sharing its own experiences with the Palestinian negotiators, was
obviously the right course and received strong backing from Peres.

Rabin and Peres each met with Arafat several times during the winter
of 1994–1995. Their aim was always the same: to impress on him that
without a marked improvement in the performance of his security
forces, there could be no interim agreement. These direct communications were complemented by a secret envoy who shuttled between

Rabin and Arafat. Early in 1994, Rabin had asked a former senior Shabak official, Yossi Genosar, to discreetly relay messages between Arafat and himself. The content of these messages had to do with specific security matters: warnings, demands, and proposals for cooperation between the sides. Genosar communicated with the defense establishment through the prime minister's military secretary, Danny Yatom, and from time to time involved senior military figures in his contacts.

Genosar's mission yielded a helpful by-product. Since the "chemistry" between Rabin and Arafat was not exactly warm, Genosar, who had a solid rapport with both of them, and was also economically active with the Palestinians, was able to "translate" each personality to the other, which gradually made for a better understanding between the two leaders. He was also able to draw a reliable picture of the internal problems facing each side and thus helped erode the mistrust between them. There's no question that he contributed to Rabin's understanding of Arafat and his problems. And Arafat, for his part, gradually began to take steps designed to heighten the mutual trust between the two men, especially in the field of security (such as arrests of suspects).

Peres's meetings with Arafat were not what you would call pleasant. Yet Peres was able to balance his fight for Israel's positions with a deeper appreciation of the Palestinians' needs. In working with Arafat, he always distinguished between the chairman's more peculiar mannerisms and his ability to make decisions—which, we had learned long ago, was critical to the progress with the Palestinians.

Important decisions were made by Peres and Arafat during those months. From the moment Peres was convinced that it was possible to achieve a full interim agreement, he became the driving force behind the process. He was intimately familiar with the details of the Yamit talks, spent considerable time talking with Rabin privately, and met with Arafat from time to time to make the decisions that became turning points in the negotiating process.

One of those milestones came on March 9, 1995, a week and a half after we concluded the Yamit exploration talks, which I summed up in a personal letter to Peres with a proposal for a package deal. In return for the Palestinians executing a comprehensive security and *antiterror policy*, the talks on the Interim Agreement would be accelerated toward completion on a target date of July 1, 1995. The agreement would require cooperation in all spheres—though primarily security—and would be implemented gradually. My proposal also cited Israel's redeployment from all the cities in the West Bank (the populated areas), with special security arrangements to be applied in Hebron, as the first stage of transferring the area to Palestinian control. Thereafter, a "further redeployment" from unpopulated areas, to be effected in stages over two years (half the interim period), would be tailored to Israel's security needs.

Peres's March 9 meeting with Arafat was a good one, as it based itself on all aspects of the Yamit talks. When it ended Arafat announced the Palestinian Authority's comprehensive security policy. It included the statement that the Palestinian Police was the only security organ permitted to operate on the ground; a systematic policy for thwarting terrorism and other forms of violence; a prohibition on citizens carrying arms not licensed by the Authority; and a commitment to intensify security cooperation with Israel. On the same occasion, Peres announced that the two sides would make every effort to conclude the Interim Agreement by July 1, 1995. After initial hesitation, Rabin had approved this target date, though he continued to rehearse his pronouncement that "no dates are sacred." I myself am an avid proponent of target dates, even if they're unrealistic, because they help negotiators bypass wearisome and superfluous debates over who is right and who is righter, move directly to the actual bargaining, and reach agreement within a reasonable amount of time.

The March 9 meeting essentially moved the negotiations from the exploratory stage to the pragmatic one. Before it ended, Arafat raised the three demands that came up at each such meeting and had never received a satisfactory response: the release of Palestinian security prisoners, the lifting of the closure on Gaza and the territories, and a total freeze on building settlements. Each of these issues was of great import to the Palestinian public, but they were not taken seriously enough by us because we regarded the conclusion of the Interim Agreement as a historic breakthrough and therefore often concentrated more on the negotiations than on the situation on the ground.

So to a certain degree we scoffed at the Palestinians' complaints about such "banal" issues as closure and the prisoners. In retrospect this was a mistake, for to have been more forthcoming on these issues would have created more goodwill, which would have helped other discussions, as well as our relationships in general.

Dividing the West Bank into Areas

For the next four months, our meetings continued to focus on two main issues: following through on the defense policy that Arafat had announced on March 9 and exploring the principles behind the future security arrangements in the West Bank. On April 16, when we saw that the Palestinian Authority's security performance was indeed improving, Uzi presented Israel's basic security doctrine, based on the differences between the West Bank and the Gaza Strip both on the ground and in the Declaration of Principles. It called for a gradual transfer of internal security powers to the Palestinian Authority while leaving Israel in control of

1. External security (in this case meaning the Jordan Valley)

2. The settlements, the areas surrounding them, and the roads traveled by Israelis (including the bypass roads then being paved for the settlers' use)

3. The defense of Israel proper along the Green Line (the pre-1967 border between Israel and the West Bank)

Except in the areas of security control, whose size would be decided by Israel, the IDF would redeploy in stages, with a first redeployment from populated Palestinian areas, on the eve of the Palestinian elections, and several further redeployments.

The Palestinians presented a completely different security concept, as outlined by Abdel Razak Yihye on May 19.

"Permit me to say," he began, "that your view of security lacks a political dimension. Security will come with an improvement in the relations between the two sides. Your doctrine admittedly gives you more control in the field. But it will only lead to a deterioration in relations, and thus detract from security.

"We are proposing to divide the West Bank into three areas: one to be under our control; one to be under yours (as permitted by the Declaration of Principles); and a third, extensive area to be administered jointly. We insist upon freedom of movement for Palestinians on the roads. If they must continue to pass through checkpoints while going from place to place, you will continue to humiliate them and poison the atmosphere. Remember: the quality of our people's daily life is what counts."

Uzi was irked by the insinuation that Israel was poisoning the public mood. "We're not starting from scratch!" he snapped. "Your performance in Gaza and Jericho has been unsatisfactory. Only recently has there been an improvement—and that only under pressure from us!"

"We have indeed all made mistakes," Abu Ala conceded. "But we must draw the necessary conclusions for the next agreement. If you crosscut the West Bank, there won't be any security!"

"We're talking about a gradual process, as we decided in Oslo," I said. "It's taken you nine months to get a handle on security in Gaza. In the West Bank, you will have to be in control from day one; otherwise the agreement will collapse. So it's not just the agreement that's important but how the sides grasp its implementation.

"As to coming to terms with the redeployment and its gradual implementation," I added, "perhaps we should return to a quiet and exhaustive discussion, far away from here."

"We're for it," Abu Ala replied, "and we'll ask the chairman about it tonight."

This was the genesis of what became known in our group as Operation Spaghetti: two rounds of thoroughgoing secret talks in Italy on the concept of the redeployment and the security annex to the Interim Agreement.

Meanwhile, through the rest of May and June, the "Savir team" consulted with Rabin, Peres, and the heads of the defense establishment on the details of our security doctrine and the redeployment. The discussions usually opened with my general survey of the negotiations and presentations by Uzi, Yoel, and Oren Shahor in their re-spective spheres. In every negotiation some friction exists between the "desk men" and the negotiators, who must suffer the tribulations of actually dealing with the other side. So there was much irritability during these discussions. Yet I developed a deep respect for the peo-ple, mostly the generals, who could debate issues fateful to national security without fear of offending their superiors. Rabin, Peres, and Shahak permitted absolute frankness and enabled us to express our misgivings and frustrations.

The dividing line between political and strictly military issues in these deliberations was much finer than some of the participants were willing to admit. Oslo had fundamentally been an ideological-political decision, but its implementation required security solutions. Similarly, security doctrine was intimately bound up with a political vision of the permanent settlement. Rabin confined himself, in the presence of the generals, to encouraging military thinking about Is-rael's long-term security interests.

As a whole, these deliberations were marked by the amount of time Rabin devoted to them, the detail in which subjects were explored, the quality of the preliminary staff work, the high level of the often bitter debates, and the operative decisions that emerged from them. Toward the end of each meeting, Peres would usually treat us to a broader perspective on the issues, then Rabin would sum up the ses-sion. Often they saw things in a similar way. Both insisted on pre-serving Israel's basic security interests, as perceived by the military, but they were keenly aware of the need to accommodate politically our Palestinian partners. A lopsided agreement, they knew, would fail. Peres would usually call for a little more generosity on ideologi-cal grounds, on the issue of free movement, for instance. Rabin leaned toward the pragmatic—assessing Arafat's ability and necessary strength to accept our demands. But their conclusions were almost identical. At times of crisis, it was Peres who encouraged us. He was absolutely confident that we were on the right track. And it seemed to me that he reached decisions more quickly because he viewed the negotiations as dealing with the problems of the past, while the real challenge was to build a regional coalition to face the risks and op-portunities of the future. Details were Rabin's forte.

The partnership between a man who was able to see the forest and another who usually focused on the trees was a boon to the decision-making process. During the consultations on the Interim Agreement, we all sensed the development of a unique and unexpected rapport between the two. If, at the start of the process, Rabin had a tendency to circumvent Peres and sometimes even rudely cut him off, as the negotiations continued, the two leaders began to treat each other with impressive respect. They constantly exchanged notes and always met privately both before and after the general sessions. Actually, the real decisions were taken in private, between them. And in time the military members of the forum, who were naturally closer to Rabin, expressed growing admiration for Peres as the man whose long-range strategy was the clearest—and therefore drew all the others along in its wake.

The negotiators among us—Uzi, Yoel, Oren, and I—wanted to protect the political leadership from decisions about the tactical needs of the negotiations. This was our expertise. But above all, every one of us sensed in Rabin and Peres the great weight of one hundred years of combined experience in handling the affairs of state. Those of us who were present when important and even historic decisions were made were greatly impressed by the advantages of that experience.

I personally felt a steady rise in Rabin's attention, trust, and backing. I can't claim to have had a strong rapport with him. He could often be bluntly intimidating during our deliberations. Yet he valued the fact that the team worked together harmoniously. And he appreciated our frankness about the tactical challenges of carrying out our mandate.

As a team we insisted that the political echelon lay its goals out before us. "We'll find a way to get our aims across," I told Rabin, "but it's essential that you spell out what kind of agreement you want."

In this respect, a revealing session took place at the beginning of June, when Uzi first laid out the IDF's security map for the Interim Agreement. The map showed four of the seven Palestinian cities in the West Bank—Jenin, Nablus, Tulkarm, and Kalkilya—colored in brown as the areas that would be under Palestinian military control before Palestinian elections. Two cities—Ramallah and Bethlehem—were also marked in brown, but as the areas from which the IDF would redeploy somewhat later, as ways were found for the settlers to drive through or around them. Hebron, marked in white, was a special case that would essentially remain under Israel's full military control. The six cities in brown were islands in a lake of Israeli-controlled territory. That would change gradually with the further redeployments and the expansion of Palestinian jurisdiction.

A lively discussion followed this presentation, in which everyone had a chance to speak his mind. When Rabin asked Shahak for his opinion, he replied, typically: "This map is the way in which we will be able to offer the best security solutions, given the fact that the settlements will remain intact. The IDF bears responsibility for the settlers' safety, and we must be able to say to them—and it's best to start talking with them now—that their security is being protected." (Indeed, much of the security arrangements we planned and negotiated were related to the settlements.)

When my turn came to speak, I said that I accepted the basic concept but feared that distinguishing among the Palestinian cities was out of the question. "Arafat can't go to elections if the main cities aren't treated equally," I warned. I was referring mainly to deferral of the redeployment in Ramallah and Bethlehem but also to our position on Hebron.

"If we evacuate Hebron, the place will blow up!" cried Rabin. "The worst extremists on both sides are living there."

Peres was no less vehement. "What does Arafat want? For everything to explode here? No one has ever given him what we did!"

I told them I was confident Arafat would accept our security demands. But he would not be able to get different treatment of the West Bank's cities past his supporters. Holding elections in three of these cities in the shadow of the occupation was as undesirable as it was impractical, I said. An extreme opening position in negotiations does not always yield optimal results.

But others felt very differently. Gen. Ilan Biran, head of the IDF's Central Command, expressed his misgivings about ever redeploying from Ramallah and Bethlehem at all. "The Palestinian Authority will be five minutes away from Jerusalem," he said. "So I agree that redeploying from four cities prior to the elections is enough."

Then Rabin steered the discussion onto a surprising track. "At any rate," he said, "we must begin thinking about withdrawing the IDF from its permanent bases in the countryside. That means we're talking about relinquishing our control over sixty-five percent of the Palestinian population. There's no reason not to dismantle our bases in that area. If we can create a third category, in which the Palestinians will have civil powers over the countryside but we'll retain responsibility for security, then our proposal will be more reasonable and congruent with the Declaration of Principles."

Rabin asked Uzi and Yoel to explore the notion of a third area. As to Ramallah and Bethlehem, he asked the deputy chief of staff, Gen. Matan Vilnai, to check on how long it would take to pave bypass roads around them. In Hebron, he decided, our position would be the one proposed by the military—that the IDF would remain in place—though we would allow for special arrangements on the day of the elections.

Yoel summed up the prime minister's decision in a detailed document suggesting the creation of a third area. Thus our proposed map would contain a brown area (A) under Palestinian civil and military control; a yellow one (B) under Israeli military and Palestinian civil control; and a white one (C) under exclusive Israeli control. When Rabin saw this document and the attached map, he asked that the yellow area be expanded to take account of lands owned by Palestinians and various ties between villages. But it was not to include any roads traveled by Israelis. This would constitute, for the first redeployment, approximately 25 percent of the West Bank as the A area; 25 percent as B; and the rest as C.

We were therefore ready for the second stage of the "Battle of the Redeployment." It had already been agreed that we would hold these talks in Italy. So Peres called home our ambassador in Rome, Avi Pazner, and asked him to find a location for the talks. He was to act with complete discretion and in conjunction with the Italian foreign minister, Susanna Agnelli, with whom Peres had a good relationship. Pazner returned to Rome and reported to us that Agnelli suggested conducting the "operation" (like everything else in Italy) in a familial fashion. She would ask her brother, Peres's old friend Gianni Agnelli, owner of the Fiat car company, to place the company's seminar center near Turin at our disposal. That way Fiat's security people and the managers of the seminar could handle everything. Naturally, we agreed.

The staff of Fiat was told that people from the Middle East would be coming to close a huge business deal, so the center would have to be cleared of all its lecturers and students. We asked Fiat for two small executive jets for the eight people in the two delegations. At the last minute they sent only one, which, they said, was sufficient for all eight passengers.

On May 26 a courteous driver from the Foreign Ministry named Chai Ozan collected the Palestinians at the Hyatt Hotel. We drove to the meeting point by the western entrance to the airport in our own cars. There Chai told us that he had talked with his Palestinian passengers in fluent Arabic and taken them for lunch in nearby Petach Tikvah. Closed security vehicles took us directly to the Fiat plane on the tarmac.

We sat in tense silence all the way to Turin, where we were directed to separate cars. There was certainly no lack of space in the center, which had four floors, dozens of classrooms, and small but pleasant bedrooms. In the middle of them all was an elegant dining room that looked out on an exquisite garden, where we could take Norwegian-style walks. Stella, my secretary, was our liaison with the local staff, which provided us with a steady supply of pasta and unlimited amounts of espresso to make up for our lack of sleep.

In the afternoon we gathered in a small meeting room on the ground floor and immediately handed the Palestinians draft copies of the Security Annex to the Interim Agreement. All eight participants began poring over the document, as the Palestinians made notes in the margins. The annex, which contained nine sections, emphasized the Palestinian Authority's policy on fighting terrorism. It called for confiscating arms upon Palestinian takeover of every city, placing terrorists on trial, and otherwise systematically preventing terrorism and incitement to violence. It clearly articulated Israel's responsibility for security in the West Bank, other than in the cities to come under

Palestinian control. It proposed the creation of a third zone, in which Israel would be responsible for security and the Palestinians for civil affairs (the area of the villages). And it stated that the further redeployment, to expand the area under full Palestinian control, would be effected gradually, in line with the security situation.

The next morning Abu Ala responded to the document with moderation—as he usually did at first, to suggest that he took our positions seriously—and asked for certain clarifications. The crux of the debate shifted to the size of the zone in which Israel and the Palestinians would have joint responsibility (Area B). But we declined to discuss the size of any of the three areas and said that we would present a map of them only after the principles of the security doctrine had been agreed upon. Among ourselves, I suggested that we not reveal the map until the end of all the negotiations, so as to avoid raising an issue that might lead to extended confrontation, since Palestinian expectation went far beyond what we intended to offer territorially in the first stage.

We then moved to an adjoining room and began schematizing our basic concept of the areas on a white board, without revealing their boundaries. This angered the Palestinians, particularly Asfour.

"According to Oslo, we're to receive *all* the security and civil powers on the eve of the elections!" he said. "Stop confusing us with legal terms. Most of the West Bank must be transferred to us!"

Yoel replied with a detailed explanation of the gradual transfer of security powers. But the Palestinians were not satisfied. We therefore suggested that they come back to us with their response to our comments on the Security Annex, confident that the side that presents its draft first always enjoys an advantage. At the Turin talks we also agreed to combine the Gaza-Jericho Agreement with the Interim Agreement.

When we took a break on Friday, Yoel's English typist, Pamela Levin, who observed Jewish traditions, organized a candle-lighting ceremony for our delegation. After she lit the Sabbath candles, Uzi said the *Kiddush* blessing over the wine as the Palestinians looked on from the side. When the ritual was over somebody suggested that we sing a song together, since we couldn't say a common prayer. We sang

Shimon Peres with his new press spokesman, 1985.

Leo Savir and Shimon Peres, June 1985.

Yossi Beilin and Uri Savir in Washington, October 1984.

Abu Ala and Uri Savir in Oslo.

Mona Juul and Terje Larsen.

Abu Ala, Terje Larsen, and Uri Savir at the
Oslo Plaza Hotel, December 1993.

Uri Savir (seated, right) and Abu Ala (seated, left) initialing the Declaration of Principles, Oslo, August 19, 1993; with Foreign Minister Johan Jørgen Holst of Norway and (back row, left to right) Hassan Asfour, Jan Egeland, Mona Juul, Terje Larsen, Yoel Singer, and Yair Hirschfeld.

The first handshake between an Israeli minister and a senior PLO official—Shimon Peres and Abu Ala—with Johan Jørgen Holst, August 19, 1993.

Abu Ala and Uri Savir shake hands after initialing the Oslo Declaration of Principles, observed by Johan Jørgen Holst and members of the Norwegian, Palestinian, and Israeli delegations.

A historic moment: Yitzhak Rabin and Yasser Arafat shake hands at the White House in front of President Clinton after signing the Declaration of Principles, September 1993. *(Les Stone/Sygma)*

On the way to Cairo in a small private jet, March 18, 1994.
Left to right: Uri Savir, Amnon Shahak (celebrating his
fiftieth birthday), Yoel Singer, and Jacques Neria.

Cairo, Febuary 9, 1994: Abu Ala and Uri Savir signing the agreement on
the Allenby Bridge and Rafah passages. Standing: Faisal Husseini, Yasser
Abd Rabbo, an unidentified Palestinian bodyguard, Nabil Shaath, Yasser
Arafat, Hosni Mubarak, and Shimon Peres.

King Hussein of Jordan, Prime Minister Yitzhak Rabin, and
Uri Savir during the initialing of the Jordanian-Israeli
Peace Accord, November 1994.

Abu Ala and Uri Savir negotiating the Interim Agreement on
the West Bank in Eilat, August 1995.

Lunch sessions at the Patio Hotel in Eilat during the Interim Agreement negotiations, August 1995: General Uzi Dayan, Uri Savir, Oded Eran.

Uri Savir in Eilat with the heads of Palestinian Preventive Security, Mohammed Dahlan and (sitting in background) Jibril Rajoub.

Negotiating the Interim Agreement with Yasser Arafat, Taba, August 1995.

Abu Ala, Yasser Arafat, Shimon Peres, and Uri Savir during the initialing of the Interim Agreement, September 23, 1995.

President Bill Clinton and Uri Savir in the Oval Office on the day of
the signing of the Interim Agreement, September 28, 1995.

Trilateral committee meeting at the Jerusalem Laromme Hotel, October
1995: Abu Ala, Uri Savir, Dennis Ross.

March 4, 1996: A suicide bomber kills thirteen in front of the Dizengoff Center in downtown Tel Aviv. *(Motty Kimchi/Sygma)*

Uri Savir, Aliza Savir, and Abu Mazen at the Passover Seder hosted by American ambassador Martin Indyk, April 1997.

Abu Ala and Maya Savir, November 1994.

Maya Savir and Mona Qurei at Maya's wedding, January 15, 1998.

"Everybody Loves Saturday Night"—which wasn't strictly appropriate, but we sang it anyway, in three languages. At dinner, Pamela announced that it was her birthday. Although she would have preferred to celebrate it with her family, she added, she was honored to be present on this occasion. We sang "Happy Birthday," again in three languages—and Abu Ala made a short speech on behalf of both delegations. A lively conversation ensued between Pamela and Hassan Abu Libdeh about a mother's feelings on the loss of a child. Pamela wondered if they might be different among Israelis and Arabs. Hassan replied, with utmost courtesy and restraint, that they were quite the same. "Only fanatics, on both sides, pay homage to violence," he said.

That night Uzi and I invited Abu Ala for a walk in the garden. We explained to him that there was no hope of getting Rabin's approval for a second Palestinian area unless Israel retained responsibility for its security, though not its civil affairs.

"I understand the need for security," he said. "But it's out of the question that most of the West Bank's population will continue to live under Israel's full military control!"

Once again he proposed cooperation in this sphere—though he stressed that the Declaration of Principles promised the Palestinians exclusive control of their own people. Uzi and I shared with him our fear that violence would break out between the settlers and the Palestinians. And if it did, we added, only the IDF was capable of handling it.

"In time both sides will adjust to the new situation," I told him. "And then it will be possible—as our draft states—to extend your responsibility for security."

"I'll talk with my colleagues and take this up with the chairman on my return. When it comes to security, we're prepared to meet your needs," said Abu Ala. "But bear in mind, that's only if we're convinced your real intention is to maintain security, not just to deprive us of our land."

After that talk we knew a tough negotiation awaited us. But at least the parameters of an interim agreement had been fixed as Israel's retention of military control over most of the West Bank, without prej-

udice to the Palestinians' ability to gradually expand the area under
their control. This was the crux of the Interim Agreement: the Palestinians would yield more easily on security powers than on territory.
Creating an area of joint control during the interim period and gradually transferring additional territory to them was the basis for a
bridging formula. Now its components had to be negotiated.

Rabin scheduled a consultation on June 1. He was satisfied with
the Turin talks and so far would back up the delegation's tactics. He
also decided that Gen. Oren Shahor, the new coordinator of activities
in the territories (replacing Gen. Danny Rothschild), should join the
team and that the broad issue of the transfer of civilian powers should
be placed on the agenda.

We flew back to Turin the same day. This time the Palestinians arrived with their comments on the draft of the Security Annex. The
gap between us was considerable. They insisted on joint security re-

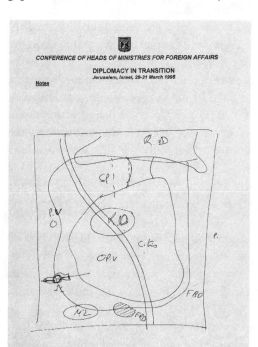

The redeployment of
cities, sketched during
Yamit Hotel negotiations,
January 1995.

sponsibility for Area B and marked Area A to include all seven Palestinian cities *and* the villages in the countryside. What's more, they demanded that the redeployment be defined as "irreversible." They also brought along a new preamble to the Security Annex. Abu Ala took the trouble to note that, if we accepted it, they would be more forthcoming about the body of text. The preamble emphasized Palestinian freedom of movement within the West Bank and "safe passage" between the West Bank and Gaza.

"We will not allow you to control freedom of movement within the autonomous areas," he declared, "and will not agree to having IDF checkpoints within the West Bank."

The Palestinians wanted to be sure that civil responsibilities would be transferred to them after the elections, in an accelerated manner, in most of the West Bank. Abu Ala was attempting a sophisticated maneuver. He confined himself to a verbal response on our detailed questions, without committing himself to a precise position, and anchored most of the Palestinians' interests in the preamble to the annex on security.

At this point Yoel and I tried to integrate the first section drafted by the two sides. This draft served as a basis for future negotiations on security principles (with the gaps noted in parentheses) alongside our draft of the Security Annex (with general Palestinian comments still in the margins). Conceptually we made progress as the Palestinians agreed to three zones in the West Bank—a Palestinian area (A), an Israeli area (C), and an area to be controlled jointly in a manner to be decided through negotiation (B). So we had the beginning of a joint document.

We returned home with a sense of accomplishment. Someone had carried a tennis ball into the plane, which we tossed from side to side as my secretary, Stella, who had picked up a few words of Italian, tried to explain to the pilots that our car deal had evidently been closed. Then Abu Ala and I did our impressions of Peres and Arafat while Uzi taught Hassan Asfour to sing "My Yiddishe Mama"—Fellini-like moments in an Agnelli-owned plane. Clearly, we needed to relax after so much tension. But we were also reverting to the common language of humor that bespoke a deeper human partnership. Humor, in fact, increasingly became a replacement for sleep and an expression of a bond and common language that had to be repressed during the long and nerve-racking negotiations.

Upon our return, Rabin and Peres concurred that the hour had come to tell the Palestinians from exactly which cities we intended to redeploy. It was also time to reveal our demand that all the Palestinian villages would fall into Area B and not A, as they had assumed.

As Stella feared that the managers of the Yamit had begun to wonder what we were really doing on their premises, we asked our Norwegian friends, Terje and Mona, to find an appropriate apartment for us somewhere along the coast. They offered us the home of the Norwegian political attaché (in Herzeliah, just north of Tel Aviv), who was then on leave in Oslo. It was there that we met on June 23–24 to reveal the redeployment map to the Palestinian negotiators.

We had reached another moment of truth. Until then, the gaps in our positions had been over our respective responsibilities in the three areas of the West Bank. Now began the battle over the size of these areas.

As Mona came to collect us for the drive to the villa, where the Palestinians were awaiting us, it was agreed that the Palestinians would sleep there while we returned to our homes. When Mona left, we sat down for our first discussion on the redeployment. The banter stopped, the smiles vanished, and the air grew tense. In the background we could hear the voices of our drivers, who had become good friends. Abu Ala stalked into the kitchen and ordered them bluntly to be quiet. It was a sign of how raw our nerves were—and we hadn't yet begun.

I opened by explaining that on the eve of the elections for the Palestinian Council, the IDF would redeploy outside the municipal boundaries of Jenin, Tulkarm, Kalkilya, and Nablus—to be known as Area A. On a subsequent date, dependent upon the completion of by-pass roads for Israelis, the IDF would redeploy from Ramallah and Bethlehem. Hebron would be treated as a special case, because Jewish settlers were living in the city, and we proposed that a committee be appointed to design special arrangements for free elections there.

The areas of the villages (Area B) would be administered jointly.

Israel would be responsible for security, the Palestinian Authority for civil affairs.

All the unpopulated areas, together with areas containing Jewish settlements (Area C), would remain under Israel's exclusive control.

After the elections Israel would gradually transfer to the Palestinian Authority, at its own discretion, security powers in rural Area B and the unpopulated areas C that were not deemed of importance to its security. This would not, of course, include any of the settlements.

The four Palestinians took notes and then asked for a break. They whispered furiously in the negotiating room while we waited in a corner of the lounge decorated with Norwegian ornaments. This time we sensed an inevitable crisis. Though we could not anticipate what impact the crisis would have on both sides, we believed that the looming date of July 1—the target for completing the Interim Agreement—would pressure the Palestinians to make progress. Finally our partners stood up and announced that they were ready to respond. Abu Ala spoke forcefully.

"We are prepared to implement the Declaration of Principles in collaboration with you," he began. "But what you are proposing deviates from the agreements we have signed. You want ninety percent of the territory and almost one hundred percent of the responsibility for security. You do not commit yourself to what you will do in the future, and you are limiting our freedom of movement. We will not accept this. Essentially you're trying to legitimize the status quo with minute changes on the ground. Now you're exercising control as occupiers, and we can resist you as such. But you will not obtain our consent to perpetuate this situation by slightly different means. We are proposing the genuine change promised by the Declaration of Principles.

"We are ready to cooperate in fighting violence. But the area of the cities will have to be enlarged to include a number of villages. In no way can we accept a distinction between one Palestinian city and another. In all the other populated areas (B), you may retain responsibility for the security of Israelis, but we must enjoy full powers, including security over Palestinians. We are prepared to field there a Palestinian police force that will inform you of its activities but *not be subordinate to you*. We will not let our policemen be humiliated by placing them under your authority.

"As to the future, after the Palestinian elections, we are demanding a precise timetable and a detailed map on the continued transfer of territory. We have no intention of postponing matters related to the Interim Agreement to the talks on the permanent one. Were we to accept your approach, which leaves most of the territory and security powers in your hands, the West Bank would turn into a field of contention. This is not our purpose. The interim period must be a bridge of cooperation to the permanent settlement."

There was a long pause after his reply. I knew it was imperative to express our firm opposition to their demands. So I said only that we had heard their views and would report them to Rabin and Peres. We were at a stalemate, for the gaps between us were far too wide for negotiations to start. I asked to speak with Abu Ala alone, and we went off to a small side room, where we sat opposite each other.

"Your proposals will not be acceptable," I told him. "We will not give you so much responsibility for security. We simply don't trust you yet. What you have proposed will sabotage the negotiations. Were we to accept it, the whole West Bank would explode."

Abu Ala responded with unusual vehemence.

"You want security, and I understand that," he began. "But we will not stand for your control of our land under the guise of security needs—and certainly not in the absence of a commitment on how the process will continue. The mistrust is mutual, I assure you. You may try to force your approach on Arafat. And if you use your strength to push him into a corner, he may have no choice but to accept your approach. But remember: if you do that, you will isolate him. A one-sided agreement will not stand. You must find a way to protect your security *and* balance the agreement—if security is indeed your only interest. On land, we will not yield."

"If you're accusing *me* of striving for a one-sided agreement, you can find yourself another partner!" I replied angrily. "What you're demanding will lead to a deadlock. And *you'll* be the losers. The onus is on you, and I suggest you come back to me with other ideas."

Without another word, Abu Ala stood up and shouted for his driver. Then we all shook hands with chill correctness and left. In reporting to Rabin and Peres, we recommended waiting for the Palestinians to make their move. The future of the security doctrine in the West Bank hung in the balance.

On June 28 Abu Ala and I met in the Dan Hotel in Tel Aviv. Our anger had abated somewhat, and he suggested that we postpone talking about the size of each of the three areas. Right now it was necessary to agree on the exact nature of Area B and the further redeployment. I told him that because of public expectations that the agreement would be concluded by July 1, it was best for Peres and Arafat to meet and announce that significant progress had been made. After all, nobody knew that these issues were even being discussed. First, however, we two would have to accept an outline of the agreement. And that would be impossible without reaching an understanding on the nature of the area with joint responsibilities (B).

Abu Ala agreed to a summit. Then he suggested that the Palestinian Authority be responsible for public order in Area B and Israel be responsible for combating terrorism and the safety of the Israelis passing through it. I asked him what would happen if the activities of the two sides clashed, and he replied that we could regulate them through a District Coordination Office in each district.

"We believe there can be a division of labor between the two security forces, but not a division of responsibility," I said. "Israel must have *overriding* responsibility for security. If we can agree on this term, and on this principle, the rest of the details can be worked out." But Abu Ala refused and wanted to leave that decision to Peres and Arafat.

When the meeting was over, Rabin called. His urgent interest was prompted by the concern that if there was no sign of progress by July 1, we might have to deal with disorders in the West Bank. I told him we were still stalled. So Peres was again charged with breaking a deadlock.

He met Arafat on Saturday night, July 1, at the Israeli base at Erez, on the northern border of the Gaza Strip. The press was there in full force. The Civil Administration's offices had been renovated but still looked like a military headquarters in every way. Our soldiers peered curiously at Arafat when he came in surrounded by several body-guards. The meeting took place in a small conference room. Only Abu Ala and I participated with Arafat and Peres in the initial conversation; others waited in a larger room nearby.

Peres offered Arafat coffee, fruit, and Mediterranean-style pastries. The chairman asked for tea and barely ate at all. Peres sipped black coffee and munched on a piece of fruit. Abu Ala and I were less disciplined.

When the formalities were over, and the photos had been taken by the press, Peres expressed his appreciation for the discreet work of the security committee and the special partnership between Yoel Singer and Sa'eb Erekat on the election issue. The transfer of civil powers, he said, could be discussed by Oren Shahor and Jamil Tarifi. Arafat responded—as he always did when the subject of civil powers came up—by talking about finances.

"You must give us the power to collect indirect taxes too," he said. "We need money, and the donations don't help. Our policemen aren't being paid!"

We had decided that this taxing power would be transferred to the Palestinians only at the end of the negotiations, to serve as leverage. So Peres's reply was evasive. He quickly changed the subject by describing the grim mood in Israel because the terrorist actions had still not ceased.

"It's true your performance has improved, but the attacks go on," he said. "We're approaching the implementation of a very difficult move. I'm for it. You know, Mr. Chairman, that I am against the Jewish people controlling the fate of another people. But we must convince our people of that; we must start out cautiously. We must not generate friction between our two peoples in the West Bank. There are extremists on both sides. And you must think about the first elections ever to take place in the history of the Palestinian people. No other nation would offer you what we are. Several months ago, you told me that you were being reduced to the mayor of Gaza City. Now we're moving on to the four to six main cities of the West Bank. This is a historic development, Mr. Chairman, but you must consider our security interests."

Abu Ala, who was taking copious notes, glanced at me with a sour smile. He felt that Peres was leading Arafat to the conclusion Israel desired. Then Peres went on to explain our demand for overriding responsibility for security in Area B. Arafat tried to dodge the issue.

"Look," he said, "if this is a matter of English terminology, leave that to Abu Ala."

"Abu Ala is too rigid. Fire him," said Peres with a broad smile. "He and Uri are too fond of conducting negotiations without ever reaching agreement. I'll fire Uri, too."

Arafat laughed but still avoided the question of "overriding responsibility" in Area B. At that point Peres asked for Uzi Dayan to come in and review the security situation. I left the room, and Uzi stayed for some two hours. When he emerged, he told us that he and Peres had exerted considerable pressure, but Arafat would not budge. Then Yoel was called in to look over the formulas that Abu Ala had begun drafting. He too told the Palestinians that many things were possible but the term "overriding" had to appear.

By the time I was called in again, Peres and Arafat had been closeted for six hours.

"Look, Mr. Chairman," Peres said testily, "we won't get anywhere unless our soldiers know that they're in charge in the B area. Otherwise there will be clashes in the field." Indeed, most of our efforts, struggles, and ultimately resources (bypass roads) were related to the security of the settlements and the movement of the settlers in the West Bank. Peres was adamant: "So you agree? Okay? *Okay?* Otherwise Rabin and I won't be able to proceed toward an agreement!"

Arafat stared mutely, apparently in anguish, at a paper lying before him, which had been handwritten by Peres and that included the notion of overriding security responsibility. He understood that Peres was not going to yield. But he seemed to feel that Israel was striving, by means of its security powers, to carve up the West Bank. He sat for about an hour without saying a word. From time to time Peres stood up and impatiently paced about the room. Finally Arafat said that he wanted to consult with his advisers and suggested that we schedule a continuation of the meeting. Peres seemed greatly annoyed but consented. He then suggested the press be informed that "general

progress" had been made and that the contacts between the two leaders would continue in the coming days. This was stated in separate
communiqués, but the press understood there were problems.

The meeting resumed three days later, after Abu Ala had sent me
a fax with compromise formulas that included the word "overriding."
The Palestinians understood that their only recourse was to demand
a quid pro quo for that magic word, because there was no getting
around it. In his fax, written by hand on the stationery of the "Office
of the President" and sent on the night of July 2–3, Abu Ala arrived at
a logical balance, from his standpoint. Israel would have overriding
responsibility for Area B, and the Palestinian Authority would be in
charge of public order through a number of police stations. Furthermore, the continued transfer of territory would have to be ensured by
a definitive timetable, and the transfer of state lands to the Palestinians would be ensured.

At the request of Chief of Staff Amnon Shahak, that night I prepared our response with Uzi, Yoel, and Danny Yatom. The following
day, July 4, we met with Rabin before going down to Erez. He was
outraged by Abu Ala's demands.

"He wants us to commit ourselves, now, to give him gradually the
entire West Bank! Well, he can forget it!"

Whenever he was angered by the Palestinians' position, Rabin
would drop a hint—almost a warning—that we must not give in to it.
Disregarding his irritation, I proposed that we compromise on mid-
July 1997 as the date when we would complete the transfer to the
Palestinians of the rest of the areas that were not of security value (the
further redeployments). Rabin said that mid-1997 was acceptable to
him, but he forbade us to say how much territory we would transfer
to the Palestinians then. "We may have to open the map of the further redeployments someday, but certainly not now," he said.

Peres was not pleased by Rabin's tone. He felt that whenever he
conducted the negotiations personally, Rabin rewarded him with in-
gratitude. I assumed Rabin felt that, because he was not doing the
talking himself, he had to signal the people around him that he was
nonetheless in full control of the negotiations.

Be that as it may, Rabin's instructions and Abu Ala's groundwork sufficed to turn the July 4 meeting into a setting for compromise. The meeting began as a private talk between Peres and Arafat, after which Abu Ala and I were asked to join them. The compromise formula read: "In Area A [the cities] the Palestinian Authority will have full security and civilian powers. In Area C [nonpopulated] Israel will have full security and civil powers. In Area B [the Palestinian villages] Israel will have the *overriding* responsibility for security for the purpose of protecting Israelis and fighting terrorism and the Palestinian Authority will have civilian powers and be responsible for public order." Peres suggested that the issues still in dispute—how the Palestinian Police would function in Area B to maintain public order and the whole matter of Hebron—be solved by special committees working as part of the broader negotiations. He also agreed to complete the further redeployments in mid-1997. (The Palestinians wanted February 1997.) In the meanwhile, IDF and Palestinian Police officers would begin coordinating the redeployment.

When Peres and Arafat went out to meet the press, they issued a general statement that revealed no details. They did note, however, that they had directed Abu Ala and me to complete the negotiations by July 25. We felt we had achieved a breakthrough, since we had determined the responsibility for security in the three areas of the West Bank.

From that meeting Peres drove to a July 4 party given by the American ambassador, Martin Indyk. There he and Rabin phoned Warren Christopher to report on the breakthrough. "I knew last night how it would turn out," Rabin mumbled to Indyk.

The only one whose assessment was stone-cold sober that night was Yoel Singer. "I hope you realize that the real work is beginning only now," he had whispered to me in Erez.

"Will we finish by July 25?"

"We'll sign on September 13, just as we did in '93—not a day before."

As events would prove, even that forecast was optimistic.

Israel will have the overriding responsibility for internal security in order to protect Israelies and fight against terrousm.

Consequently movement ~~of~~ on the roads of Palestinians armed police or its activities in villages that don't have permanent police stations, will ~~be~~ ~~can~~ ~~to~~ ~~be~~ confirmed ~~~~ through by the DCO

Draft, in Shimon Peres's handwriting, on Israel's overriding security responsibility, presented to Yasser Arafat at Erez, August 4, 1995.

7

DISMANTLING
THE OCCUPATION

AFTER THE CONCEPT COME THE NEGOTIATIONS ON AN AGREEMENT.
After all, we were talking about transferring security and civil powers
in the West Bank to the Palestinian Authority and establishing the
ground rules for the elections to the Palestinian Council. Yoel Singer
was right: we were now just beginning the work of dismantling the
occupation under optimal conditions of security. The way was open
for the most wide-ranging and intricate set of negotiations yet to take
place between Israel and the Palestinians.

First we decided that all the working groups would proceed simultaneously. They were divided into committees on security (including
a subcommittee on Hebron), the transfer of powers, the elections,
the legal annex, the annex on cooperation, and the body of the agreement itself. Between the July 4 meeting at Erez and the start of the
actual talks, we worked on building our respective delegations and
finding a place to meet. Again we agreed on Italy. The Italian government offered us a military installation, and a point team had already worked out all the arrangements. Then Arafat changed his
mind. He wanted his chief negotiators to be closer to him. So we
agreed to meet in the Ganei Moriah Hotel in Zichron Ya'akov, a
quaint Israeli town near Haifa overlooking the Mediterranean from
Mount Carmel.

THE FURTHER REDEPLOYMENT

We reported there on July 16. The talks continued for about a week and didn't get us very far. Actually, we had great difficulty adjusting to such large delegations, which included about a hundred people each to spread out the work among experts in various spheres. Abu Ala exploited the situation by presenting, for the first time, a draft of the body of the agreement in which he emphasized Palestinian jurisdiction on most of the West Bank after Israel's further redeployments. It became the prime subject of our talks. The Declaration of Principles stated that security powers would gradually be transferred to the Palestinians through further redeployments in the West Bank except for the settlements and security locations, but it did not specify the size of these security locations. We held that such areas would have to be determined by Israel's own considerations and could not be defined in advance.

We talked to Rabin on this point over the weekend. He feared that showing the Palestinians a map of specified security locations would only spark a crisis, because, again, they were expecting to receive far more territory than we were prepared to offer (which would have been at this point roughly 50 percent of the West Bank, according to the army's assessment of what were essential security areas, given the need to secure the settlements, too). He therefore preferred to avoid the issue now and agreed to postpone a confrontation on the amount of territory to be transferred. On our side there were even those (especially in the IDF) who were concerned that carrying out the further redeployment altogether would strip us of our greatest leverage in the talks on the permanent settlement. I pointed out that the further redeployment was an improvement over the Camp David agreements, where we had to redeploy in one stage. At any rate, we would begin conducting serious talks on the permanent settlement on May 4, 1996—fourteen months before the last redeployment. The map of the permanent settlement, on which we would show greater flexibility than in the further redeployment that we would have to reveal to the Palestinians in the course of those negotiations, would at any rate neutralize the importance of the interim arrangement, so for tactical reasons we decided to postpone the battle over the further redeployment while trying to make progress on other issues.

The problem with all this was getting Abu Ala, a consummate tactician who knew how to protect his own side's interests, to agree. Back in Zichron Ya'akov, we found that the Palestinians had stiffened their position on all the civil issues on the agenda. Their message was unmistakable: you tell us what we can expect of the redeployments in the future, and we'll start making progress in the present.

No progress was made in Zichron Ya'akov.

This was bad enough, but what really irked us there was the noisy presence of a large group of Israeli demonstrators from the West Bank and their allies on the radical right. Not only could we hear their roar inside the conference rooms but they made it difficult for us to get in and out of the hotel. The Palestinians complained that the demonstrators pounded on their cars with their fists. I once had to be smuggled into the hotel at one in the morning in a small security vehicle while my driver negotiated his way through the crowd and was treated to a hail of curses. We had encountered small groups of right-wing demonstrators before, but never anything of this size or vehemence. And never once were we privileged to encounter a demonstration by the supporters of peace, which left a few members of our delegation—including me—quite bitter. We had a deep ideological commitment to the peace process and felt that demonstrations in support of peace should have been going on at this critical juncture in Israel's history. They did not take place, to any significant measure, until much later in the year.

At the same time, the setting in Zichron Ya'akov also made for some poignant experiences. At dinner one evening in the hotel dining room, I sat with Uzi Dayan and Abdel Razak Yihye, who was staring wistfully out the window at the sea, exquisite at sunset.

"You see down there?" he said, pointing to the shore. "That's Tantura, where I was born."

"Ah, really?" I said with some discomfort, for talk about birthplaces always reminded us how much this struggle was essentially over the same land—and thus how important it was to divide it once and for all.

An odd smile crossed Abdel Razak's lips. "Look at what a fool I've been," he said. "From Tantura I went to Jordan, from Jordan to Syria, then to the Palestine Liberation Army [he had been its commander], the Gulf, Egypt, Beirut, Tunisia, Amman, the West Bank, and now up on this mountain. Thirty-five years of wandering, when I could simply have walked up the mountain to have dinner with you here."

"In that sense, we've all come a long way to this table," I said.

During that week some of us also made a different journey in the interests of progress. On July 21 President Mubarak invited Peres and Arafat to Alexandria to brief him on the talks. Abu Ala and I were asked to join them.

We sat in a large room around a long rectangular table, with Mubarak at the head and Peres and Arafat on its sides. Mubarak was accompanied by his two foreign-affairs advisers, Foreign Minister Amr Moussa and Osama el-Baz, two impressive men who did not always see eye to eye. We believed that the brilliant el-Baz was more committed to the present process and that the suave Moussa was the proponent of a peace strategy in which Israel's status and role were rather minor in comparison with a strong regional leadership role, which Egypt would claim. The further redeployment was the focus of this discussion. Abu Ala raised it before Mubarak, who had undoubtedly been well briefed by Arafat before we arrived.

"The security issue and the redeployment are the heart of the matter and the basis of any settlement," Abu Ala said. "Hebron is admittedly a problem, because its residents and their relatives are scattered throughout the West Bank. Things are moving along on Area B. But my hope is to reach agreement on the further redeployment from C."

This bothered Peres, who wanted our hosts to understand that we would not be able to accommodate the Palestinians by defining the extent of the further redeployment, and therefore was putting on quite a show.

"Look at what you're getting," he said to Arafat. "Kalkilya is nine kilometers from the sea and half a kilometer from our city of Kfar Saba. Bethlehem and Ramallah are just a few kilometers away from Jerusalem. No other country would do what we're prepared to do. Mr. President"—he turned to Mubarak—"would you agree to another authority governing two to three kilometers from Cairo? You would not! The Palestinians and others thought that 'Gaza first' would be 'Gaza last.' They thought we were trying to trick them. And here Rabin and I are saying: 'Trust us about the further redeployment too. Don't negotiate about it now. We've committed ourselves to complete the redeployments by the middle of '97, and we'll keep to that. When we give our word, we keep it. So take our word for it!' "

"But what if your government changes?" Arafat retorted. "Who will guarantee it won't?"

"We'll win the next election despite what anybody says. Mr. Chairman, do you see what we're offering? What country would do that? The Libyans? The Serbs? The French? The Iraqis?"

At that point Moussa intervened to try to defuse the tension.

"I suggest we allow the teams on the further redeployments and Hebron to keep working," he said. "I understand from Uri that there are various proposals."

Peres continued to emphasize Israel's sacrifice. "We're spending a billion shekels on new army bases and bypass roads for the settlers. We're serious people!" When he felt that he had made his point, he seconded Moussa's suggestion that the teams continue to work on that issue.

In Alexandria some progress was made on a key issue. The Egyptians proposed (apparently at Abu Ala's initiative) that the elections in East Jerusalem be held in a post office. Israel had insisted that the voting in Jerusalem be done by mail (like absentee balloting). The Palestinians wanted the polling stations to be in the holy places or UN facilities, but Peres rejected that. Compromising on a post office would enable each side to say it had won. The arrangement seemed closer to our conception of absentee balloting, but the Palestinians could claim otherwise.

When the discussion shifted to the thirty-nine Palestinian women we were holding as security prisoners—a subject the Palestinians raised again and again—Peres explained to Mubarak that some of them had been convicted of murder and no decision about them could be made unless they were pardoned by the president of Israel. Instantly Mubarak (who was famed for his spontaneity and very fond of President Weizman) picked up the phone and asked an aide to get Ezer Weizman on the line.

"Ezer, how are you?" he sang into the receiver. "I have Peres and Arafat sitting here, and they send their regards. I'm really calling with a request: we want your consent to free the Palestinian women."

We didn't hear the reply, but Mubarak let out a boisterous laugh, wished Weizman the best, and told us that he had agreed to help out. This conversation opened the way for including all the women in the prisoner release clause of the agreement. But meanwhile, Peres asked Mubarak not to make this known.

That night, when Abu Ala and I met with our delegations back in Zichron Ya'akov, I reported that the meeting in Alexandria had been helpful. Abu Ala thought otherwise. "Nothing was decided on the most important issue: the further redeployment," he objected. "We'll have to keep working on it."

The Palestinians announced that they did not want to remain in Zichron Ya'akov, where right-wing demonstrations were continuing. So we decided to move to Eilat. On the way, we stopped for two days at the Dead Sea, but the talks there were fruitless and ended after a terrorist attack on a bus in Ramat Gan, in which six people were killed. The Palestinian Authority was sincerely fighting terrorism, said our military people, but there had been no way to contain it. The upshot of the contacts between the security people on both sides was to intensify both the pressure on the terrorist organizations and the cooperation between Israel and the Palestinian Authority. Nevertheless, we were convinced that Hamas and the Islamic Jihad would try even harder to prevent us from concluding an agreement. Unfortunately, we were right.

We reached Eilat on August 1 for the final phase of the talks. We took over the Patio Hotel, near the main road with an entrance through a back alleyway. Security outside the hotel was the responsibility of the Israeli Police. Inside it was the joint task of men from our Foreign Ministry's Security Department and the Palestinian Preventive Security, each side manning a desk at the entrance. We arrived from the

Eilat airport by bus to find a handful of photographers waiting outside the hotel, which they were not allowed to enter. The protesters
who had surrounded Zichron Ya'akov avoided the swelter of Eilat.

Some two hundred negotiators and support staff moved into the
hotel. The third (lobby) and fourth floors were allocated to the Israeli
delegation, the first and second floors to the Palestinians. Each delegation had a number of offices filled with all the requisite equipment.
The Palestinians had a smaller support staff, with only a few secretaries but many bodyguards, who stood outside the rooms of the senior members.

The delegations—unlike those in Oslo—were cross sections of
both societies, with equally full ranges of political views. We had, for
example, about thirty standing army officers who lived in settlements
and, like many of the others, were experiencing their first encounter
with Palestinians as equals. The Palestinian delegation included PLO
people who had served in Tunis, academics and other experts on specific subjects, members of the new administration in Gaza, and officers and men of the security services, including former terrorists who
had spent time in Israeli jails. The Palestinians, too, reflected a broad
political spectrum, from dogmatists who were skeptical about the
Oslo process to its fervent supporters. The meetings were the first
major encounter between two societies seeking to create a new relationship in all spheres of life. Abu Ala and I had decided to allow no
one to leave the hotel except on weekends or with special permission,
in order to create a group dynamic that would enhance common creative solutions.

On Monday I met with the members of our delegation to discuss
strategy and analyze the subjects under negotiation. As usual, our
people expressed their annoyance with the Palestinians' negotiating
tactics. "They've changed their minds again"; "they claim they don't
have a mandate"; "they're sticking to an extreme position"; "they're
stalling for time"; and so on. "They" were still the enemy. A degree of
tension marks every negotiation, but now it was heightened by the
need, new to so many, to relate to the Palestinians as equals. Some of
our people found this difficult after twenty-seven years of occupation
and deep resentment toward the PLO. During our long nocturnal

meetings, Abu Ala used to tell me that his people groused about us in similar terms: "They, the Jews, aren't interested in an agreement; all they really want is to continue the occupation." He, too, had to explain that hanging tough is in the nature of a negotiation.

During the first week, Israelis and Palestinians usually ate separately—except for the senior negotiators and security people, who already knew each other. The committees worked simultaneously, with several lawyers whom on our side Yoel directed with élan. On the negotiating floor, one door was marked LANDS, another SECURITY, a third HEBRON SUBCOMMITTEE. You could walk through the halls and see the peace process unfolding.

At night the senior negotiators would meet in small groups, and toward the early morning hours I would sit with Abu Ala alone. His mind was still fixed on the further transfers of territory. One night I told him that I understood his priorities, but even if we negotiated for a thousand years, Israel would not reveal its map for the last phase of the further redeployments.

"You expect us to enter into an agreement without knowing what its consequences will be? With all the future decisions left in your hands?" he asked. "Well, then, if it depends upon me, there won't be any agreement!"

Thus once more I told Peres that he had to solve this problem with Arafat. He agreed to call the chairman, complain about the lack of progress in Eilat, and tell him that the Americans shared his impatience. He called during a dinner given by Martin Indyk and Terje Larsen, who were interested in arranging a summit at Taba. Arafat, against the advice of his delegation, agreed to meet there on August 10.

When he heard of that decision, Abu Ala was furious. "You're working here with a delegation representing the Palestinian people," he told me the next day. "If you come to an agreement with us as equals, it will hold up. Only those issues we can't solve together should be passed on to the decision makers, at the *end*."

I understood his anger but knew that if we didn't solve the matter of the further redeployment now, we would have great difficulty making progress on anything else. Despite our personal trust, Abu Ala suspected that Israel was hoping to pay a minimal price for regional acceptance while continuing to control (albeit more moderately) the lives of the Palestinians in the West Bank. Before Arafat arrived at Taba, he offered me a deal.

"You'll remain in twenty-five percent of the West Bank and transfer seventy-five percent to us through the last phase of the further redeployment. Your twenty-five percent will be the area of the settlements and specified security locations. I want to take your security interest into account."

I told him there was no way we could accept that, since we had no idea what the security situation would be in the middle of 1997.

Arafat and Peres met in Taba on August 10 in the presence of Yasser Abd Rabbo, Abu Ala, Abdel Razak Yihye, Uzi Dayan, Yoel Singer, and me. Peres arrived in a militant mood. He felt that Abu Ala's demand that Israel relinquish most of the West Bank by the middle of 1997 was excessive, and would make the whole deal more difficult to carry out given Israeli public opinion. But Abu Ala was not impressed by arguments about Israeli public opinion. He wanted to protect his people's primary interests for the future. Arafat showed more understanding.

Before the summit, Uzi and I had prepared our position calling for the transfer of further security powers to the Palestinians every six months, over eighteen months, without defining the amount of territory involved in each of the three phases. In Taba, we presented it to Arafat, and to the amazement of the Palestinian delegation, he accepted it. He understood, perhaps better than any of the others, that the journey toward full Palestinian autonomy and subsequently permanent status had to be resumed quickly. Thus he ascribed less importance to guarantees about the future than to what could be accomplished in the present. His greatest concern at the moment was to galvanize Palestinian public opinion. So he decided to confront Hebron rather than anguish over future redeployments. In return for conceding on the further redeployment, Arafat demanded that we agree to the presence of a Palestinian police station in Hebron. If Peres would give him that, he implied, the rest of the agreement could be worked out swiftly.

On the spot, Peres decided to cut a deal with Arafat and flew to Jerusalem to talk to Rabin and Shahak. Rabin scheduled a meeting in his office at eleven that night. Uzi, Yoel, Oren Shahor, and I accompanied Peres to that session, which was attended by the commanders of the IDF and the Shabak and ministers Moshe Shahal, Yossi Sarid, and Ehud Barak (whom Rabin had recently appointed minister of the interior).

In Jerusalem, Peres began by explaining the understanding reached on the further redeployment, and Rabin expressed his satisfaction. Then Peres asked that the discussion be limited to the subject of a police station in Hebron, because he had to return to Taba and give Arafat his answer that night. He also pointedly noted that Arafat was being bombarded by his colleagues because of his concession on the further redeployment. It was a smart move to yield to Arafat on an issue of importance to Palestinian opinion in exchange for his concession on a matter that both sides considered far more important in strategic terms but that was obscure to those unfamiliar with the detailed talks. Nonetheless, the military objected to a Palestinian police station in Hebron. They claimed that two security forces in one area would create havoc and expressed their concern over the unsettling reaction of the Jewish settlers to the entrance of Palestinian police into Hebron. Rarely had I seen Peres so determined to reach a decision against the opinion of the army and his colleagues.

"I'm fed up with your fear of what the settlers will say. What gall!" he bellowed. "You want 150,000 Hebronites to remain under our control because of 400 Jews? There's a limit to arrogance and a limit to timidity. I'm telling you that we can break Arafat, if that's what you want. But then we'll be left with Hamas, an intifada, and terror. We've made a decision to strive for a political settlement. Today we must decide who's in charge in this country: the government or a handful of settlers. And to you generals, I say: you too must weigh this matter from the standpoint of security. Enough of this dread of how the settlers will react!"

When Peres finished, the room was silent. He was crimson with rage. Admirably, he had cast aside all consideration of his own popularity, for it was obvious that, before the night was out, someone would leak to the press that "Peres has sold Hebron out." Rabin, meanwhile, sensed that the discussion had shifted to political issues and asked everyone but the ministers to leave the room. We waited outside without uttering a word. Ten minutes later the ministers filed out. Peres was walking quickly. "We're going back to Taba," he said. His proposal had been accepted unanimously.

By the time we reached Taba, it was 2:00 A.M. Peres spoke with Arafat privately and told him of the ministers' decision. Arafat thanked him and suggested they meet again the next morning. The Palestinians postponed the continuation of the talks until early afternoon, and when we gathered, Abu Ala avoided me.

When the two leaders sat down again, Arafat told Peres that on the previous night, following an item broadcast by Israel Radio about a compromise on Hebron, a delegation of Hebronites had arrived at the hotel asking to meet with him. They threatened that unless Hebron was treated exactly like all the other cities, and the IDF redeployed from it, they would boycott the elections. Arafat also explained again that the Hebronites are a special breed: hard and obstinate. Peres suggested that he explain the compromise to them himself. But when he tried, they ignored his case about Israel's security interests and the need for stable coexistence. In the meantime we had reports from our own sources that the tension in Hebron was real. So Peres agreed to postpone a decision on the city. The joint communiqué issued that day said only that the two sides had discussed the matter.

We also agreed (after consulting with Dennis Ross) on the formation of a trilateral Israeli-Palestinian-American committee to discuss economics, public opinion, and policy. The remainder of the "package"—including the understanding on a phased redeployment to be implemented over eighteen months and the division of authority in Area B agreed upon on July 4—was summed up in a document. Peres suggested it be signed at a formal ceremony, because he wanted to bring it before the full cabinet for approval. Arafat consented.

"But this isn't an agreement! It's only a small part of it, why should it be signed?" Abu Ala complained.

Arafat ordered him to sign nevertheless. "Fine," he huffed, "but not in front of the cameras."

Thus for the third time, after Oslo and Cairo, Abu Ala and I sat down to initial a document. At two in the morning, Peres and Arafat convened a press conference and read out the understanding related mainly to the three stages of the further redeployments. The Israeli cabinet met the next day, and Peres laid out the points agreed with Arafat. In response to the ministers' questions, Yoel, Uzi, and I explained the details of the understanding. Then the floor was opened to discussion, and Ehud Barak expressed misgivings about the pace of the further redeployment.

"If we don't keep our leverage for later on," he protested, "how can we be sure we won't have to pull back into relatively small areas of the West Bank by mid-1997, before the crucial decisions are made about the permanent settlement?"

I tried to explain that in the Camp David Accords, the redeployment to "specified security areas" was supposed to have been done in a single step, after the elections to the Palestinian Council. So by having three stages of future redeployments, we were keeping more leverage. What's more, we were not defining the size of the territory that would remain in our hands.

"What do you want?" Rabin asked Barak. "We're talking about a real achievement, and you're portraying a concession!"

Barak chose to abstain. The rest of the ministers raised their hands in favor of the Taba understanding.

Uzi, Yoel, and I knew we had scored a coup in the negotiations, for the Taba understanding left the future more or less open and gave us important leverage over its outcome. Nevertheless, we returned to Eilat aware that much of the detail work still lay ahead. We also knew that the Palestinians were now bristling with resentment toward us for having gone directly to Arafat. The time had come to bring in the Americans more actively.

Throughout the talks, I had been updating Ross by phone. He made a point of encouraging the negotiators and expressed his appreciation that we were solving our problems without the United States' active intervention. Whenever Ross visited Israel with Warren Christopher, or on his own, he would meet with Abu Ala and me to hear about the talks. The appearance of his "peace team" at the Yamit Hotel, for example, prompted the two sides to hold a "dress rehearsal" of what each would say and how we would articulate the gaps between us. As a result, the atmosphere of these trilateral meetings tended to be relatively stiff. Nevertheless, the Americans were delighted, they said, by the "chemistry" between the two delegations and the degree of creativity they displayed.

By mid-August, however, I felt it was important to involve the Americans as a lever in the Eilat and Taba talks. By then both Abu Ala and I were talking with Ross almost daily, often taking turns on the same cellular phone. Ross also made a point of speaking often with Arafat. Like me, he was concerned that pressure on Arafat from other members of the Palestinian leadership who were not involved in the negotiations would delay the Interim Agreement. He constantly urged Arafat to keep moving forward. He also sent Edward Abington, the American consul-general in Jerusalem, to see the chairman. And he sent his close friend the U.S. ambassador Martin Indyk—a highly effective and popular envoy who was outspoken about the desirability of the process—to Rabin and Peres. This network of ties was to be of great importance in the final, decisive stages of the talks.

At the same time, the Americans continued to prod the donor countries, in coordination with Norway and the European Union. They were particularly concerned about the support of their own Congress, where informal representatives of the Likud were conducting a vigorous campaign against further aid to the Palestinian Authority—especially among the Republican leadership and the Jewish lobby AIPAC. We sometimes felt that our embassy in Washington wasn't acting forcefully enough to counteract this influence. If I suffered from a "Palestinian warp" during that period, Itamar Rabinovich, our ambassador in the United States, was equally beset by a Syrian one. Yet the directives cabled to the embassy by Rabin and Peres were definitive: it was imperative to step up the campaign in Congress in favor of aid to the Palestinians. In one of these cables, which was coordinated with the Prime Minister's Bureau, we explained bluntly that aid for the purpose of raising the standard of living in Gaza was part of the fight against terrorism. At the same time, we were invoking Congress as part of our strategy in Eilat, especially the fact that it was going to publish a report on the Palestinian Authority on October 1, 1995.

In August, Ross came to Israel on a private visit and flew down to see us at the Patio Hotel. He spoke separately with Abu Ala, Uzi, and me and was able to get a clearer impression of our progress and especially of the atmosphere of the talks. Ross had rich experience in negotiations, including the complex disarmament talks with the USSR. But he told us that never had he seen anything that could compare with our negotiation center in Eilat.

TRANSFERRING CIVIL POWERS AND DISMANTLING THE CIVIL ADMINISTRATION

The media covering the talks were concerned mainly with Israel's security and outward signs of Palestinian autonomy. But the core of the evolving Interim Agreement was the transfer of the civil powers. This task was given to Gen. Oren Shahor, who in February had become the coordinator of activities in the territories, against the advice of the negotiating team, who worried about his lack of experience in the territories. In the end this proved to be his greatest virtue, because it enabled him to conduct productive talks on dismantling the Civil Administration in the territories under him. Hassan Asfour continued to refer to Israelis who "think like before [Oslo]" and Israelis who "think like after." Shahor had no sentiments about the bureaucracy that ruled the lives of the Palestinians, and he was free from the habits of control that vexed many of the others in our delegation. He spoke his mind bluntly to Israelis and Palestinians alike. Though he moved on to the General Staff, he was not "one of the boys."

His opposite number, Jamil Tarifi, a wealthy businessman from El-Bireh, was likewise an exception among the Palestinian leadership but enjoyed Arafat's support because of his widespread economic activities and connections. In the beginning Shahor and Tarifi founded their own "club," but gradually they integrated into the team, both personally and in terms of their policy.

I asked Rabin to encourage Shahor, because I believed that most of the work in Eilat would be on the transfer of civil powers. I imagined that our people would bargain furiously over exactly which powers Israel would retain. I was right about the niggling but wrong about the pace. Shahor moved forward quickly from the moment the Eilat talks began. He and I would meet with the heads of the working groups, hear their reports, and implore them to concentrate only on what was important.

These negotiations, over the powers Israel had exercised for a whole generation, opened an entire world before me. Over the years Israelis had cultivated a self-serving myth that ours was an "enlightened oc-cupation." I knew this was a contradiction in terms, but I did not know—and I think few other Israelis did—how thoroughly we had invaded the lives of our Palestinian neighbors. We repressed this knowledge as we may have been the first conquerors in history who felt themselves conquered. Our self-image as a humane society and history's eternal victim, as well as Arab antagonism, blinded us to what was going on in the territories. What I discovered in the Patio was that a West Bank Palestinian could not build, work, study, pur-chase land, grow produce, start a business, take a walk at night, enter Israel, go abroad, or visit his family in Gaza or Jordan without a per-mit from us. The apparatus for managing this octopus was huge.

Some of these restrictions stemmed from legitimate security con-cerns. But many were the products of inertia and a burgeoning bu-reaucratic monster with a bottomless budget to feed on. During twenty-eight years of occupation, about a third of the Palestinian population in the territories had, at one time or another, been de-tained or imprisoned by Israel. And the whole of the population had, at some time, been grossly humiliated by us. Some wounds may never heal. Now the bureaucrats and officers who ruled the Palestinians had been asked to pass on their powers to their "wards." This proved excruciating for them, both conceptually and emotionally. In Eilat we were dismantling the occupation, but some of our people could hardly bring themselves to change.

Some of these administrators found it almost unbearable to sit down in Eilat with representatives of their "subjects." We had been engaged in dehumanization for so long that we really thought ourselves "more equal"—and at the same time the threatened side, therefore justifiably hesitant. The group negotiating the transfer of civil powers did not rebel against their mandate, but whenever we offered a concession or a compromise, our people tended to begin by saying: "We have decided to allow you . . ."

Throughout the negotiations, I wrote Shimon Peres personal letters that described the scenes around the bargaining table. Of the talks on civil affairs in Eilat I wrote, "All in all, I have the impression that the civil negotiating teams are made up of people living in the settlements, many are lawyers, and many simply aren't interested in dismantling the administration."

The personification of the occupation, according to many Palestinians, was an officer in the Civil Administration named Moskovitch. If Moskovitch approved, you could build. If Moskovitch didn't approve, you could not, and until Moskovitch approved, you could tear your hair out. Moskovitch had become an institution in himself. When I finally met him—a thin, religiously observant, amiable man—he in no way impressed me as tyrannical. "Moskovitch is a good man," one of his superior officers told me. And this was just the problem—a good man carrying out the orders of an unfeeling bureaucracy makes an impossible situation, for there is no way under such conditions for goodwill or common sense to function.

I also intervened in some of the negotiations on the subcommittee level, primarily to demonstrate my involvement but also to become more familiar with the issues, so as to recommend to Rabin and Peres where we could compromise and where we could not. I usually agreed with Shahor in these meetings that some Israeli interests related to security or the permanent settlement could not be compromised, for example, regarding water. But the control of many powers that had simply become habits clearly had to be ditched.

Eleven powers had been agreed upon in the Cairo talks led first by Gen. Danny Rothschild and then by Shahor and Jamil Tarifi on an early transfer of powers. Another twenty-nine still had to be negotiated at Eilat.

At about 3:00 A.M., on one of the first nights of the civilian power talks, I decided to sit in on a relatively simple negotiation—or so I thought—on the transfer of powers over the nature reserves in Areas A and B that had been developed by Israel since 1967. I found myself in a stormy debate between the two cochairmen of the subcommittee, and my colleagues quickly explained to me what the uproar was about. Our side insisted that the Palestinians promise to maintain the reserves in their present state, but the Palestinians refused to make any such commitment as a matter of principle. Some members of our delegation, representatives of Israel's Society for the Protection of Nature, were appalled by the Palestinians' approach. I then sat down in place of the chairman of our group and began negotiating with his Palestinian counterpart.

"Do you wish to destroy the nature reserves?" I asked him.

"That's none of your business," he snapped. "You are transferring our land to us, and we'll do with it as we please! Don't think for a moment that nature is unimportant to us. But we will not bow to your dictates on this subject!"

Suddenly, in walked Abu Ala, who had been summoned as a counterweight to me. After he received a quick briefing in Arabic, the negotiation continued.

"Abu Ala, it's your right to decide what you will do with the nature reserves," I said. "But we have an interest in your maintaining them. Perhaps you're of the opinion that we never had a right to develop them in the first place. But I disagree. I say we're returning an asset to you. And just as you must not destroy archaeological sites, you must not destroy nature or do harm to animals."

"It's true that you know how to treat *animals* well. And it's also true that we, as Palestinians, are interested in preserving nature. But we'll do that in our own way. What's more," he said, "I hate rabbits

and personally intend to see to it that every last one of them is destroyed!"

The Israeli nature reserves man sitting on my right didn't realize
Abu Ala was joshing. "Then you won't get the reserves back!" he
barked.

"My friend"—Abu Ala laughed at his own joke—"you needn't
worry about the rabbits, not even the Palestinian rabbits!"

Abu Ala then proposed that the nature reserves be protected by
Palestinian law.

"I'm glad that passing such a law is your top priority," I said. "But
to the best of my knowledge, it doesn't exist yet."

"You will not set standards for us," he replied. "That is a matter of
principle."

"Fine," I said. "Let's issue a communiqué stating that you refuse to
protect the nature reserves. That will certainly do wonders for your
fine public relations abroad."

From my left and right came vigorous nods of approval. "If we give
in on this, tomorrow they'll do whatever they like in other areas!"

It was time for a compromise. "Why don't we agree that you will
maintain the reserves according to international conventions on nature reserves?"

"Is there any such thing?" Abu Ala asked.

I looked at our experts, who didn't believe that there was an actual
convention. But there were international agreements. Then a young
lady, a skillful lawyer on Abu Ala's staff, said: "How about saying that
we will maintain the nature reserves according to established scientific standards?"

I agreed, adding that it's truly important, on a matter that knows
no political borders, to work in cooperation. Abu Ala seconded that
sentiment, then added: "But cooperation must extend to all the nature reserves, ours and yours."

I had no objection to that. So another committee for cooperation
was established, and the easiest of our problems was solved. Similar
debates took place regarding almost every other issue, as to how to
transfer powers to the Palestinians while protecting our long-term
interests. The most intricate problems had to do with infrastruc-

ture—electricity, water, and, obviously, land. But before tackling them, the teams discussed matters such as transportation and health. The transportation subcommittee, for example, debated the right to post road signs for both populations in the West Bank. In the end it was decided that each side would post the signs in the area under its responsibility—even though in some areas that would result in confusion. But this was inherent in an interim agreement.

In discussing health, we insisted that the Palestinian Authority commit itself to a list of vaccinations and bear the costs of emergency treatment for Palestinians in Israeli hospitals. After much debate we compromised: the Palestinians would, like Israelis, pay for treatment in our hospitals. Vaccinations would be given according to the recommendations of the World Health Organization. Here too a discussion that could have been the basis for far-reaching cooperation, with heartening implications for peace, had turned into a confrontation.

We fought down to the last minute over lands, water, and electricity. Rabin had agreed to transfer state lands (those not owned by private citizens) to the Palestinian Authority, but only on condition that the rights of Jews who did own land would not be prejudiced. The Palestinians vehemently objected to this condition. They said they intended to establish courts to hear Palestinian appeals on the illegal confiscation of land. Our people argued—and with good cause—that we could not trust the objectivity of a Palestinian court. What's more, the status of lands should be left to the permanent settlement talks.

I tried to talk to Abu Ala privately about this, but he was adamant. He again told me, as an example, about the land that had been stolen from his father, stressing that when the old man had tried to show an Israeli court a document proving his ownership, he was dismissed with contempt. The soil of the Holy Land had once again become the object of vehement confrontation. We realized this especially when the Palestinians announced that if we claimed these lands, they intended to claim property within the sovereign State of Israel. The rows on this issue, which often spilled into the hallways, were fierce and highly emotional. In the end, the Palestinians compromised by agreeing to establish a legal commission, with equal representation from both sides, to decide on appeals regarding alleged illegal expropriation, transfer, or sale of lands. That kept the lid on Pandora's box—for the moment.

Brutal exchanges took place over construction plans. In the Gaza-Jericho Agreement, we limited the Palestinians to planning and building within the confines of the existing towns by requiring any expansions to be approved by a joint committee, a lopsided understanding that could never be enforced. In Eilat we tried to be more realistic and set down definitive criteria for construction, especially where it reflected on security issues (for instance, prohibiting building in the vicinity of an IDF base), and a sweeping statement to the effect that planning and construction would not inflict damage upon the settlements or their infrastructure. This was a positive step that reflected Shahor's understanding—and that of Rabin and Peres—that we must no longer suppress Palestinian economic development by restricting planning and construction.

As to powers over land in the area under full Israeli control (Area C), the Palestinians demanded that we keep the status quo in all non-military activities. "The settlements have been frozen by the decision of your government," they said. "The rest of C is security locations. So why should you go on developing the parks, forests, and so on?" Rabin accepted this logic, and it was agreed that although Israel would retain powers over the parks, forests, and nature reserves in Area C, their future development would be in coordination with the Palestinian Authority. The rest of the land and building rights in C remained under Israel's control. Some forty thousand Palestinians would live in Area C, and power over such matters as education and health had already been transferred to them. So the agreement stated that the Palestinian Authority was "accountable" for all Palestinians in the West Bank and Gaza.

The struggle over exactly what would be transferred to the Palestinians, as a function of each and every power, went on day and night. Basically, two approaches were in conflict. The Palestinian position was that what's ours is ours and we won't share it with you—except, perhaps, through cooperation based on reciprocity. The Israeli approach was that we are entitled to decide which powers, or parts thereof, to relinquish—and only on condition that doing so did not prejudice Israeli long-term interests. The solution was usually a compromise. But reality was stronger than theory, and the powers were usually divided according to which party controlled the area.

On two points we realized that cooperation was absolutely essential—and probably for a long time to come. Electricity was the only issue on which agreement was postponed. We were adamant that every high-tension wire would remain under Israeli control, so as to protect our interests in the settlements and army camps. The worst battles were waged on water, between Noah Kinarti, an old friend of Rabin's who was also his adviser on settlement affairs, and Nabil Sherif, a veteran Palestinian expert on water issues.

Kinarti was rough, rigid, and suspicious of Peres and me. At first he consulted only with Rabin. During the initial meeting he insulted the entire Palestinian delegation by saying that a Palestinian uses a quarter as much water as an Israeli does (implying that we were cleaner). Abu Ala alone chose not to be offended and at mealtimes he repeatedly asked Kinarti whether it was all right for him to drink the water.

"Just a few drops," Kinarti would reply.

When I suggested to Kinarti that he consider a less abrasive style of negotiation, he said, "Let me do it my way. We'll reach an understanding in the end. Because without an understanding on water, there won't be an Interim Agreement."

In response to this tactic, Abu Ala decided to try rigidity too. He demanded that Israel recognize the Palestinians' water rights, a legal term that would entitle them to an equitable share of the subterranean water table as well as water from the Jordan River. Kinarti, however, talked only about the present amount of water allocated to the Palestinians, the possibility of locating new sources of water, and a joint supervisory apparatus that would prevent the piratical sinking of new wells. Peres had raised the issue at the July 21 meeting in Alexandria with Mubarak and Arafat; there he said, "When it comes to water, Mr. Chairman, your people treat the issues by sailing back in history and talking about water rights."

Arafat replied, "Mousa [Moses] is more important than Ibrahim. Mousa not only drank the water of the Nile, he was saved from it."

"Well then, while you're on the subject of Moses, perhaps you can create water by striking a rock with a rod. Please feel free to do so," Peres replied.

Mubarak laughed. "Today only Shimon can get water out of a stone!" he quipped.

"Let's be realistic," Peres continued. "We won't take a drop of water from you. I suggest that all the water you now have will remain at your disposal, and we'll try to help you out by finding new water. There's a risk that the potable water will be polluted by sewage, especially in Gaza."

He then suggested a pragmatic solution: desalinizing water for Gaza. "With the aid of the donors, we can set up a joint committee on purification and try to increase the yield of the eastern subterranean reservoir of the Jordan Valley. But under no circumstances will we jeopardize the water under our control."

In the final stage of the water negotiations, Kinarti was joined by Agriculture Minister Ya'akov Tsur and Oren Shahor. Abu Ala established a rapport with them, and Kinarti even built a good working relationship with Nabil Sherif. Our mutual "incarceration" in the Patio was creating the most surprising relationships. The solution to the water issue was ultimately agreed between Peres and Arafat, to the satisfaction of both sides, by compromising on all the details—amounts, rights, and finding new sources of water—but mainly by establishing a joint water committee.

I learned two things from these water talks. When I got to know Kinarti better, I found that under his rough exterior was a warm, caring, and astute man who had lost a son in uniform and was genuinely striving for peace. But it was too much to ask the Palestinians, who had no opportunity to know him better, to understand this. The other lesson was about water itself. Amounts may seem objective, but there are as many views on this subject as there are experts—from the alchemists, who forecast a dry and perilous future for Israel, to the scientists, who put their faith in technology for solutions. The solution to this problem must be regional, and therefore the best source of water is peace.

After transferring its powers to the Palestinian Authority, Israel's Civil Administration for the territories was meant to be dismantled. However, it was decided that in order to supply the Palestinians with the necessary services to follow from the Interim Agreement, the Civil Administration would be transformed into a Liaison and Coordination Center to supervise the cooperation anchored in the agreement. I feared that what would emerge from this makeover was more of the same on different stationery. So I preferred that most of the old administration be absorbed by various government ministries, to execute cooperation directly with the Palestinian ministries, and that the Foreign Ministry play a more prominent role in the coordination efforts. To some extent these views became part of the agreement's special annex on cooperation.

I remained concerned, however, that since the Liaison and Coordination Center was to become the chief instrument of daily contact with the Palestinian Authority, we might not achieve the cooperation necessary to create the kind of bilateral relations vital for a stable peace. The transition from Palestinian dependence on us to mutual dependence was difficult for the Israeli establishment. I was learning that the struggle to free Israel from the occupation was one thing, while the struggle to free Israelis of an occupier's mind-set was another. In a way, the same was true of the Palestinians, who after living through years of occupation found it hard to cooperate with us on a totally new basis.

I wrote to Peres about this problem: "The Interim Agreement will not succeed unless we're wise enough to change our attitude toward the Palestinians in all working contacts, including the army, the Civil Administration, and the ministries." I told him, for example, how my secretary Stella Shustak had become the standard recourse for our Palestinian colleagues who were stopped at checkpoints on their way to the negotiations, and sometimes delayed there for hours. One evening a frantic Abu Ala phoned Stella from the Erez checkpoint. The soldier on duty had refused to let him enter Israel from Gaza, though he had presented his VIP pass (a special pass issued by both sides for designated Palestinian dignitaries, in order to facilitate their passage in and out of Israel) because his driver didn't have one. Stella and I tried to reason with the officer on duty, but he stood fast.

"I don't care whether this is Abu Ala or anyone else," he said. "Those are my orders!"

In the background I could hear Abu Ala ranting in exasperation. Grabbing the phone, he told me in a voice shrill with rage: "Dozens of Palestinians are passing by here, and you insist on humiliating me in front of them. One day I'll have a heart attack from you!" Nothing I could say would calm him. Meanwhile Stella had reached the chief of staff's office on a different line. It took another hour, but Abu Ala finally got through. I was embarrassed for him and far more so for us.

It's always possible to explain malevolent behavior toward Palestinians as a function of the fear of terrorism—and not without justification, given the Palestinian Authority's ineffective efforts to combat it. But part of this malevolence stems from a deeper erosion of norms in human relations. Few understood that if we could not treat the Palestinians with respect as equals, across the full spectrum of relations, they would repay us in kind in the fields where we are interdependent.

Just how important it was to develop amicable relations on the road to peace became abundantly clear in our human attitudes laboratory at the Patio Hotel as the relations between us began slowly to improve. One by one, members of the various committees and subcommittees started taking their meals together. The closest ties were between people dealing with logistics. My driver, Oded Anavim, who often arrived with material from the Foreign Ministry, became fast friends with Palestinian drivers and bodyguards, and they spent much of their time sharing "war stories." Oded told me that one of the Palestinian drivers had been a "real terrorist, though today he supports peace." Much of this intimacy developed in the workout room, where gym clothes often exposed the terrible physical wounds of Israelis and Palestinians alike. Negotiators would sit beside each other on exercise bikes or in the sauna and talk about how they had been wounded.

One night I went for a swim in the pool, where I found the two security chiefs, Jibril Rajoub and Mohammed Dahlan, along with Sufian Abu Zaide and Hisham Abdel Razek—who were leaders of the Ex-Prisoners' Club, a support network for Palestinians who had spent time in Israeli jails. After a few laps, the five of us sat on the edge of the pool. All four of them spoke fluent Hebrew, sabra slang and all. "We learned it in prison," one of them explained. A quick calculation revealed that these men, all in their forties, had together spent sixty years in Israeli jails. Over and over they spoke of the plight of their comrades, who had carried out violent attacks on the orders of those with whom we were now negotiating—including, of course, Arafat. They warned that unless there was a mass, albeit gradual, release of security prisoners, they wouldn't be able to support the agreement. But they did promise to recruit at least the freed Fatah prisoners into the Ex-Prisoners' Club and engage them in peace activities. I told them that on this issue there had to be a political decision, given the domestic repercussions on our side. We sat and talked until dawn.

Soon thereafter, I spent an evening with Israeli families that had lost loved ones in terror attacks. They were very bitter and asked us not to release the detainees who had murdered their children. They also wanted us to demand, as a condition of the agreement, that the Palestinian Authority extradite to us murderers of Israelis. Their pain was sharp, deep, and utterly understandable. Justice Minister David Liba'i had been recruited to their cause and came down to Eilat to meet with Abu Ala on the question of the extradition. Abu Ala was uncompromising in his reply.

"That's out of the question," he told Liba'i. "You wouldn't agree to extradite your people to us either. If you agree to reciprocity then we will accept it. If not, I am prepared to guarantee that we will arrest murderers and place them on trial."

Ultimately the agreement reflected Rabin's realistic view that the Palestinian Authority had to arrest and try murderers, or extradite them to Israel.

The Palestinians had a hard time overcoming the habit of legitimizing the murder of Israelis as part of what they had perceived to be an armed struggle against the occupation. Terrorism was clearly the greatest threat to the success of the talks. And the terrorists knew it. On August 21, Stella woke me with a chilling statement. "There's been a terror attack," she said. "Turn on the TV."

A bus had been blown up in Jerusalem, taking the lives of five people. Uzi Dayan and Yoel Singer reached my room immediately, and I asked them to inform everyone of a pause in the talks. When I called the Prime Minister's Bureau in Jerusalem, Peres (who was then in a meeting with Rabin) told me that they were demanding that the Palestinian Authority do everything in its power against terrorism. But they were also intent on distinguishing between the Palestinian Authority and Hamas and not allowing the latter a veto right on the process. Then he told me to suspend the negotiations until the funerals had taken place. We would not play into the hands of the terrorists by stopping the process. I asked for permission to keep the delegations at the hotel, so that reconvening the talks would be simpler. He agreed.

The Palestinians in the hotel remained closed in their rooms, and it was just as well; we could hardly face them as though nothing had happened. No one doubted that the people with whom we were living and working in Eilat were opposed to terrorism and knew how much it damaged their interests; that terrorism was also directed at them. Nevertheless, Palestinians had killed Israelis that day, and all the fear, grief, and anger on our part—and embarrassment and perhaps sadness on theirs—made for a suffocating atmosphere in a once-bustling hotel that had suddenly fallen silent.

In the afternoon, Abu Ala and the other leaders of his delegation asked to come to my room to express their condolences. Abu Ala, Abdel Razak Yihye, Hassan Asfour, and Jamil Tarifi sat in a circle with Uzi, Yoel, Oren, and me and offered formal statements of regret. We described to them the details of the killing, and they returned to their rooms. In the evening, like everyone else in Israel, we braced ourselves to watch the news. I sent Stella to ask Abu Ala whether he wanted to bring some of his colleagues to join us. When they arrived we sat together, overcome by the anguish of the bereaved families. Not a word passed among us, and we parted.

The talks were resumed the next afternoon, after the last of the funerals. Two days later Abu Ala phoned from his room and asked me to watch the evening news in Arabic with him.

"What's happened?" I asked anxiously.

"Come," he said.

The news showed the funeral of a seven-year-old girl who had been shot and killed by our soldiers that day. The camera zoomed in on the small coffin and the grieving family, then panned the angry crowd. Our Palestinian partners constantly told us that neither side had a monopoly on suffering. The pain was as awful on their side as it was on ours. Would our growing awareness of this shared tragedy, I wondered, be the first step toward reconciliation? We had learned that it was not enough to transfer authorities and to involve officers and officials in cooperation. The people had to be involved, too. Abu Ala and I met in Eilat with Mona Juul, who at Norway's embassy in Tel Aviv continued to promote her country's role in the peace process. We agreed toward the end of the negotiations to create a "people-to-people program," organized and financed by the government of Norway. It was time to get Israelis and Palestinians to talk and work together. Peace requires popular participation and the eradication of prejudice. For peace to become habitual might take a generation or more, but we had to start somewhere. The Interim Agreement was the appropriate occasion, and Norway the ideal partner.

The talks continued around the clock. We would usually start very slowly, break for lunch at about 10:00 A.M., and keep going until an hour's break for dinner at 6:00 P.M. Then came the nightly sessions, which lasted till early morning.

THE ELECTION, COMPOSITION, AND POWERS OF THE PALESTINIAN COUNCIL

Yoel Singer and Sa'eb Erekat held very detailed talks on the elections as well as the size and makeup of the Palestinian Council. Creating a new legislative body, defining its powers, and drafting an elections law was fascinating work to the Palestinians. We had decided to confine our role to safeguarding the format of the elections and of the council's prerogatives. In time, however, as a result of the close personal relationship between Yoel and Sa'eb, our involvement became broader. They even traveled together to Scotland to supervise local elections there and see what they could learn.

Yoel and I recommended that our leaders approve a 250-member elected legislative council, much larger than the 100 members that the Palestinians were asking for. Our aim was to reinforce the supporters of the peace process and encourage a pluralistic system. Our recommendation was rejected, and an 83-member council (later to be expanded to 88) was decided upon.

The Palestinians aspired to a separation of powers between the executive and legislative branches. Our approach was relatively flexible. Above all, we wanted to encourage open-mindedness within a society rife with tension between the champions of a centralized regime and those who wanted to emulate the Israeli model. We agreed upon three things: the establishment of an executive council (for all purposes, a cabinet); a larger council with legislative powers; and Arafat's title as *ra'ees* (which could be translated variously as "chairman" or "president," to satisfy both sides). Erekat wanted to create the position of chairman (or speaker) of the legislative council, which ostensibly was not in line with the Declaration of Principles. But Peres complied with this request and persuaded Rabin of the value of the post in creating more pluralism. Abu Ala would be chosen as the first chairman of the new Palestinian Council.

Almost the only irritant in these talks was how the elections would be run in East Jerusalem. But Yoel and Sa'eb conducted their negotiation with great care on this sensitive issue. The solutions they reached were technical and pragmatic. Jerusalem was outside the autonomous area, which had been among the prime conditions for pursuing the original Oslo talks. Yet they managed to ensure that the Palestinian residents of Jerusalem would not be ignored in the electoral process, as stipulated by the Declaration of Principles. This was a tour de force for Yoel and Sa'eb, because nothing would have been easier than to turn every last detail of their talks on Jerusalem into a threat to the negotiations as a whole.

They agreed that the Palestinian residents of Jerusalem would indeed vote in post offices, using special containers that were a hybrid of a mailbox and a ballot box. The Israeli Police would be responsible for maintaining order, and international observers would transport the boxes into the autonomous area for the vote count. Each Palestinian candidate living in Jerusalem would be required to have a second, binding address outside the city, making it possible for Israel to claim that no Palestinian Jerusalemite was standing for election. In the end, the only point that remained open was whether it would be necessary to place a stamp on the envelope containing the ballot. The creative compromise was to rubber-stamp the envelopes. Representatives of the international observers team, provided by the European Union, flew to Eilat to be briefed on their role—which was by no means marginal given the need for transparency in the electoral process.

The New Legal Status of the Authority

The subject of the legal status of the new Palestinian Authority was dealt with professionally and harmoniously by lawyers from the Office of the Military Advocate General and the Palestinian Ministry of Justice. They drafted an intricate formula providing for Israel's jurisdiction over criminal cases in Area B that enabled us to take the steps necessary to maintain our security while the Palestinians remained responsible for public order. For the first time, Israelis would be subject to Palestinian tax laws when trading in Areas A and B.

Economic Relations

The Israeli Treasury, represented by its director-general, David Brodet, continued to think mainly about the interests of the Israeli economy. Admittedly, the Treasury made great efforts to persuade the donor states to increase their aid to the Palestinian Authority. It also faithfully transferred to the Palestinian Authority the taxes collected by Israel on its behalf. But when it came to planning economic relations that would enhance both Palestinian prosperity and future economic cooperation among Israel, the Palestinians, and Jordan, its policy was inadequate. Domestic short-term economic interest dominated our decisions, partly because decision makers were unfamiliar with technical economic details. Another problem was our policy that security considerations would dominate the free passage of goods and manpower.

We did not look carefully enough at the economic understandings because we assumed that most of the Palestinian Authority's economic problems could be solved through massive investment from the donor states. That was a serious mistake, for we failed to see that in the absence of stable arrangements for the movement of goods (which would not be disrupted by closures) and without legal arrangements to protect investors, the private sector would not invest in the Palestinian economy. Without such investment, along with the tax-generating activity that would result, the governments of the donor states would be forced to keep the Palestinian Authority afloat. Those who warned against this result were Foreign Ministry officials Oded Eran and Yossi Amrani. Amrani, a junior diplomat, wrote an excellent paper on the danger that our military occupation would be replaced by economic domination, and he recommended that Israel be far more generous toward the Palestinian Authority. We agreed with the recommendation but unfortunately did not adopt it because the prevalent view was to preserve Israeli economic interests rather than take into account the benefits of economic stability both to ourselves and to the Palestinians. The problem was exacerbated by the Palestinian leadership's own impulse toward economic centralization and the lack of modern economic institution building. There were also allegations of corruption—mostly for political payoffs. As in the political field, economically the emerging Palestinian society was torn between those copying the regional economic model and those who aspired to the development of a more Western market system; between those who established monopolies and those who advocated competitiveness. The autonomy developed into a unique blend of governance whose future remained unclear. In the short run, however, the situation was bleak.

Terje Larsen understood the economic predicament extremely well. He had spent three years as a UN undersecretary-general in Gaza and was realistic about its needs. He tried to convince the donor community to invest more in infrastructure projects and social services, as these would strengthen the needy and contribute to political stability. He attempted to convince us of the foolishness of the closure policy—that we were creating a pressure cooker in Gaza—and he worked candidly with the Palestinian leadership on the creation of economic institutions. He enjoyed excellent relations with all leaders—yet they ignored his advice.

Had all sides fully accepted his advice, the economic situation, and therefore political stability and security, would have benefited. Perhaps the main reason for our misjudgment was our faith that the political process itself would inevitably lead to healthier economic relations. All of us believed that, if the main operation succeeded, both patients would live a better life. The economic annex of the Interim Agreement basically did no more than extend the existing economic agreement reached in Paris that was part of the Gaza-Jericho Agreement.

At the same time, the security committee, headed by Uzi Dayan and Abdel Razak Yihye, and the subcommittees under it worked relentlessly on such questions as the quantity of arms that would be carried by the Palestinian Police, the policemen's entry into the area and the ground rules for the period of overlap, and the difficult matter of Israel's right of "hot pursuit" into Area A. Rabin and Shahak were specific in their instructions. The sine qua non, they stressed, was to combat terrorism and create a framework for cooperation, not to argue over every road and hilltop, since the Palestinians had accepted our basic security doctrine.

By making steady progress on all main components of the agreement, toward the end of August we reached the endgame, which was played out mostly in Taba. At 2:00 A.M. on Thursday, September 1, I wrote a report to Rabin and Peres detailing the remaining cluster of significant disagreements. This served as the basis of a preliminary discussion in the chief of staff's office later that morning, immediately after we landed in Tel Aviv. At this meeting, Gen. Ilan Biran presented the IDF's map of the Interim Agreement, which we decided to put aside until the end of the discussion. Then, as Biran was offering various options for flexibility in the final stage, Shahak's secretary entered the room and gave me a note that read: "Dr. Horn is asking for you on the phone."

Dr. Horn was our family physician, and I left to take the call with foreboding. When she asked me whether I was sitting down, I lied but immediately understood what was coming.

"Uri, Mother died last night. I'm terribly sorry."

My mother was eighty-one years old and in good health for her age. She was independent, full of energy, and followed my work closely, with pride and concern. I visited her on Saturday nights and had seen her on the previous Saturday as usual. I tried to remember when I had last spoken with her from Eilat, and couldn't. I was later told that she had gone to the hairdresser the previous afternoon, then came home, went to bed, and died in her sleep. The cleaning woman found her the next morning and called Dr. Horn.

I passed a note to Shahak and went home. The first thing I did was call my sister, Yael, in the States, and she immediately left for Israel. Aliza and Maya were with me. The funeral took place on Sunday afternoon. I was cushioned by their love but nevertheless felt an indescribable loneliness and pain. Rabin and Peres came to the funeral, along with our entire delegation. During the seven-day mourning period, which we spent in my parents' house, I sank into memories of childhood and thoughts about my deep bond with my parents. Many came to console me. I was close to exhaustion.

It was Uzi, more than anyone else, who kept in touch with me from Eilat that week. He told me that Peres and Arafat were trying to make progress on the Hebron imbroglio without success. Terje and Mona had returned from Oslo and stayed with us all week. Abu Ala phoned and then visited at the end of the week, when he had returned from Taba and Eilat. We sat alone in the living room, and I told him about my parents' lives and how much they valued the pursuit of peace. Before he left I removed from the library an old copy of the Koran, which my father had used while studying Arabic in Cairo in 1947, and gave it to him.

Before leaving for Eilat again on September 10, I was told that the guard at my house in Tel Aviv was being reinforced and that I was now to have a personal bodyguard. My name had appeared on a blacklist prepared by settlers in the territories.

Back at the Patio, many members of the Palestinian delegation expressed their condolences. In the evening I met with the members of our delegation for an update. The time had come to prepare for the conclusion. At first I wondered if I could hold up physically. Like the others, I had gone without much sleep for about half a year. But my head was clear, and I was able to concentrate on every detail of the negotiations. That steady concentration on a key preoccupation sharpens one's thinking was an impression shared by most of the veteran negotiators.

Yoel and Sa'eb had drafted a document on the probable timetable for the rest of the talks. It posited a target date of September 17–18, so we could sign the agreement before the start of the Jewish holidays on September 24. The two were now in charge of wording the full agreement, and all the committees were relaying their joint drafts to them. They also solved a long list of outstanding problems by themselves, out of a thorough understanding of the mutual and conflicting interests of the sides, and did an excellent job of integrating subjects into various places in the draft. In addition, Yoel supervised a group of Israeli lawyers who worked around the clock checking every last word and punctuation mark and repeatedly proofreading the latest drafts.

But Abu Ala was trying to give us the impression that he was ready to negotiate forever. We were engaged in a war of nerves. He and many of his colleagues still seemed to resent our having "twisted Arafat's arm" at the August 11 meeting on the further redeployment. He tried to tackle the subject indirectly by demanding an absolute freeze on settlements. He insisted, for example, that no settlement be allowed to expand more than fifty meters beyond the last house. He even quoted Rabin's comment to Arafat (during one of their meetings a year earlier) about building fences around the settlements—though Rabin was talking about security needs, not about preventing their natural growth.

On Hebron, we got nowhere. The Palestinians continued to raise the same demands, from opening a Palestinian police station to removing the Jewish settlers from the city. Abu Ala even tried to undermine the agreement on security responsibilities in Area B by demanding that the Palestinian Police be given greater powers under the rubric of "maintaining public order." We would not budge on any of these points. Toward the end of the second week of September, we ticked off about sixty issues that remained to be solved. Yoel, who was usually very tolerant about the time required for negotiations, suggested that I cut a deal with Abu Ala on a final date for signature. Otherwise, he said, we might be tied down in Eilat forever. We had effectively exhausted our negotiating momentum. Our job now was to decide on one cluster of issues to trade off on a quid pro quo basis and another to be decided by Peres and Arafat. At the end of that week, we received instructions from Jerusalem about how to divide the topics. The decisions on Hebron and Rachel's Tomb in Bethlehem would be left for Peres and Arafat to handle. After receiving that answer, I asked Abu Ala to my room and told him that time was running out, especially in regard to the American Congress. So I suggested informing Dennis Ross that we intended to sign the Interim Agreement in Washington on September 22. Rabin, who was initially against a second signing ceremony at the White House, yielded to Peres.

Abu Ala called Arafat and returned with his approval of the Washington ceremony, and we called Dennis Ross to share with him our decision. Abu Ala suggested that we meet alone in his room the following night and try to solve most of the issues still in dispute. Compromise toward the end of a negotiation requires a good measure of mutual trust, because a certain degree of flexibility is always saved for the end. After months of bargaining, we now had to put our cards on the table, and I didn't really know whether Abu Ala was ready for that.

During the course of the day, both sides held internal consultations to organize their strategy for the remaining talks. Abu Ala had succeeded, through a combination of panache and coercion, to unite all the members of his delegation behind him. In those final days, security people like Rajoub and Dahlan, Tarifi and other businessmen, academics and influential officials in the Palestinian Authority all bowed to his authority. My job, as head of our delegation, was easier. Each of my senior colleagues essentially ran his own team. We worked through mutual coordination, full integration, and common tactics.

When I reached Abu Ala's room that evening, a bodyguard showed me into the adjoining conference room, where most of our private talks and those of the Steering Committee had been held. The piles of position papers that had cluttered the table during the previous weeks had disappeared. Now the table was covered with a white cloth, and in the center lay my father's Koran, in its red binding. I sat down to wait. Abu Ala walked in wearing a white shirt, took a seat, knit his brows, and announced: "The time has come to finish."

We sat there all night, while Uzi met separately with the Palestinian security people, Oren Shahor met with Jamil Tarifi, and Yoel Singer worked with Sa'eb Erekat. In the morning we found that we had solved about half the questions on the agenda. Among the decisions reached that night was that the further redeployment would be concluded eighteen months from the convening of the Palestinian Council and that there would be twenty-five Palestinian police stations in Area B. Abu Ala was adamant about defining the redeployment and the agreement as "irreversible," and on this matter of principle I agreed with him. We were not leaving the Palestinian cities in order to reoccupy them. So we agreed to say in the preamble that the new relationship established between the two parties is irreversible.

During the following week Yoel and Sa'eb worked with Dayan and Yihye, Shahor and Tarifi, and Abu Ala and me. By its end we had put together a 410-page draft of the Interim Agreement. But much work still lay ahead for Peres and Arafat. They would have to tackle not just the three toughest issues—Hebron, Rachel's Tomb, and the map of the redeployment—but a relatively long list of less sensitive problems that had cropped up as we prepared the final draft. In a letter containing my recommendations on their coming session in Taba, I wrote to Peres that about twenty-five issues still had to be resolved. "You can expect to have a hard time of it," I warned him. "At this last stage, Arafat will want to come across as a man who has battled for his people's rights down to the last second."

During the preparations in Jerusalem, Peres convinced the IDF that security would be better if we came to a just compromise on Hebron. So Shahak and Ilan Biran worked on a plan that divided responsibility for security in Hebron between the Palestinians, who would control most of the city, and the IDF, which would control the Jewish Quarter and nearby areas. The plan would be implemented within nine months, conditioned on the completion of a bypass road around Hebron and the adjoining town of Halhul. Rabin gave the plan his blessing on September 15. We would remain in control of the bypass road, the large settlement of Kiryat Arba directly east of Hebron, the Jewish Quarter of Hebron and its immediate environs, the Cave of the Patriarchs, the road connecting the Jewish Quarter with Kiryat Arba, and a connection to the southern section of the bypass road. Rabin requested that at the outset of the talks only Peres, Biran (sitting in for Uzi Dayan, who was on personal leave to attend to family matters), and a few other senior security people meet with Arafat in Taba. Their mission was again to stress the need for vigorous action against terrorism as a condition of implementing the agreement.

The longest week of the negotiations began on September 17 at the Hilton Hotel in Taba. Our delegation was housed on the eighth floor, the Palestinians on the ninth, and the negotiating room on the tenth. At one end of that room was a long rectangular table where the official talks were held. At the other was a small sitting area where internal consultations or private talks between Peres and Arafat took place.

The windows looked out on the Red Sea and the Jordanian mountains beyond. The hotel was filled mostly with Israelis, who wished Peres and the rest of us well whenever we appeared in the lobby. They were joined by legions of journalists from all around the world.

After the opening conversation, in which the Palestinian Authority's activity against terrorism had been raised, Peres asked Biran to present Israel's new proposal on security arrangements in Hebron, which he defined as a far-reaching compromise. Arafat, who had arrived with the leaders of his delegation and Yasser Abd Rabbo, began by asking why the twenty thousand Palestinians living immediately around the Jewish Quarter should remain under the IDF's control. I was relieved to see Biran, who was hardly experienced in the art of negotiation, display hitherto hidden diplomatic skills. He addressed Arafat with great deference—assertively but with an understanding of his needs—and explained our requirements in great detail. When the Palestinians asked to change the demarcation line in the city, Peres turned them down flat.

Then Arafat questioned another point. "We can *not*," he stressed, "accept the status quo in the Ibrahim Mosque" (the Cave of the Patriarchs, which was under Israeli security control).

Peres suggested a number of formulas, all of which boiled down to keeping the status quo. Arafat rejected every one.

Finally it was decided that Abu Ala and I should work out the appropriate formula. We moved to the sitting area and began one of our exchanges.

"You know we can't be any more flexible," I told him.

"Perhaps you've forgotten this is also a Muslim holy place. And considering that a Jew massacred Muslim worshipers there, we insist on at least some security presence."

"That's not possible!" I said, knowing that given the enormous sensitivity of the place, responsibility for its security was indivisible.

"And we won't agree to the status quo!"

In the end, we decided to agree not to agree and to say so in the text of the Interim Agreement. That way the status quo would be anchored in the agreement. But we also agreed to form a committee to explore security arrangements and issue a joint recommendation

Paragraph 11: Each side explained its position regarding the Tomb of the Patriarchs. Since they were unable to reach an agreement about it, they have agreed to keep the present situation as is. *Will Continue*

Paragraph 12: Six months after the redeployment, the high level committee on Hebron will begin to discuss the above mentioned arrangements in order to seek an agreement.

Negotiations over the Tomb of the Patriarchs, September 1995.

within three months of the redeployment from Hebron. Arafat approved that formula and passed me a slip of paper on which he sketched two vehicles. Then he asked for a break. I had no idea what to make of the sketch.

We went down to the hotel bar, where Peres met with a crowd of worn-looking journalists. An hour later we returned to the negotiating table. Peres expected Arafat to open the discussion, because it was he who had asked for a break. Arafat merely looked at him and remained mute. The silence lasted for quite a while before Peres busied himself by writing something on a piece of paper. Arafat looked at the sheet in expectation. Sitting beside Peres, I began reading what he was writing with such inscrutable aplomb. It was a poem to Avi Gil about Avi's obsession with the Internet! Summoned from the other end of the table, Avi read it and managed, somehow, to keep a straight face. Meanwhile, the tense silence continued. Finally, after more than half an hour, Peres calmly turned to Arafat and asked: "Mr. Chairman, why are we waiting?"

"I want to know if you've given thought to the proposal I passed to Savir."

Surprised, I took the sketch out of my pocket. Peres glanced at it and, like me, had no idea what it meant. Arafat explained that it was a sketch of a joint patrol and that he proposed it be stationed at the entrance to the Cave of the Patriarchs. Peres replied that the matter had already been settled. Arafat wanted it reconsidered.

"Mr. Chairman," Peres exploded, "I have made you the best offer we can, which is probably better than you expected. If you're interested in more, you won't get it from me. I'm leaving!"

As Peres pushed back his chair to go, Arafat tried to calm him and suggested that our new proposal and the understanding reached by Abu Ala and me be worded by Yoel and Sa'eb. The issue of Hebron was resolved. If goodwill is lacking between negotiating parties, any charged issue can blow up into an affair with vast repercussions. This one could easily have turned into a battle between Judaism and Islam. Instead, the commitment to partnership led to a compromise formula. Details were left to the security subcommittee.

For three days and three nights thereafter, the remaining issues were placed on the table. They included the dispute on water, which was solved, in Kinarti's presence, by fixing the amounts due to the Palestinians. The Palestinians then raised the disconcerting issue of the prisoners, in the presence of Sufian Abu Zaide and Hisham Abdel Razek, the leaders of the prisoners' lobby. The compromise was to release all the women prisoners and any others who fell into specific categories, such as those who had completed two thirds of their term or had been sentenced to less than ten years. The exact wording of the understanding was left to Police Minister Moshe Shahal in Jerusalem. It was also agreed that there would be a second, later stage of prisoner release.

Peres stuck to his tactic of roaring at Arafat's aides, this time in the chairman's presence. He was especially blunt with Sa'eb Erekat whenever the latter tried to intervene in the discussion with legal or other comments.

"Let it be, Sa'eb. That's really not important," Peres would say, or "Sa'eb, you don't need this!"

Yet he would lavish praise on Arafat. "You're lucky to have this man as your leader," he told the members of the Palestinian delegation. "Look at what the mufti achieved for you through extremism in 1948. Nothing!"

Throughout those three days Peres was like a bear, growling, biting, and, as a result, not very popular with the Palestinian delegation. He threatened. He banged his fist on the table. Once he even stormed out of the room, slamming the door behind him, leaving us

© Tammy Soffer

all stunned. He had decided that only in this way could he push the talks to conclusion.

On the third night, Yoel and Sa'eb presented the long list of secondary issues still to be resolved. It was four in the morning by then. Arafat suggested continuing the session the next day, but Peres was implacable. He read issue after issue—as the exhausted Arafat sat looking bemused, almost apathetic—and formulated the compromises himself. The next morning Arafat's spokesman, Marwan Kanafani, told the press: "I forced the chairman to sleep for a few hours when I feared he was about to keel over onto the negotiating table facing Shimon Peres."

But Arafat's hour as a first-rate negotiator came at the very final stage. The issues that remained open were Rachel's Tomb, the passage of Palestinian policemen from Area A to Area B, and the map of the Interim Agreement.

Israel's proposal for security arrangements at Rachel's Tomb was detailed by Biran. It called for the IDF to retain responsibility for the tomb itself, the road leading to it from the southern Jerusalem neighborhood of Gillo, the roofs of a number of buildings around the tomb, and the adjacent parking area. The outer envelope of this enclave would be patrolled jointly.

Arafat said no. "The residents of Bethlehem will never accept this!" he cried. "*I* can't accept it! There's a Muslim cemetery next to Rachel's Tomb, and the holy site is in Area A. I myself am one of Rachel's descendants, you know."

Then he again tried to reopen the discussion on the Cave of the Patriarchs. The meeting dissolved into bedlam, and we decided to postpone the decision on Rachel's Tomb to the next day.

After a short break for dinner, we returned to the tenth floor to reveal to the Palestinians, for the first time—twenty-four hours before the proposed conclusion of the talks—the full map of the Interim Agreement. Biran presented the map of Areas A and B, which together constituted 22 percent of the West Bank. The Palestinian cities that constituted the A area were 3 percent of the territory. Arafat glared at it in silence, then sprang out of his chair and declared it to be an insufferable humiliation.

"These are cantons! You want me to accept *cantons*! You want to *destroy* me!" he screeched and strode out of the room.

Minutes after we had returned to the eighth floor, Israeli journalists came pouring out of the elevator shouting that Marwan Kanafani had issued a statement saying the talks had collapsed and Arafat was about to leave. Peres suggested that I approach Arafat while Avi Gil phoned Dennis Ross to inform him of the crisis. (During that week, Ross was in phone contact with us every few hours.) Before going up to the ninth floor, we asked both the Egyptians (by phoning Osama el-Baz in Cairo) and Yossi Genosar to talk with Arafat. Clearly we wanted to prevent the talks from crashing over the map—a crisis that could have lasted for weeks.

Finally I went up to Arafat's room, and he asked everyone else to leave. Sitting opposite him, I quietly told him that our map was perfectly congruent with the Declaration of Principles. He replied that he could not agree to cantonization. "It's impossible!" he pronounced. Then I suggested that, working with his aides, he outline his requests for creating territorial continuity, and we would discuss them with Biran. After Biran came to the room and likewise talked to him, it was agreed that the two delegations would reconvene to discuss possible revisions.

Arafat returned to the tenth floor, bringing the map the Palestinians had prepared in the Patio. It showed 40 percent of the West Bank as autonomous Palestinian territory after the IDF's first redeployment, and provided for Israeli access to each settlement. Peres looked at the map, refused to discuss it, and asked General Biran and General Samia (head of the subcommittee dealing with maps) to spread ours on the table again. "Where do you want continuity?" Peres asked. Arafat pointed to a number of places. Biran added them, wherever possible, extending the Palestinian zone in about ten places to create passages between Areas A and B. Then Peres said, "That's it. I can't add any more," and sent the cartographers to remark the map. Arafat did not object. By agreeing to redeploy at first from 27 percent of the West Bank, we had shown reasonable flexibility. The entire session took thirty minutes.

When it ended, Abu Ala stood up and announced that he was going to his room to make a call. He had not intervened at all during the discussion on the map and now looked pale with rage at our arm-twisting negotiating style. The rest of us dispersed to plan the final day of the talks, Friday, and the initialing of the agreement. Yoel and Sa'eb worked without rest to word the final mutual concessions.

Suddenly Stella came rushing toward me. "Arafat wants you to go to Abu Ala's room immediately," she said. "He's collapsed."

I dashed to Abu Ala's room to find him lying on the bed, deathly pale, trembling and dipping in and out of consciousness. Arafat sat holding his hand and looking shattered. I leaned over the bed and whispered, "It's okay, Abu Ala. You're going to be all right."

By the time the doctor had taken his blood pressure and found it unstable, Peres and Avi had reached the room. We were sure that he had suffered a heart attack and immediately called an ambulance to take him to the hospital in Eilat. Peres and Avi accompanied him there. As Abu Ala was carried out, I began feeling ill myself, probably from a combination of exhaustion and anxiety about my friend. The talks stopped. We were too concerned to go on.

I returned to my room to pull myself together and wait for a phone call. It was Stella who finally told me Avi had called to report that Abu Ala was in stable condition and had collapsed of exhaustion, not a heart attack. The photo of Abu Ala being carried out on a stretcher with an oxygen mask over his face made front pages the world over. His son Ala was summoned urgently from Abu Dis, and we stayed in close contact with his doctors.

We resumed negotiations that night, so as to initial the agreement by the following noon. I suggested to Peres that Yoel and Sa'eb do the initialing this time. I could not imagine doing it in the absence of my longtime partner who, more than anyone else, had struggled for some nine months to conclude an agreement that many people, on both sides, deemed impossible. At every step, Abu Ala conducted his side of the talks with tenacity and rigor but always fairly and with an understanding of our security needs.

After hearing the report on Abu Ala's condition, Arafat was back to his old self. He thanked Peres for helping Abu Ala and returned to brinkmanship. First he raised the settlement freeze. After all, he reminded us, Rabin had committed himself to a maximum of fifty meters beyond the last house.

"We can't negotiate a freeze with you," Peres told him. "That was a unilateral Israeli decision, and our government made it before the Declaration of Principles. But I'm prepared to send you a copy of that decision as an accompanying letter." Peres also persuaded Arafat not to have the size of each settlement marked on the map, so as to avoid a fruitless debate over what constitutes a settlement.

The teams continued working. The eighth and ninth floors were a document factory, with dozens of people scurrying between rooms. In one of those rooms the teams began tracing the changes on the map of the West Bank and putting the finishing touches on the map of the special arrangements in Hebron.

By Friday morning there were only three issues that required Peres's and Arafat's intervention: the passage of Palestinian policemen from Area A to Area B, upgrading the status of territory from B to A in the future, and the security arrangements at Rachel's Tomb. There were also a few minor civil and legal issues that required further negotiation, and of course it was necessary to finish revising the maps. Yoel and Sa'eb forecast that it would be impossible to finish all the work by late that evening, when the Sabbath began. We would have to continue working on Saturday night in order to finish by Sunday, the eve of the Jewish New Year.

For the weekend we checked into the Princess Hotel, just over the border in Eilat, and decided to get some rest. But late in the evening, I gathered together the junior staff, who had worked hard for months and rarely received the credit they deserved. Instead of resting, we celebrated the upcoming conclusion of the negotiations with a party that lasted till dawn. Throughout the negotiations, my devoted staff—including Bureau Director Rafi Barak, executive assistants Ido Aharoni and Eran Etzion, the indomitable Stella Shustak, who managed my office, the English drafters Aviva Meir and Pamela Levin, and my secretaries Meira Alouf, Revital Dankner, and Avital Hershkovitz—worked tirelessly to assure that the complex operation ran smoothly. Avi, Yoel, Ilan, Oren, and I spent Saturday with Peres in his suite, walked a bit, and planned the closing hours of the talks. When the Sabbath ended, we returned to Taba.

Sa'eb, Yoel, and I worked out a satisfactory formula for turning part of Area B into Area A parallel to the further redeployment (except for areas related to the permanent-status talks). We considered this formula very positively because it enabled Israel to keep certain villages close to the Green Line or to settlements in the West Bank under its security control until the permanent settlement. But we didn't want the Palestinians to know that we were pleased, and we weren't sure that the cell phones in Taba were secure. So when Peres updated Rabin on this formula, the conversation turned out to be a bit strange.

"Yitzhak, this is Shimon," he began. "We've reached an agreement on transferring parts of B to A." (Here he described the formula.) "The boys say it isn't so good, but we recommend accepting it."

"I don't understand," said Rabin. "If it's not good, why accept it?"

"Yitzhak, I'm speaking from Taba."

"*I know,*" Rabin replied.

"Yitzhak, remember that I'm speaking from *Taba.*"

"You just said that. I know!"

"And that's why I'm recommending the formula."

"Ah," said Rabin, who finally realized the reason for Peres's odd, backhanded recommendation. He approved it.

On Sunday morning, the day before the Jewish New Year, we again convened in the conference room. Biran explained the arrangement for Palestinian policemen to travel from Area A to Area B (from the cities to the villages), pointing out that they would need our permission, as between police stations.

"Yes, of course," said Arafat, "they will coordinate with you."

"No, Mr. Chairman," Biran corrected him. "You know the difference. They will have to ask our permission, via the District Coordination Office. Otherwise there will be chaos regarding the movement of your policemen and our troops."

"That's why both sides must coordinate," Arafat said.

"The coordination will be done by approval in the DCO," said Peres. "What's the problem?"

Arafat flew out of his chair. "What do you think?" he snapped. "That my policemen will be subordinate to you? That you'll humiliate my security people? That we'll ask your permission to move to a Palestinian village in B to deal with a robbery or a family spat? That's not an agreement. I will not be shamed by you! I am not your slave! I'm not your slave!" he shouted and stormed out of the room.

"It's always this way before the end of a negotiation," some of our people murmured to each other. But then we saw the Palestinians' luggage being carried downstairs and began to wonder whether this wasn't a genuine crisis.

Kanafani came up to me and said, "Listen, this time he's really leaving."

"Peres is leaving too," I said. "We've had it with these crises."

"Forget the games now," Kanafani said. "Come with me. Perhaps you can persuade him to stay."

I followed Kanafani to Arafat's suite, where the chairman was shut up in his private room. I knocked, entered, and sat down next to him by a small, round table. He was in much more of a lather now than he had been over the map three days earlier. "I didn't understand it that way," he said, his voice hoarse. "You really want to humiliate me. Well, I prefer that there be no agreement."

"Look, Abu Ammar," I began softly. "You've come this far; it's a pity to break now. I give you my word that even if the talks go on for a hundred years, Rabin and Peres will not be able to change their stand on this point. What you want will destroy the balance on the ground."

Arafat remained silent for several moments. Then he called in Abd Rabbo and they spoke in Arabic. Abd Rabbo was hardly one of Arafat's moderate advisers, yet he too was clearly trying to persuade the chairman to be more flexible.

"Mr. Chairman," I said, "knowing my mandate for a compromise, I'm sure we can find a less offensive way of saying it in the text, and after three months we may change it to notification."

Arafat agreed and I thanked him. Yoel replaced the word "approval" with "confirmation." When I spoke to Biran, he conceded that after the first three months of joint control in Area B, only a prior announcement of police movements would be necessary in areas agreed upon by the sides.

All that was left now was the problem of Rachel's Tomb. When we reconvened on the tenth floor, speaking rather heatedly and in Hebrew, Biran told Peres that he was adamant about stationing soldiers on the rooftops around the tomb.

"Switch to English," Peres told him.

Then Biran turned to Arafat. It was his turn to explode. "Look," he said, "if we do things your way, I won't be able to provide security. You've already agreed. We've gone a long way toward accommodating you on the redeployment from all the cities. From Hebron now, too. I must maintain minimal conditions at this holy site!"

As Biran seethed, Arafat surprised us again. He had apparently been impressed by the outburst, because he walked over to Biran, shook his hand, and said, "I agree." Then he actually embraced the astonished general.

The Interim Agreement was now complete. After Peres and Arafat rang Christopher and Ross to update them, a photographer was brought in to take a picture of the two delegations as a memento for the negotiators and support staff.

On the previous day, Abu Ala had returned to the hotel and was warmly embraced by colleagues from both delegations. We could see that he was moved by the reception, and he immediately walked over to Peres to say, "Thank you from the bottom of my heart for going to the hospital with me."

"The important thing is that you're well," Peres replied.

"Peres saved my life," Abu Ala whispered in my ear. "He sat next to me in the ambulance and said, 'Hold on, Abu Ala. We all need you.' I'll never forget that."

On Sunday afternoon Abu Ala and I sat down, this time in front of the cameras, and initialed the Interim Agreement (which came to be known colloquially as Oslo II). Then Peres and Arafat made brief speeches, and Arafat wished the Israeli people a happy new year, in Hebrew, "*shana tova.*" Before the press, Biran praised the document by saying, "It was impossible to reach a better agreement than this one, but we couldn't have settled for less." He had said it all.

The interim agreement included 410 pages and 8 maps. Its language was as complex as its outline and the reality it was about to change. Yet its basic principles were clear.

Area H1
Area H2

0   1 km

©*Tammy Soffer*

In Stage One (October–December 1995):

1. The IDF was to leave six Palestinian cities in the West Bank (except Hebron) and turn them over to the Palestinian civil and security authorities.

2. Simultaneously, the IDF was to leave all of its positions in the 465 Palestinian villages, yet retain its overriding security responsibility to fight terror and for Israelis.

3. The Palestinian Authority would, upon Israel's military redeployment, receive security and civil responsibilities for the Palestinian cities (3 percent of the West Bank) and civil and public-order responsibility for the Palestinian villages (24 percent of the West Bank) to be exercised through twenty-five Palestinian police stations (as outlined on the maps).

4. Israel would retain civil and security responsibilities in 73 percent of the West Bank (the unpopulated area) and about 10 percent of the Gaza Strip (mainly in the areas of Israeli settlement, as previously agreed in the Gaza-Jericho Agreement).

5. Israel would retain all security responsibilities regarding the entrance and exit of people and goods to and from the West Bank and Gaza.

In Stage Two (January–April 1996):

1. Free and democratic elections for an eighty-eight-member Palestinian Council, as well as for the chairman of the Palestinian Authority, would be held in all of the West Bank and Gaza. (They took place on January 20, 1996.)

2. Two months after the inauguration of the Palestinian Council, the representative organ of all Palestinians—the Palestinian National Council (PNC)—would pass by a two-thirds majority a resolution nullifying all the clauses of the Palestinian Covenant that call for the destruction of Israel and otherwise contradict the various agreements with Israel.

4. Six months after signing the Interim Agreement, Israel would leave the last major Palestinian city—Hebron—and turn over most of its area to Palestinian security and civil control. Israel would retain security control of an enclave inhabited by Jewish settlers, the roads on which they travel, the Cave of the Patriarchs, and some adjacent areas.

In Stage Three:

On May 4, 1996, the negotiations on the permanent settlement between Israel and the PLO would begin and cover such issues as settlements, Jerusalem, refugees, borders, and relations with other
countries. These negotiations were to be concluded by May 4,
1999.

In Stage Four:

Israel would redeploy from unpopulated territory of the West Bank
within eighteen months of the inauguration of the Palestinian Council, except for Israeli-defined specified security locations. These further redeployments would be carried out in three stages of six
months each. Simultaneously, Israel would transfer to the Palestinian
Authority security responsibilities in the area of the Palestinian villages (Area B), except for areas related to permanent-status issues.

Israel's security responsibilities would include defense against external threats, full responsibility for Israelis living in the settlements,
and full responsibility for Israelis traveling in the West Bank and
Gaza Strip. The Palestinians would be responsible for carrying out
security actions designed to fight terror (such as confiscating illegal
arms) in areas under their security control.

The agreement also outlined the specific legislative responsibilities of the Palestinian Council, which could not contradict the accord. It noted that the Palestinian Authority would not conduct
foreign policy, except on specified issues handled by the PLO (such as
international aid). The Palestinian Authority would also be part of
the Israeli customs system.

Israel and the Palestinian Authority would establish an array of
committees for cooperation in implementing the agreement. These
would include a senior monitoring and coordination committee to
oversee the implementation.

Yet above all this was a historic agreement, putting an end to Israeli
rule over the Palestinians, an end to the notion of a greater Israel, and
a beginning to cooperation and reconciliation between two peoples

who had decided to divide the land on which they lived for the sake of a common destiny of peace, security, and economic development.

We flew back to Israel to reach our homes just minutes before the New Year holiday began. Only later in the week did a large delegation travel to Washington for the official signing there. The Palestinian delegation, which flew via Cairo, was joined by Abu Mazen. At the last minute it was decided that he, rather than Abu Ala, would cosign the agreement for the Palestinians. This offended Abu Ala, because Abu Mazen had not been associated with the talks at all. He hadn't even entered the autonomous area until two months earlier— a year after Arafat and most of his colleagues from Tunis had arrived. In fact, Abu Mazen would hardly have known what was going on had Abu Ala not kept him abreast of developments. So during the signing ceremony, Abu Ala surrounded himself with his family and kept apart from the rest of us. He didn't even eke out a smile when President Clinton mentioned the two of us in a speech as people without whom the agreement would not have been reached.

By contrast, the chemistry between Rabin and Arafat was extraordinary that day. In his speech that afternoon at a reception hosted by Clinton, Rabin even publicly teased a laughing Arafat by saying that by giving so many speeches, he was becoming Jewish. Rabin, Peres, Arafat, and Abu Mazen signed the agreement inside the White House, in the presence of President Clinton, President Mubarak, and King Hussein. This time, all maps were signed.

At the cabinet meeting before the flight to Washington, Rabin complimented Peres for the way he had handled the negotiations, and Peres complimented the delegation. Two ministers abstained in the vote, but Ehud Barak backed the agreement unequivocally and was sent by Rabin to cull a majority in the Knesset.

Since most of the delegation had not gone to Washington, we decided to hold a thank-you party for all 150 of its members. Rabin and Peres agreed to come and express their gratitude. Two Jordanian comedians were scheduled to perform. We printed up a special certificate for each of the delegation's members. This time I prepared a written speech. I wanted, personally and on behalf of the delegation, to thank Rabin and Peres for allowing us to be part of a monumental effort that would change the history of the region. And I wanted to express our appreciation for their courageous decisions, which not only moved us forward toward peace but liberated us from the burden of ruling over another people. The party never took place. It had been scheduled for November 6, 1995. By then Yitzhak Rabin was gone.

III

Struggle

8

PEACE AND VIOLENCE

YIGAL AMIR, A TWENTY-SEVEN-YEAR-OLD LAW STUDENT WITH DARK, curly hair partly covered by a black skullcap, participated in the demonstrations that denounced the government for handing over the Land of Israel to bloodthirsty murderers of Jews. "Rabin is a murderer, Rabin is a traitor" was the chant. Like many others, he had absorbed the messages of hatred proclaimed by the leaders of the radical right. Yet Amir was not satisfied with demonstrations and screaming epithets. For months he had planned an independent action to destroy the peace process.

Yigal Amir lived in the Tel Aviv suburb of Herzliya. His mother ran a kindergarten, and his father was a scribe of devotional texts. On the bookshelf in his room stood Frederick Forsyth's *Day of the Jackal*, a thriller about the race by the French security services to stop an assassin hired to kill Charles de Gaulle. The Jackal is stopped just as he is taking aim at the president.

Amir intended to do better.

In March 1994 he had taken part in a hunger strike during which he had said, "Peres and Rabin are snakes; they should both be killed. The country will be saved only if someone gets up and kills them, then there'll be elections and Bibi [Binyamin Netanyahu] will be in power."

The Israeli right felt, perhaps even more strongly than the left, that Oslo II was a historic development, but a disastrous one from their point of view. The left, which supported the agreement, was now studying its wording and maps and to a lesser extent its historic significance. The right, which understood that the redeployment in the Palestinian towns meant the Palestinization of the West Bank, hoped to stop the process through mass street protests organized by leaders of the various parliamentary and extraparliamentary opposition groups.

When the agreement was submitted to the Knesset for ratification, on October 5, 1995, tens of thousands of demonstrators gathered in Jerusalem's Zion Square. The list of speakers was headed by the leader of the opposition, Binyamin Netanyahu, who defined the agreement as an "act of surrender" and a "danger to the existence of the State of Israel." Netanyahu stressed that it would be ratified by a *non-Jewish* Knesset majority—that is, a majority that included Arab-Israeli members. (Among the narrow majority of 61 members out of 120 were 6 Arab Israelis.) Ten percent of Israel's population is Arab, most of whom live in the northern part of the country. In effect, Netanyahu was delegitimatizing Israel's Arab citizens when he said, "Rabin counts on all the anti-Zionist Arab parties that support the PLO."

The argument by Netanyahu and his colleagues that the ratification was not supported by a Jewish majority was gaining hold among those who at best questioned the identity of Israeli-Arabs or were racist, or both. Elyakim Ha'etzni, a leader of the settlement movement, said, for example: "The government is a faction that grabbed power with the aid of a terrorist organization." In other words, the Rabin government was illegitimate and did not represent the people of Israel. Yigal Amir himself would testify at his trial that "the prime minister was elected by the Arabs; twenty percent of those who voted for him were Arabs. Are those Arabs to decide the future of my country?"

At that same demonstration on October 6, 1995, leaflets were distributed, apparently by supporters of Kahane Chai, that depicted Rabin in SS uniform. "Rabin is a Nazi," they shouted. Children of settlers wearing yellow Stars of David bearing the word SETTLER mingled with the demonstrators. The Holocaust images were being used to spread anxiety, to imply that Oslo meant extermination. Rabin was depicted as a "traitor," "murderer," "Nazi," and "illegal prime minister." Netanyahu disapproved of the slogan "Rabin is a

Nazi." "It does not become you," he told his followers at the rally. But the writing was on the wall.

That same evening an angry mob attacked the prime minister's car—in which he was not traveling at the time—and spat on it. Two young men, members of Kahane Chai, broke off the Cadillac emblem and in an interview published in *Yediot Aharonot* on October 10 they boasted, "If we managed to get Rabin's Cadillac emblem, we can get Rabin."

During that period I observed Rabin at staff meetings on the redeployment. His reaction to the demonstrators was a mixture of anger and dismissal. All along he had shown restraint toward the right, including the settlers, but remained undeterred by them. That was perhaps his finest hour as a leader.

On the day of the Knesset vote, he called us in for a meeting while the mob roared in the streets. The prime minister opened the discussion in the presence of the upper echelons of the security establishment, Peres, Yoel, and myself.

"We will begin the evacuation of the Civil Administration offices next week, at least two offices in the Salfit area, and I would like to reach four. The order will be decided by the chief of staff. Before the redeployment begins, I would like Shimon and the heads of the security services to meet with Arafat and demand that he improve his performance in the war against terror. We can also propose that he choose a date between January 20, 1996, and April 1996 for holding the elections, in case he wants to wait until the Hebron redeployment is completed."

Rabin sounded resolute and determined to continue the process and made it clear that the turmoil in the streets, the threats and incitement, had not affected him. During the course of the discussions, it was evident that the partnership between him and Peres was becoming stronger as a result of the road they had decided to take, and the violent threats against them both. They were aware that they were leading a historic change, while being engaged in its details in a practical and pragmatic way. They were about to implement a most complex security move: withdrawing the IDF from Palestinian-populated centers while working with a less than ideal partner but with a clear objective in which they firmly believed.

The following night Peres and the heads of our security establishment met with Arafat, who had once again come to the Erez checkpoint with the heads of the Palestinian security and intelligence apparatus. Some of our officers were critical of Arafat because his people were placing far too much emphasis on their talks with the Hamas leadership, which were taking place in Sudan with our approval. They said that it was not sufficient for Arafat to attempt to convince his ideological opponents to become a political nonviolent movement but that he should at the same time take concrete steps against terrorist elements on the ground. Arafat's people replied that they were working night and day to prevent terrorism. They complained about the character of our coordination with them, which in their view took the form of unilateral demands rather than true cooperation between equals. Peres and our security people stressed that everything depended on whether the Palestinians acted systematically to tighten security coordination, particularly on the West Bank. In fact, our security people made the redeployment conditional upon reinforcing security activities and cooperation. Arafat agreed to everything we asked but still pursued his "divide and rule" strategy vis-à-vis Hamas.

At this meeting the redeployment timetable for the various towns was agreed upon. The Palestinians asked that the first step, IDF withdrawal from Jenin, be completed as soon as possible and also that all women prisoners be released, including two whom President Weizman had refused to release because they had been involved in murder, which violated our commitment in the Interim Agreement. In the wake of this meeting, the start of the redeployment process was decided upon contingent on a more resolute Palestinian antiterror policy and improved security cooperation. Operation Diary, as the redeployment was called, was under way, and to supervise its successful execution Rabin determined that the negotiating teams should establish a steering and monitoring committee to be headed by Abu Ala and myself. We decided to convene the committee every two weeks.

We met for the first time in Abu Ala's office in A-Ram near Jerusalem and decided that as a result of lessons learned from the Gaza-Jericho Agreement, we would supervise the implementation of every clause in the agreement as well as ensure the smooth functioning of the dozens of subcommittees established under its terms.

We had no doubt that the Interim Agreement stood no chance of succeeding without full cooperation between the two parties in all spheres. The Palestinians complained about the intermittent closure in response to terrorist attacks. "You are harming the process," said Abu Ala. "That, too, is part of an atmosphere that will affect security." In these discussions we dealt with the oversight of the Palestinian election process, and more specifically with the arrival of dozens of international observers. The level of transparency that the Palestinians were prepared to adopt was impressive. They had originally wanted the observers as a barrier against our intervention, but now the observers became a tool for assuring the credibility of the elections.

We also addressed coordination between the parties in the organization of Christmas festivities, with all their inherent security problems, so that Gen. Ilan Biran and Gen. Haj Ismail found themselves occupied with the celebration of Christ's birthday under Palestinian control. "After all," said someone at the table, "Jesus was born in Area A!"

A far less congenial subject was the transport of stolen Israeli cars to areas under the Palestinian Authority. Stealing vehicles in Israel and moving them to Gaza, often with the help of criminal elements in Israel proper, had become a thriving industry. Criminals on both sides quickly learned to cooperate in this area.

Biran led the redeployment, a complex operation in which the IDF had virtually no previous experience: voluntary withdrawal, enabling those who had been controlled by the IDF to take responsibility for security matters that would have ramifications for our own security. This called for not only hard work at the staff level but shattering the tradition that on security matters we would rely only on ourselves.

Biran organized a short seminar to which he invited the Oslo team to explain the Interim Agreement. It dealt, among other things, with "reeducation"—a change of attitude from one of control to one of cooperation. The approach of inspiring a more humane attitude through a course of lectures was not very creative, but the intentions were the best. These objectives were daunting, at least in the short term, but eventually they would be part of the developing process. In a sense, the Interim Agreement called for more cooperation than the Permanent Settlement would because of the large area under the control of two armed forces. The enemies were the extremists on both sides, and indeed cooperation improved.

I vividly remembered the announcement broadcast during the Six-Day War that the IDF had taken Jenin. Twenty-eight years later, on October 17, 1995, the IDF withdrew from Jenin. The Palestinian officers in uniform entered the town and raised the Palestinian flag to tumultuous applause. The IDF forces conducted themselves honorably as they left Jenin while Palestinians hurled stones at them, harsh scenes for the Israeli public to stomach. The bitterness of the mobs was not surprising, but the insensitivity of the Palestinian leadership toward Israeli public opinion continued to amaze me. Israelis might accept Palestinians' management of their own affairs, but not stones thrown at IDF soldiers, which turned the peace into a new kind of confrontation.

Arafat failed to understand the effect of these scenes. He was obsessed with his own domestic predicaments, and we ourselves did not attempt to enact a dialogue with Palestinian public opinion for similar reasons of self-centeredness. As the weaker party, Arafat should have recognized the importance of inspiring Israeli opinion, as President Sadat and King Hussein had done before him. Our own rhetoric toward the Palestinians was a combination of support for the process and a somewhat condescending, didactic approach. Therefore throughout most of this period of historic transition, picture and words were often not synchronized, which led to the public's confusion.

We now sought the fruits of peace in a wider area. The decision to end the occupation of the Palestinian towns created a new attitude toward Israel in almost the entire Arab world, as well as in the rest of the world. As director-general of the Foreign Ministry, I felt the tangible results of this turnabout as Israel's status steadily rose. We now had diplomatic relations with 162 countries, and our embassies, which had been asked to reap the economic harvest, reported increasing interest in the Israeli economy. Not a week went by without the visit of a foreign prime minister or foreign minister to Jerusalem. The State of Israel had left the West Bank towns, but more important, it had emerged from the international wilderness to which it had been exiled for twenty years.

In the Middle East, our legations in Oman, Qatar, and Tunis commenced diplomatic activities.

A new high was reached at the second regional economic conference in Amman, a year after Casablanca. Another economic conference was held simultaneously in Jerusalem under the auspices of the financial newspaper *Globes*, attended by thousands of businessmen and businesswomen, many of whom crossed the bridge from Jordan to be there. The emphasis of the Amman conference was on projects for regional development, especially joint projects with Jordan, such as an airport in the Aqaba-Eilat area, a tourist riviera in the same area, and joint projects on the shores of the Dead Sea.

If the Casablanca conference had set a precedent, the feeling at Amman was of permanence. There was talk of establishing a Middle East regional bank and an Israeli-Palestinian-Jordanian-Egyptian economic planning body in Amman. We were about to appoint a first diplomat to a Middle East organization.

Politicians were far less visible in Amman, as the conference was attended mostly by businesspeople. The theme was clearly the emergence of the New Middle East, of an era of cooperation and competition for the benefit of the people of the region. The conference's closing announcement contained an explicit reference to the cessation of the Arab boycott, and a number of Arab businessmen went on to attend the Jerusalem conference. Peace with the Palestinians and the international openness toward Israel had reinforced the current situation in Jerusalem. This was our strategy on the issue of Jerusalem: the creation of stability that would benefit those who governed the city and in time would effect a solution in the permanent status negotiations.

I also crossed the bridge from conference to conference. At the Allenby Passage, I visited the Palestinian terminal on which we had negotiated so hard and long only a few months earlier. The arrangement made a very positive impression. I walked over to Passport Control to see how the Palestinian police officer was working with the "unseen, unheard" Israeli behind him. The director of the Israeli border crossing, a likable and intelligent man, unlocked the door to reveal the mysterious Israeli and we found the position empty! Probably this was pure chance, but it may also have been that whoever had said back in Cairo that an unheard Israeli is a contradiction in terms was right.

Yitzhak Rabin and Shimon Peres, with their hosts, King Hussein and Crown Prince Hassan, were the heroes of the conference. They met with heads of state and businessmen and were warmly received. After months of negotiations, decisions, and ferocious opposition, both Rabin and Peres were well satisfied. They knew that "without Oslo there could be no Amman," without a solution to the Palestinian problem there could be no strengthening of the regional status that was bringing international investment and security to Israel. The Oslo Accords and the Casablanca and Amman meetings were the key to the long-term strengthening of both our economy and our national security. Yet many were still mesmerized by one clause or another of the agreement, and others still wanted to rule the Palestinians and the West Bank endlessly for the sake, as they conceived it, of security, or for reasons of ideology. These people failed to see that economics, technology, science, and international relations determine the real power of countries, more than land. Amman frightened the extremists on both sides, hypnotized by the past and by hate.

Toward the end of the Amman conference, Peres, joined by our ambassador, Shimon Shamir, and me, went on a stroll through the Jordanian capital. The people in the street greeted him warmly, with cheers and handshakes. This was not what we encountered on Israeli streets, where the right fulminated as if with their very bodies they might stop the "great surrender." While Rabin was meeting the heads of Arab states and their businessmen, the demonstrators and rabble-rousers were shouting that our country was led by traitors.

In October, outside Rabin's home, Kach (the racist movement that was created by Rabbi Kahane and was officially outlawed after the Hebron massacre) held a Pulsa Dinura ceremony, a religious curse of death, calling upon the Avenging Angels to harm the prime minister. The majority of the right's protest activities were organized by the so-called Action Headquarters, an ad hoc structure composed mostly of antigovernment elements.

According to the press reports at the time and a recent Israeli television documentary, Knesset member Tsahi Hanegbi led this right-wing unrest as Likud's representative. In September he appeared in disguise at an annual popular event, the festive Jerusalem march, and shouted, "Rabin is a traitor." Nahum Barnea, a well-known columnist for *Yediot Aharonot*, the leading Israeli daily, described the incident and added: "Hanegbi is Netanyahu's right-hand man. With his special talents he will run to crown Netanyahu prime minister or drag him down into the gutter, or possibly both." The right-wing theme was that the government was a fifth column jeopardizing the country by capitulating to its enemies, the murderers of Jews.

Netanyahu himself declared that the government was "endangering the existence of the state." Elyakim Ha'etzni, a lawyer from the settlement of Kiryat Arba, prepared to put "the government on trial like the traitor Pétain" (who had been sentenced to death in France). Moshe Feiglin, who headed the Zu Artzenu protest movement, called Rabin "a murderer . . . whose days are numbered."

It was amid this chorus of hatred that Yigal Amir laid his plans, as we worked on redeployment in two additional towns, Tulkarm and Kalkilya.

According to the press at that time, the head of the General Security Services had spoken with the leaders of the opposition parties, including Netanyahu, in August and cautioned them about joining forces with extremist elements of the religious community. They dismissed the warnings as intervention in political matters. When Rabin visited the United States on October 20 for the fiftieth anniversary of the United Nations, unprecedented security measures were taken to protect him from extremist Muslim groups. But Rabin was also advised to beware of Israeli terrorists.

In that hostile atmosphere, Rabin and Peres felt isolated. The left had not taken to the streets but chose to avoid confrontation. It had already begun to enjoy the fruits of the peace process. Some even complained about aspects of the agreement and criticized Rabin and Peres for decisions made or not made, for implementation that was too slow or too fast, or for statements with which they disagreed. These critics had no conception of the courage with which Rabin and Peres had forced the great decisions of 1995, decisions that would determine Israel's future. These autumn months were an occasion not to take peace for granted but to take a stand in the streets, as Americans had done during the Vietnam War and French had done during the withdrawal from Algeria. This passivity of the left germinated into the eventual electoral loss to the right, at precisely the moment of the left's ideological victory. The streets belonged to the opposition, and I was frustrated when my friends asked me, "Why don't you make a greater PR effort?" It was they who should have constituted the PR effort that they were seeking while Israel was engaged in a fight for its soul.

The contest was not between leaders but between Israelis themselves. One man who grasped this was a French citizen, Jean Friedmann, a sixty-year-old Jewish businessman and a friend of Shimon Peres. At the beginning of October, he persuaded Peres to let him and the former mayor of Tel Aviv, Shlomo Lahat, organize a rally supporting the process and the government as a response to the violence of the right.

Peres urged Rabin to go along. The prime minister wondered at first: "Would people come out of their homes?" But he overcame his skepticism and agreed in the end.

On their return from Amman, Rabin and Peres discovered that Friedmann and Lahat were taking their work seriously; the papers were full of announcements of the forthcoming rally: "Whoever comes has an influence. A mass rally with the participation of Prime Minister Yitzhak Rabin and Foreign Minister Shimon Peres in Malkhei Yisrael Square, Tel Aviv, Saturday night, November 4, 1995, 7:00 P.M. Yes to Peace, No to Violence."

Yigal Amir also read the announcements. On the Thursday before the rally, he attended a lecture on the organization of the computerized catalog at Bar-Ilan University and the next day told his brother that Saturday evening would be his big opportunity.

On the evening of November 4, he loaded his pistol with hollow-nosed bullets, cocked it, then took a No. 284 bus from his home in Herzliya to North Tel Aviv.

That Saturday afternoon we met our good friends Mona and Terje as usual at Cafe Basel. Maya was eager to attend the rally and tried to persuade Mona and Terje to join us, but they had a dinner engagement with Chairman Arafat in Gaza in honor of Portuguese President Mário Soares. "We will make a contribution to peace in our own way," said Terje, so we arranged to meet again later that night.

Aliza, Maya, and I then returned to our home near the sea on Frankfurt Street and picked up the "rally equipment" that Maya had prepared. She was wearing a short-sleeved "Peace Now" T-shirt, as she had from the time she had taken part in demonstrations as a child. Wearing our sneakers, we almost ran to the square, eager to see whether people had taken to the streets. I was anxious about the turnout, knowing that the rally would be a test of support for Oslo. From a distance we saw Malkhei Yisrael Square, in the heart of Tel Aviv, full to overflowing. Rivers of people filled the side streets, and huge posters hung from the balcony of City Hall reading: YES TO PEACE, NO TO VIOLENCE.

Maya was exuberant: "I told you so, I told you!" she shouted, as we joyfully joined the enormous crowd. The demonstrators were upbeat but quiet. We met friends we hadn't seen for months. Many strangers congratulated me on my role in the process, something I had rarely experienced before.

There was a feeling of gratification in the air. People were smiling as though they had emerged from hiding and discovered that there were many just like them who supported peace with the Palestinians. It was a "happening," part rally and part reunion, as people hugged one another in familial joy. As the rally opened, we moved closer to the stage, where singers were performing and the ambassadors of Egypt and Jordan were addressing the crowd. Yitzhak Frankenthal, whose son had been killed by terrorists, spoke in support of giving peace a chance. And then came Peres and Rabin, who spoke in an unprecedented show of mutual appreciation, each mentioning the other as his partner in peace. The audience took them to their hearts.

Rabin's words were unforgettable: "You are proving today that the people really do want peace, not violence. Violence corrodes the foundations of Israeli democracy. It must be condemned and isolated. It is not Israel's way. The people of Israel want peace and support peace," he said.

"Peace is first of all in our prayers, but it is also the aspiration of the Jewish people, a genuine aspiration for peace. There are enemies of peace who are trying to hurt us, in order to torpedo the peace process. I want to say bluntly that we have found a partner for peace among the Palestinians as well: the PLO, which was an enemy and has ceased to engage in terrorism. Without partners for peace, there can be no peace."

Finally Miri Aloni, with Peres and Rabin at her side, led them and the entire crowd in "The Song of Peace." Rabin put his arm around Peres. It seemed that the stormy relationship between the two leaders had at last become a genuine partnership, that only together could they carry the burden.

The rally ended with "Hatikvah." At official events I usually mumble the words of our national anthem, but that night I sang it with all my heart as I looked around me with a special feeling about being an Israeli, of being part of a country that had struggled so hard for peace. Most of the crowd were young, and I believed I was seeing Israel's first "Peace Generation." What surprised me was the sight of many crocheted skullcaps, which we had become used to seeing at demonstrations by the right.

The crowd began to disperse at 9:00, and we decided to walk north on Ibn Gvirol Street to see if we could greet Peres on his way out. As we crossed the square, Maya held us up for a few moments while she signed a political petition. We hurried her along and made our way toward the steps, which Peres and Rabin would descend on the way to their cars, surrounded by a large crowd of demonstrators and security men. A number of young people shouted encouragement to the two leaders. As we drew closer, our spirits were as high as I could remember throughout the years of negotiation. Then came the horror.

Yigal Amir had reached the vicinity of the square and removed his skullcap. He wanted to look like a driver of one of the VIP cars. Wearing a dark blue T-shirt, he stood throughout most of the rally at the foot of the steps, waiting for Rabin and Peres. As we approached these steps, we saw, from a distance of about thirty feet, Peres walking toward his car when suddenly people were shouting, "Rabin! Rabin!"

"There's Rabin," I said to Aliza and Maya as he made his way down the steps with his wife, Leah, behind, separated from him by security men. It was 9:47 P.M.

Suddenly, three sharp reports were heard.

"What was that?" Maya shouted.

"A motorcycle, I think," I replied.

There was a sudden commotion, and people began running from the steps. I saw an ambulance drive into the street from the north and then realized that what we had heard were gunshots. We were unable to get any closer as the police had surrounded the area.

Not knowing what else to do, we ran home to watch the news.

"Are you sure they were shots?" Aliza asked.

"I think so."

We passed crowds of happy people, completely unaware of what had happened only a few yards from where they were standing. We reached a line of cars and stopped at the first one to listen to its radio. Uri Avneri, a veteran left-wing peace activist, was in his red car.

"Shots were fired in the square," we told him.

From Avneri's car we heard an Israel Radio report that "shots were heard in Malkhei Yisrael Square at the end of the mass pro-peace rally. There was apparently an attempt on the life of the prime minister," but not a word about his condition or even whether he had been hit.

That's a bad sign, I said to myself, and we ran toward home as fast as we could.

On the way we were stopped by Dov Gilhar, a reporter for the military radio, who was running in the opposite direction. "I don't know," I mumbled in reply to his question, "I think Rabin has been shot."

We reached home at 11:00 and switched on the TV. Friends began calling, saying that they had heard a rumor that Rabin had been shot but that his condition was not serious. Others had heard that he was seriously wounded.

We switched from channel to channel and then heard Sky News announce, "Prime Minister of Israel Rabin died today after being hit by an assassin's bullets." It was 11:10 P.M.

Maya and Aliza wept. My head was spinning.

I switched to Israel Television in the foolish belief that British TV had been mistaken, and then Yitzhak Rabin's picture appeared on the screen over the caption "1922–1995" and Eitan Haber read the official announcement: "The Government of Israel announces with shock, great sorrow, and deep grief the death of Prime Minister and Defense Minister Yitzhak Rabin, who was murdered by an assassin this evening in Tel Aviv."

The people surrounding Haber wept, cried out in disbelief. People returned to the square in confusion, unable to absorb the news. Some had already lit candles.

On the TV screen was the picture of the slight young man who had been arrested by the police. It was Yigal Amir.

As I write, it is still too soon to tell whether Amir succeeded in killing the peace as well. Those who sang "The Song of Peace" sit on the opposition benches today, while some of those who chanted "Rabin is a traitor" are in power.

But Amir was not alone, and his pistol was not the only weapon aimed at the peace process. "Yes to Peace, No to Violence" was the demonstration's rallying cry. "Yes to Violence" was the slogan of those on both sides who sought to destroy the process, mostly, so they declared, in the name of God.

Terje Larsen called from Gaza in deep shock. His voice shook as he told me that he had been with Abu Mazen and had gone to see Arafat after the dinner for Soares, to tell him of the assassination attempt and later of the death of the man he had called "my partner." "Arafat wept and so did I."

Avi Gil was on the way to the Ministry of Defense when I located him. He had been told that Peres was convening a cabinet meeting and a press conference. I also reached the ministry within minutes. The night seemed unreal. When I arrived, I found many of the Ministry of Defense and the Prime Minister's Bureau staff in tears as Peres made the official announcement.

The cabinet meeting had been convened earlier. Peres was now acting prime minister, and it was decided to hold a cabinet meeting the next day to appoint him prime minister. The ministers had tears in their eyes. Truncated and confused eulogies were uttered.

I walked with Peres to his car. He did not look at me. I sensed that he was in a state of shock. As we reached the car he whispered, "You're coming to Jerusalem with me."

I got into the car beside him. He remained mute for a few minutes, and I did not know how to break the silence. Without moving his head he said suddenly, "I am on my own. He is irreplaceable."

We reached Jerusalem at four that morning. I entered the Foreign Ministry situation room. Messages of condolence and notifications of participation in the state funeral were flooding in from all over the world. In my office we set up a center to deal with the mourners from abroad. There had never before been a day of such deep global emotional identification with the State of Israel. In the past, part of the world, particularly the Western world, had shared our fears, our tears, and our joy, but this time there were almost no exceptions, and most important of all, it was perhaps the first time that at least part of the Arab world displayed empathy toward Israel and not simply the common interest to which we had been witness in the recent past. People were seen mourning in the streets of Gaza; Arab leaders came to the funeral, and many wept.

Peres, in consultation with the security people, had decided it was safer not to invite Arafat to the funeral. The Palestinian delegation was headed by Abu Ala and included several of the Palestinian Authority's leaders. Abu Ala came over to me at the site of the ceremony and said, his voice shaking: "He was a real leader for peace. It is a great loss, also for the Palestinian people." At the end of the seven-day period of mourning, Arafat visited Leah Rabin at her home. Without his trademark kaffiyeh on his head and accompanied by Yossi Genosar, he told the Rabin family about his partner, his friend.

This was his first visit to Israel. Leah spoke of her late husband's respect for his peace partner. She was outspoken and courageous when it came to peace.

President Clinton was accompanied to the funeral by a vast entourage, which included administration leaders past and present, members of Congress, and leaders of the American Jewish community. Clinton's parting words were "*Shalom, haver*—good-bye, friend."

After paying our last respects at the graveside, I stood with Dennis Ross. With tears in his eyes he told me about his last meeting with Rabin, whom he admired, which had taken place in the United States only a week earlier.

A private meeting between Clinton and Peres had been arranged for later that day. Ambassador Itamar Rabinovich briefed Peres and me on what he would hear from the president. "The subject is Syria," he said, "and the Americans will want you to fulfill the undertakings given by Yitzhak. It is an extremely complex issue. Rabin's assurances on a possible withdrawal from the Golan Heights were conditional upon a number of matters that Assad has not met to this day." Clinton and Peres talked in private for about an hour and a half while I met with Dennis Ross, who told me that the United States was very much interested in moving forward on the Syrian track. After their private meeting, Clinton met with Peres and a group of ministers and the negotiating team. The two leaders undertook to continue the peace process with full coordination between them. Thus on the very day of Rabin's funeral we were once again engaged in the peace process. After the meeting, at which Peres thanked President Clinton and his entourage for their identification with Israel in its grief, Clinton rose from his chair, went over to Peres, embraced him warmly, and said, "You have lost a partner. You can count on me to be your partner for peace." Late that night Peres briefed me about his talk with Clinton. He was surprised. The president had told Peres that Rabin, in his deliberations with the United States, had expressed conditional acceptance of full withdrawal from the Golan Heights, provided Israel's needs were met on the issues of normalization, security, and the timetable for implementation. Peres said that he would be committed to Rabin's position and would pursue the peace process vigorously.

In the meantime, Peres formed a government to maintain continuity.

He did not deliberate long over this. Like Rabin and Ben-Gurion before him, he decided to keep the defense portfolio himself, to appoint Ehud Barak to replace him at the Foreign Ministry, and to bring Haim Ramon back into the government as minister of the interior.

On a short trip to Brussels for talks with the heads of the European Union, Peres told me that he would like to see me in the government but he would do that after the coming elections. He appointed me the coordinator of the peace negotiations together with my positions as director-general of the Foreign Ministry, head of the team on the permanent-status talks with the Palestinians, and head of the delegation to the negotiations with Syria. All this was concluded with the agreement of Barak, who had become a new political force within a small group that influenced decision making.

Peres held meetings in Rabin's conference room at the Ministry of Defense, which was extremely difficult for him. The workload of the prime minister and minister of defense was brutal, but in addition, and unlike Rabin, Peres had no practiced partner with similar experience and a common background.

His first decision was to order the IDF to proceed with the implementation of the Interim Agreement. The peace process had to continue. By the end of 1995, on the dates pledged by Israel, the IDF withdrew from Tulkarm, Kalkilya, Nablus, Ramallah, and Bethlehem.

Israel had proved its democratic strength at the edge of the abyss. During this entire period, Rabin's murder remained the most devastating act of terror directed against the peace process.

The redeployment became possible, partly because of the shock evident among the right, and especially the religious right. Some of these religious groups attempted a moral self-examination with regard to the nationalist and religious values they were teaching their youth. Zevulun Orlev, secretary-general of the National Religious Party, said, "It is a fact that the right-wing extremists wear skullcaps and are graduates of religious educational institutions. Our opposition to the words that emanated from the national religious camp was not strong enough."

Meanwhile, the left failed to seize the opportunity of joining forces with some temporarily apologetic religious political groups, in particular the National Religious Party. Only my friend Yossi Beilin saw the importance of such an alliance; the rest of us, myself included, did not give it the priority it deserved. Many people said that "Israel after Rabin's murder is not the same country it was." In retrospect, and apart from the tragic loss of Rabin, this is probably not true; each side returned to its old ways within a relatively short time.

But at least the months that followed the murder were free from violence, demonstrations, and incitement. Even the settlers were in shock, so the IDF withdrew from the West Bank towns without incident. The face of the West Bank had been changed forever; no longer would there be full Israeli control of the Greater Land of Israel, no longer would Israel dominate the lives of the Palestinians. It was a historic milestone.

Although Israel bled from Amir's bullets, the legacy of Rabin and his partner was now being realized. We were entering perhaps the most pressing phase of the peace process: redeployment, the Palestinian elections, the fight against terrorism, negotiations with Syria, permanent-status negotiations with the Palestinians, the hopes for a new Middle East, and the battle against fundamentalism and terror. The train of history was about to rush down its track at a dizzying pace during the first five dramatic months of 1996.

As a new year dawned, we faced two main questions: would we see a new or an old Middle East, and a new or an old Israel?

9

AN OLD-NEW MIDDLE EAST

THE ASSASSINATION OF PRIME MINISTER RABIN BY A JEWISH FANATIC
inspired by the incitement of Jewish fundamentalists initially had no
impact on the peace process. Peace proved to be a stubborn impulse.
But the shock of Rabin's murder in no way tempered the resolve of
Arab fundamentalism to fight the growing "threat" of peace. It soon
became clear that the extremists—on both sides—were committed to
cultivating fear in order to reinforce the walls of hatred and suspicion
that could protect their societies from cooperating with "eternal enemies." A month after Rabin was depicted as a Nazi in a Jerusalem
demonstration, Hamas issued a leaflet in Gaza urging Palestinians to
rejoice at "the death of the Nazi." Yet Hamas represents a broad
movement and is part of a terrorist network.

The masterminds of Muslim fundamentalism, headquartered in
Tehran, had been exporting violence by means of their fanatic and increasingly desperate allies in the Middle East: the Palestinian Hamas
and Islamic Jihad movements and the Lebanese Hezbollah. At the beginning of 1996, instructions were disseminated to these movements
to embark on a round of mayhem, to kill as many Israelis as possible,
and thus to destroy the fledgling peace they denounced as an ignominious surrender. The ongoing murder of Israelis, they believed,
would drive a wedge between Israelis, Palestinians, and Syrians and
weaken, perhaps even bring down, "the government that has occupied
Jerusalem." Orders to create turmoil were issued to the Hezbollah

fundamentalists in Lebanon, who used their training camps to indoctrinate young Lebanese and Palestinians in an ideology of holy war
and sublime rewards for those who sacrificed themselves in its name.
The martyr (*shaheed*) who turned himself into a human bomb and
sowed death and terror among the enemy would receive his eternal re-
ward in Paradise. Thus both in Lebanon and in hidden places in Gaza
and the West Bank, the countdown of the human time bombs began.

Meanwhile, in Jerusalem, aware of the threat of new violence, we
were planning further breakthroughs as a means of cementing the
peace in the region. Shimon Peres, as the new prime minister, now
turned to implementing his strategy for achieving a regional peace
and building a "new Middle East." That was undoubtedly the ultimate weapon against fundamentalism and extremism. During November and December 1995, he coordinated with the American
administration an aggressive peace strategy centering on an attempt
to reach a peace treaty with Syria in less than a year. The Syrian-
Israeli peace was to be the key move in forging a *comprehensive* settlement in the region that would finally put the Arab-Israeli conflict to
an end. The plan for the Palestinian peace track was to pursue a gradual and meticulous implementation of the Interim Agreement, first
by ensuring the smooth transfer of power to the Palestinians in the
West Bank and then by holding the first free Palestinian elections.
Thereafter, the two sides would embark upon the permanent-status
negotiations and tackle the most contentious issues: Jerusalem, the
Israeli settlements, the Palestinian refugees, and the final borders.
These talks were to begin on May 4, 1996, and be completed no later
than May 4, 1999.

In mid-November, Peres had appointed me to head the negotiations with Syria (which had been conducted until then by our ambassador to the United States, Itamar Rabinovich). As I was doing my
homework on the Syrian track, I realized that I would have to change
my perspective. For over two years, I had been engaged in intense
and ingenious negotiations with the representatives of the PLO,
whom I had come to know quite well. Now I would be entering far
more structured talks with the representatives of a sovereign state
and be meeting people with a very different political background and
mind-set.

On December 14, 1995, Secretary of State Warren Christopher visited the region to lay the groundwork for the talks based on Peres's approach. A retiring man (especially by Israeli standards), Christopher sometimes gave the impression of being bored by details, but he was committed, resolute, patient to a fault, and unfazed by obstacles. I learned to respect him. He had never been given the credit he was due as "the right man at the right time." He and his peace team were skeptical that President Assad would go for the kind of "blitz" peace that Peres had in mind. But they were convinced that he was fundamentally interested in peace and would progress incrementally toward an agreement.

Indeed, Christopher enjoyed a cordial welcome when he arrived in Damascus, carrying a note from Peres that emphasized Israel's interest in having the negotiations move ahead through any modality Assad preferred—open or secret, at the level of government officials or leaders. Peres was interested in creating a positive climate that would accelerate the process. He insisted only that all the issues between the sides be dealt with simultaneously. Assad responded to the note orally in a positive tone. The result was that, back in Jerusalem, Christopher was able to announce resumption of the peace talks in a new format that would sequester three delegations—Syrian, Israeli, and American—at a location near Washington, where all the issues would be tackled conceptually and in parallel.

The negotiations would be held against the background of the earlier talks directed by Prime Minister Rabin and conducted by Ambassador Rabinovich. On two occasions, our chief of staff (first Gen. Ehud Barak and then Gen. Amnon Shahak) also held talks with the Syrian chief of staff Gen. Hikmat Shihabi, at which the Syrians strongly objected to Israeli early-warning stations on the Golan. The formula for a possible peace treaty that had been developed by the United States at that time included diplomatic, trade, and tourism relations; reciprocal but not geographically symmetrical security arrangements in agreed-upon areas; a full Israeli withdrawal from the Golan Heights; and a gradual timetable for an interconnected implementation of the various elements of the treaty.

As for the future border, the Syrians demanded the June 4, 1967, line (that is, the line before the outbreak of the Six-Day War, in which Israel captured the Golan Heights). After talking with Rabin in May 1994, Christopher had conveyed to the Syrians the United States' understanding that, conditional upon all of its needs being met, Israel would be prepared to make a "full withdrawal," which implied pulling back to the June 4, 1967, line. Actually, in official terms, there is no such line—in the sense of a cogent frontier—but rather a complex set of lines created by Syria's expansion into some parts of Israeli territory before the 1967 conflict. One of these areas was a strip of shore on the Sea of Galilee, effectively the country's main water reservoir, about which Israel was particularly sensitive. According to Christopher and Ross, however, what the Syrians wanted beyond the international border, which runs a few kilometers east of the June 4, 1967, line, was El-Hama, a well-known location with warm water springs that had been part of mandatory (British) Palestine but was occupied by Syria until 1967.

These understandings about what "package deal" Israel would agree to were solely verbal. No Israeli undertaking was ever made directly to Syria about the depth of its withdrawal from the territory occupied in 1967. What's more, the Syrians had never accepted Rabin's demands about the various other components of a peace agreement, particularly the nature of the mutual security arrangements. All of this meant that we had to begin our talks from a state of ambiguity. It was therefore our task to engage Syria in a new approach to bilateral peace, which, as Peres envisioned it, would lead to a regional system of cooperation and economic development. This peace "construct" was to have a Palestinian foundation, a Syrian roof, and a new regional economy within its walls. Roads, energy, the supply of water, trade, and tourism would link the countries of the new Middle East, and as their economies grew, the appetite for conflict would diminish.

To pursue this concept with the Syrians, on December 27, 1995, our delegation arrived at the Aspen Institute's guesthouse at Wye Plantation, Maryland—a lakeside, colonial-style house furnished in classic simplicity. On the ground floor was the plenary conference room, with a round table able to accommodate a dozen people. Our delegation slept on the ground floor of one of the wings, the Syrians

Map 6: Golan Heights

LEGEND:
- INTERNATIONAL BOUNDARY
- CEASE FIRE LINE, 1949
- PEACE AGREEMENT LINE, 10/26/94
- LINES OF DISENGAGEMENT OF FORCES, 1974
  - Israeli Forward Line
  - Syrian Forward Line

© Tammy Soffer

were in another wing, and the Americans settled in between us. The first two floors contained rooms for the delegations' offices and some recreational equipment, such as Ping-Pong and pool tables. During the day the support delegation worked on these floors, and in the evenings the Israelis and Americans played Ping-Pong while the Syrians, or so they said, were busy writing detailed reports for Damascus. By contrast, Itamar Rabinovich and I updated Jerusalem through long telephone conversations with Peres, Barak, and Shahak.

Upon our arrival, I met the head of the Syrian delegation, Walid Moualem, blessed with an impressive paunch and a generous measure of worldly wit. I came to appreciate him as a peace-seeking man who bridges the very different worlds of Damascus and Washington. Intellectually he had been shaped by Syria, where he had served in the army, written a doctoral dissertation on Syrian history, and served in the foreign service; then he had been appointed to the ambassadorial post in Washington and put in charge of the peace talks as the confidant of his omnipotent president. A tough and crafty negotiator, he knew what Damascus expected of him but also what was practical and knew how to size up the other side's position. Moualem brought considerable creative talent to his delegation. As time went by, he and I were able to develop a common language and a degree of mutual trust.

The other members of the delegation to the first round were the Syrian foreign minister's chief of staff, Michael Wabha, and the legal adviser Riad Daoudi. In subsequent rounds, two generals also participated in the talks: the chief of Syrian intelligence, Ibrahim Omar, and the deputy head of internal security, Hassan Khalil. Moualem ruled his delegation firmly and was, in effect, its only spokesman. The other officials were unfailingly polite, but they never budged from the official line, though they became more open in private conversations and tried to convince us of their and their people's desire for peace. The Syrian generals were deliberately aloof and spoke only in Arabic, which was translated by the American delegation's well-known interpreter Jamal Hallal. Always rigid during the official talks, they relaxed in private conversations with their IDF counterparts but even then held strictly to their positions.

Our delegation included Itamar Rabinovich, Yoel Singer, and myself, later to be joined, sequentially, by Generals Danny Yatom, Uzi Dayan, and Shaul Mofaz. The American delegation included Dennis Ross, Mark Price from the White House, Aaron Miller, and Toni Verstandig.

The negotiations at Wye Plantation extended over approximately ten weeks and were carried out in three rounds. Between these rounds, Ross, Moualem, and I held ten meetings in what became something of an informal back channel approved by Assad and Peres. The tone and nature of these negotiations with Syria were totally different from the talks with the Palestinians. The Syrians represented an Arab state with a proud tradition of viewing itself as a regional leader. It was clear that they were the envoys of a closed regime whose principles and values were dictated by one man. Syria had surrounded itself with a wall of suspicion. Yet its leader and his representatives were aware that the world beyond was changing in a way that would inevitably affect them too.

At our meetings it soon became clear that they wanted both to traverse that wall and to keep it intact. They sought American economic aid but wanted to block the penetration of any kind of Westernization that might come with it. They were interested in an accommodation with Israel but feared being overwhelmed by the economic strength of their Westernized, democratic neighbor. The solution they were seeking was aid without influence and peace without engagement. From our standpoint, the negotiations were a more difficult intellectual challenge than the talks with the Palestinians, because we had to adjust to dealing with a mind-set radically different from our own. On the emotional level, however, the negotiations with the Syrians were easier because, far from feeling that we were dealing with life-and-death issues of coexistence in the same land, there was a sense among both delegations that, if necessary, we could go on living without peace.

If the negotiations with the Palestinians turned with time into a dance in which each side tried to outdo his partner, who was nevertheless fastened to him, the negotiations with Syria were like a complex, multilayered chess game in which the players had to finish in a satisfactory draw. During those months, I moved between the Syrian chess game and the Palestinian dance while attempting to maintain the link between the two processes. We could hardly neglect the Palestinians, because if that dance stopped, everything else would too. In each set of negotiations, we faced one key player. The difference between them was that Assad was more focused than Arafat and imposed his authority on his negotiators far more stringently. Moreover, none of us had ever been able to take the measure of the man in direct, personal contacts, so he remained something of an enigma in our eyes, though his spirit was ever present in the talks.

The Damascene sphinx played his game cautiously and cynically, hoping that we would move a number of our pieces before he gave any hint how he was going to move his. My sense of this strange and shrewd man evolved as a result of my talks with the Syrians. Withdrawn into himself and the confines of his country, Assad (who was sixty-seven years old at the time and who has ruled Syria since 1971) is nevertheless a brilliant man, interested in everything going on in the world, including Israel. In deciding to move toward peace, he had made what was a revolutionary decision from his standpoint, yet he remained conservative in his tactics. Assad is both a strong leader and an insecure one, who fears any sign of less than total loyalty. He feared that change might pose a challenge to his Alawite regime (the Alawites being only 12 percent of the Syrian population) yet probably sensed that reforms in his closed system would be unavoidable in the wake of peace with Israel and improved relations with the United States. This was the heart of the Syrian dilemma: Assad both sought peace and was intimidated by it. He made his decisions slowly and cautiously. But we believed that this tension could lead to discourse and progress—provided we knew what might urge Assad toward relative openness and help him overcome his deep suspicion.

Before entering the talks, I read dozens of Assad's speeches and interviews and concluded that, given a lack of intellectual flexibility, one could speak to the Syrians only in "Syrian." In order to explain and advance our interests, we had to master a "language" that sanctifies the national interest and pride of sovereign decision to the point where it views every challenge to these concepts as a conspiratorial threat. At the same time, we also suffered from some important shortcomings as partners in these negotiations with Syria. Although we had developed a realistic and integrated approach to the talks, we tended to cling to a perception of peace as an expression of affection (mostly toward us) rather than a set of durable mutual interests.

"After years of hatred, we're seeking to develop warm relations with Damascus?" I chided our delegation. "But the Syrians don't enjoy warm relations with anyone!" In negotiations with our Arab neighbors, we always face the danger that our need for acceptance will push us into making trivial demands for the sake of symbolic gains rather than focusing rationally on our long-term strategic interests.

Furthermore, we have a tendency to cling to an exaggerated best-case scenario when it comes to discussing the normalization of relations and to deal with every possible contingency of the worst-case scenario when it comes to discussing security issues. In this sense, our military establishment had a powerful voice in the negotiations, even though the peace agreement would intrinsically be political. Our tendency was to aim for the best possible peace while protecting ourselves against the worst dangers of war, rather than to seek a way of creating and nurturing mutual interests. The Syrians suffered from exactly the opposite tendencies. They viewed peace as very little more than the absence of war, so when it came to the normalization of relations, they offered the most meager prescription. And when it came to security, they expressed the optimistic platitude that peace ruled out the possibility of war. They too had to move toward a realistic middle ground where we could work to create a convergence of interests. Yet Moualem started by emphasizing the need to ensure withdrawal first.

"Our journey to peace must first take off, like an airplane," he said.

"What do you mean?" I asked.

"We must know that our rights to our land will be reinstated."

"And we have to know where the airplane will land, what the nature of the peace between us will be. Without clearly knowing its destination, it's useless to speak of its takeoff."

"We will have to travel from the island of the present to the island of the future," suggested Moualem, "while defining both."

In time we were able to agree on the metaphor of a common bridge between the past and the future, our interests, and our basic attitudes as the conceptual basis for our talks. The mutual effort to build all its parts would move Syria and Israel from a state of war to a state of peace in agreed stages. This concept, together with the relatively open and creative nature of our talks, permitted us to define common interests and make progress on several substantive issues in the two and a half months of meetings at Wye Plantation.

1. THE NATURE OF PEACE

In discussing the normalization of relations, we arrived at a pragmatic approach toward building our future relationship. Rather than fill our legal archives with dozens of ignored agreements on cooperation, we agreed to concentrate on practical steps of mutual interest, such as constructing a road between our two countries rather than drafting a whole transportation agreement. We also singled out a dozen areas of normalization that were divided into three agreed main categories: embassies, tourism, and trade (such as termination of the boycott, telephone, fax, and post links, railway links, maritime trade links, and so on).

2. ECONOMIC RELATIONS

In the long-term view of peace, we felt that we had to link normalization to economic relations. But the Syrians were not interested in planning a bilateral economic relationship with Israel because of their concern that Israel's relatively strong economy would overwhelm theirs. We therefore had to create a bridge between Syria's interest in a relationship with the West and Israel's interest in an economic relationship with Syria and Lebanon as a way of cementing the peace. We were looking toward the development of Middle Eastern economies that would become dependent upon one another (without influencing the ideological nature of each economy), and upon the world, and thus upon stability. There was no better guarantee for a lasting peace and no stronger antidote to fundamentalism, which thrives on poverty and despair. We therefore sketched out an economic program to deal simultaneously with the cancellation of Syria's debt of about $7 billion to the Western economic powers, the accelerated development of its economy, the creation of economic links with Israel (mainly through infrastructure such as energy, water, and roads), the creation of multilateral economic links with other countries in the region, and the development of the Golan Heights through international investment, primarily in tourism. The partners in this program would be the United States, the European Union, Japan (possibly through a G-7 initiative), and, on the regional side, Saudi Arabia.

The Syrians were keen to engage the United States in bilateral talks on this economic package. Yet the administration was caught by surprise and relatively unprepared to mount a concrete initiative, largely because of the fear of congressional animosity. Our economic team—which included Finance Ministry Director-General David

Brodet, Yossi Vardi (a creative developer of regional projects), Oded Eran from the Foreign Ministry, and myself—held extensive talks on an economic package with Dennis Ross and his staff, as well as with the president of the World Bank, James Wolfensohn, and the vice president of the International Monetary Fund, Stanley Fischer.

While the Syrians were interested mostly in economic aid from the American administration (following the Egyptian model), they understood that inevitably the private sector would have to be recruited to the effort. We proposed the creation of a network of private-sector groups in the United States, Israel, Saudi Arabia, and Syria (with the European Union and Japan to join at a later stage) that would interact through the American group with the development of possible peacetime projects. My friend Lester Pollack of Lazard Frères, a brilliant and experienced businessman, was asked to head the American group, and the Saudis agreed to cooperate through their highly effective ambassador in the United States, Prince Bandar. A meeting held in the State Department on February 23, 1996, between Secretary Christopher and five heads of major American corporations was the first step toward building this promising new network.

3. COMPREHENSIVE PEACE

Perhaps the most important aspect of the talks at Wye Plantation was that we were able to reach an understanding that bilateral peace treaties between Israel and Syria and Israel and Lebanon would mark the end of the Arab-Israeli conflict and the beginning of a regional peace. To achieve this outcome, the United States would be called upon by the two parties to ensure the endorsement of the Israeli-Syrian peace treaty by the Arab countries and the normalization of their relations with Israel. (I received Saudi confirmation that this would indeed be their position.) The Syrians liked this concept and repeatedly told us: "You have made peace with Egypt, the Palestinians, and Jordan, and yet you remain in conflict with the Arab world per se. Only when you make peace with Syria, and only when Hafez el-Assad announces to the Arab League that he has decided to allow Israel to open an embassy in Damascus, will the rest of the Arab states follow suit." Assad's view of his leadership role in the Arab world could therefore be linked to Peres's conception of a comprehensive peace.

Yet our mostly economic view of the "new Middle East" was not identical with the Syrian one. We had an opportunity to learn about the Syrians' regional outlook during the Thursday night dinners that were devoted to dialogue on the future of the region. In these discussions, which were usually chaired by Secretary Christopher, Moualem envisioned a new Iranian stance, in which Tehran would no longer resist the processes under way in the region. He also hinted at an improved relationship between Syria and Turkey. The interesting aspect of the Syrian regional analysis was its strategic view of the effect of peace on the fundamental relations in the region. We believed that in time Syria's and Israel's regional outlooks could reach a point of convergence based on a common interest in stability and good relations with the United States.

4. SECURITY ARRANGEMENTS

The most difficult aspect of our negotiations was reaching an understanding on the security arrangements. Israel could not withdraw from the Golan Heights, in our view, without ensuring that Syria would not exploit its resultant strategic advantage to mount a surprise attack. The IDF therefore drew up a set of very detailed demands to guarantee Israel's security. These included limitations on the deployment of Syrian troops facing Israel, arrangements for monitoring the deployment, coordination between the two armies, early-warning systems, and possibly a third-party presence on the Golan. The Syrians, however, were interested in minimal and absolutely symmetrical security arrangements alongside an increased American role to ensure them.

Part of the gap in our thinking on this issue stemmed from opposing perceptions. Ours was basically that the peace would be ensured by security arrangements, while the Syrians held that security would be guaranteed by the peace. The discussions on security arrangements in which generals from both sides participated were long and not very productive.

The root of the problem was Syria's rejection of the principle of transparency regarding the size and deployment of its army in peacetime. As far as Damascus was concerned, our inquiries about the nature of their future deployment were tantamount to desecrating the holy of holies. When we asked, time and again, how Syria would deploy its troops vis-à-vis Israel after a treaty was signed, the Syrians consistently replied, "This is a decision that only Hafez el-Assad can make"—in other words, "It's none of your business." In a regime where one general rarely discusses the deployment of his soldiers with another, any frank discussion of military deployment and strategy with an archenemy—even in the context of peace negotiations—proved an almost impossible task. This was the main obstacle to the progress of the overall negotiations. These issues required not only that there be a deeper level of engagement between the delegations but also that each side hold separate talks with the United States about its projected role in guaranteeing the peace, as well as its commitments to each of the two parties.

As part of the discussion on security, we raised the irksome problem of terrorism in Lebanon (the actions of the Hezbollah) and Syria's protection of the Palestinian terrorist organizations opposed to Arafat. The Syrians argued that once peace was attained all these activities—which they defined as the struggle of "freedom fighters"—would cease. They viewed terrorism as a kind of trump card, to be held in reserve until the end of the negotiations. More important, they intended to continue cultivating relations with their current antipeace allies, especially Iran, as alternative strategic partners in case peace with Israel (and the United States) failed to materialize.

I believe the Syrians committed a serious error in clinging to this strategy since the pro-Iranian terror organizations had a definite interest in thwarting the peace. We also erred in not insisting, in the form of an ultimatum, that Syria force the Hezbollah to cease all its activities while the negotiations were in progress. In retrospect, I'm not sure that we appreciated the degree to which terrorism was a strategic threat to the peace process. We were eager to reach a comprehensive peace in the belief that it would solve the underlying political problem. The terrorists were interested in blocking a political solution and perpetuating fear, anger, and despair in the service of religious fundamentalism.

5. DEPTH OF THE WITHDRAWAL
FROM THE GOLAN HEIGHTS

The issue of withdrawal from the Golan Heights was not negotiated in the talks held at Wye Plantation. When the Syrians mentioned it in passing, implying that they took for granted that Israel would withdraw to the June 4, 1967, line, we responded that this was not the time to discuss the matter, and that we were aware that the United States had received a verbal and conditional commitment from Rabin on the issue. Technically, we agreed that the demarcation of the border should be negotiated by a working group to be set up at some time in the future. Yet it was clear to us that Syria would not agree to real peace with Israel unless we reciprocated by carrying out a full withdrawal. Our task was therefore to define, and receive the Syrians' agreement to, the precise nature of a peace, in all its aspects, that would compensate us for giving up territory of such strategic value to our national security. The final "peace border" could be determined only after we were convinced that the evolving relationship between the two countries would reduce the Golan from a vital strategic plateau into another mountain.

Israelis feel strongly about the Golan Heights as a necessary security buffer. After the first round of talks at Wye, I visited the Heights as the guest of the Golan Heights Settlers' Council. Arriving at the last settlement, just before the fence with Syria, I met my cousin Shlomit, who greeted me warmly and led me into her living room. She then read me a letter that she had written to me, describing how her five-year-old son asked why Uncle Uri wanted to give the Golan to the Syrians. She responded by explaining that in a democracy everyone is entitled to his or her views about what is good for the country. Nonetheless, she wrote, it was very difficult to explain to her little boy why he might have to give up his home.

While the tour of the Golan persuaded me that its Israeli inhabitants were far more pragmatic than the West Bank settlers, like all of us, they would have to be convinced that Syria wanted a true and lasting peace with Israel.

6. WATER

Two thirds of the water of the Sea of Galilee, on which Israel depends for its national water reservoir, comes from sources in the Golan Heights and southern Lebanon. We therefore made it clear to our Syrian counterparts that without a satisfactory solution to our water needs from these areas, there simply would be no peace agreement. We reached a general understanding that each side's water needs, in terms of both quantity and quality, would have to be met. For Israel this meant guaranteeing its existing water supply by a mechanism to be worked out in future negotiations. For Syria it meant finding a way to supply its water needs through an arrangement with Turkey, to be worked out through the auspices of the United States. To gain Turkey's cooperation, Syria would have to bring the activity of Kurdish terrorists against Turkey from Syrian soil to a halt. During this process, Turkey would essentially become, in Moualem's words, a partner in the comprehensive regional peace. Most of the discussions on water were held separately by each side and the United States. Dennis Ross was planning to hold discussions with the Turkish government on these ideas.

7. THE UNITED STATES' ROLE IN THE NEGOTIATIONS

The peace team led by Ross played the role of host, mediator, and observer in these talks in an unimposing manner and with great diplomatic skill. Ross continually emphasized what we had in common and made a point of expressing satisfaction at the progress we made. He even drew up an informal summation at the end of the second round of talks of approximately sixty points of understanding between the parties that would have to be explored in more concrete and detailed negotiations. Some people in our defense establishment believed that Ross, like Secretary Christopher, was somewhat naïve about dealing with an unscrupulous Syrian regime. And it's true that the Americans—particularly in the Clinton administration—were marked by a certain innocence that is alien to our region. Yet altogether it is precisely the honesty, decency, and businesslike approach of American diplomacy that makes the United States such a valuable and courted player in the Middle East's peacemaking effort.

If there was a weakness in the Americans' position, as I openly told Ross, it was their exaggerated involvement as mediators in the talks. I believe that the United States should have spent more energy defining its own broad strategic role in a peaceful Middle East: the direction of its future relations with Syria and Israel (we did hold very initial and informal talks on a possible American-Israeli understanding parallel to the peace agreement, covering security, economic, and political issues); the possible deployment of American troops in the region; the role of the United States as a peacekeeper; and its economic involvement in the region. The Syrians were interested in having the United States accept the double capacity of brokering the peace agreement and serving as its guarantor. But the administration was very cautious about exploring its future role in the region, especially because Congress was critical of a possible American rapprochement with Syria.

I tried, in Ross's presence, to convince Moualem to shift from the trilateral format of Wye to bilateral negotiations, which I believed would be more effective, while the United States would continue to talk to both sides separately. To help make my case, I told him a story that I had heard from Peres. A young man, it went, fell hopelessly in love with a young lady but was too shy to profess his passion to her directly. So every day he sent her a love letter. The result was that, after a year, the woman married the mailman. Moualem laughed, and I asked him to tell the story to Assad. I doubt that he did or that he thought it was necessary, for Damascus was truly less interested in its Israeli "suitor" than in the American "mailman."

As part of our talks at Wye Plantation, we tried to engage the United States in a broader peace strategy, based on a plan that Shimon Peres had developed a few years earlier. Peres's original conception, called Partnership for Peace in the Middle East, called for extending NATO to the Middle East, much as it was now being extended to Eastern Europe. At Wye we presented to the United States an informal paper entitled "Economic Partnership in the Middle East" describing a kind of economic NATO, in which development would play the key role in stabilizing the security of the region. It focused on joint economic projects, links between the infrastructures of the neighboring countries, and a plan for investment by the industrial powers in the peaceful Middle East. Open economic borders were the best defense against military temptations. In principle, the American team agreed that the idea deserved further exploration.

8. METHODOLOGY FOR FUTURE PROGRESS

In January, because of domestic political developments in Israel, we reached a turning point. As it became increasingly clear that Peres felt compelled to call early elections (which would otherwise not be held until November 1996), voices in the Labor Party were relating more to the party's primaries (for a seat in the Knesset) than to the peacemaking process. Many felt the need to express hawkish and critical views of Syria that appealed to constituents who remained skeptical of Assad's reactions to peace. Ehud Barak, the former chief of staff and now foreign minister, who was very creative and constructive in helping to forge a model for the future peace with Syria, and with whom I consulted by phone for several hours each night during the talks, suddenly began to express views very critical of the Syrians. Other Labor contenders for Knesset seats tried to gain popularity by criticizing the negotiating team itself. Micha Goldman, the deputy minister of education, called for me to be replaced because of my "ill-founded optimism." The Syrians followed the domestic scene in Israel very closely and generally attached too much importance to these statements. Assad even asked Christopher why a senior member of the Labor Party had attacked the head of the Israeli delegation. The Israeli political arena impressed the Syrians as chaotic, and they felt that Peres was unable to discipline the Knesset deputies. All this led Peres to conclude that, rather than wait until November, he must ask the country for a clear mandate to pursue his peace policy as soon as possible—and a number of optimistic pollsters encouraged him in that direction.

My own recommendation was different. I wanted the opportunity to help forge a peace settlement with Syria in 1996. Peres responded that the only way to accelerate the negotiations, which was clearly in the interest of Israel, given the Syrian negotiation tactics, was through a series of summit meetings with Assad. If Damascus agreed, he would not call early elections. That was the gist of the message that Secretary Christopher carried to Damascus on February 5, 1996. Assad replied that he knew it would be necessary to meet with the Israeli prime minister at some point, but he could not commit himself to a date. In response, Peres, who rightly understood this reply as an evasion, announced on February 11, 1996, that the elections would be moved up to May. He sent Assad another letter, again carried by Secretary Christopher, assuring him that intensified negotiations would resume after the elections, with the hope of concluding an agreement in 1996. Until May the talks could continue on a variety of issues in an attempt to reach additional conceptual understandings. Assad agreed to this arrangement. The Americans told us that he had developed a certain degree of trust in Peres's intentions, which was in itself an essential building block for the future.

In the continuation of the Wye talks, from February 27 to March 3, we struggled with the difficult issue of security arrangements—without much progress—and prepared the ground for the working groups that would begin meeting after the elections. Moualem and I agreed that in the future we would map out all of our understandings on all issues according to a time line that began with the signature of the peace treaty and ended with its full implementation. We also agreed to establish a steering committee to supervise the work of three distinct groups:

1. A committee on security arrangements, which would include a subcommittee on withdrawal and delineation of the new border

2. A committee on normalization, whose subjects would also include economic relations, water, and comprehensive peace in the region

3. A drafting committee, to be chaired by Yoel Singer and Riad Daoudi

In talks between these two lawyers, Daoudi addressed the structure of the future treaty, which he wanted to build within the body of the agreement rather than in lengthy annexes. He even ventured that the treaty should be no longer than about thirty pages; anything resembling the 410-page document we had concluded with the Palestinians was out of the question and would only complicate matters. Yoel replied jokingly that he thought the preamble alone would be thirty pages long and left the matter to future deliberations. Their exchange showed that each side had a radically different attitude toward words. The Syrians wanted to use them to express basic principles; we wanted to use them to describe a concrete reality, in great detail.

Still, it was clear that both sides meant business. Moualem believed that once the elections were past we could conclude a treaty within a few months. And I became increasingly convinced that we could negotiate a peace with Syria based on compatible strategic interests, not on an illusion of empathy. It might not radiate the kind of warmth that Israelis found so compelling, but it would serve our long-term interests and strengthen our national security. Many of my colleagues were skeptical, based on their view of Assad's caution. But I strongly believed that the dynamics of change would surprise the status quo experts and possibly the status quo leader himself.

Paradoxically, those who seemed to share my assessment that peace was within reach were the opponents of peace, who felt the need to brutally neutralize the "danger" of a settlement. The instructions sent from Tehran were followed by the agents of hatred and death. In the Palestinian arena, there was an additional motive, or excuse, on January 5, 1996, when, in Gaza, a cellular phone rigged to explode when answered killed the Hamas terrorist Yehiya Ayash (known as the Engineer), whom Arafat feared to arrest even though he was responsible for the murder of more than fifty Israelis. While I believed that such activities were seldom advantageous, given the vast network of terrorists and terror leaders, I do not believe that the killing of Ayash in itself led to what was about to occur. The motivation for terror is strategic—it is not based on vengeance.

On February 25, the day we returned to Wye Plantation for the third round of talks, a suicide bomber blew himself up on a bus in Jerusalem. It was 6:45 A.M., and the bus was crowded with people on their way to work, children on their way to school, soldiers returning to their bases. Twenty-four people were killed. One of them was Yoni Barnea, the son of my friends Nahum and Tami Barnea. Nahum is one of Israel's leading journalists and was himself on the scene that morning, covering the story, unaware that his son was among the casualties. When I told Moualem about this tragedy that touched so close to me, he mumbled that it was regrettable, but, like his fellow Syrians, he could not bring himself to forthrightly denounce violence against Israelis. They were still bound by the dogma of conflict and saw acts of terrorism as legitimate. Their response to the events of those days drove an emotional wedge between us and was, I believe, self-defeating from a Syrian point of view. Another suicide bomb struck the next day, at a hitchhiking post for soldiers in Ashkelon, taking the life of a young woman.

In our last meeting that week, held in Ross's living room on March 3, the issue of terrorism came up. Ross expressed to Moualem his administration's concern that the Iranians were using Syria as a conduit for passing on instructions to Hamas to escalate its terror attacks on Israel. Moualem asked for evidence. Within twenty-four hours, another bus was blown up in Jerusalem, on the same bus line, on the same street, and at the same time as the week before, leaving eighteen people dead.

In our Washington hotel, where we stayed on the weekends, we watched the horror on television. The familiar streets of Jerusalem covered with blood and debris were a nightmare. We were anxious to return home, to our families. When we asked for permission to do so, we were told that we would receive an answer within a few hours.

It came in the form of another bomb blast, this time in the heart of Tel Aviv. At 3:55 P.M. Israel time (8:55 A.M. in Washington), a fourth suicide bomber—twenty-three-year-old Ramez Abid, an art student from Khan Yunis—blew himself up outside Dizengoff Center, a large shopping mall in the city's center. That day was the festival of Purim, when children dress up in costumes and Israelis of all ages spend the day outdoors having fun. The mall's shops and restaurants were a magnet on the holiday, and the blast killed thirteen people and wounded scores of others. Most of the members of our delegation came from Tel Aviv, and when we received the news in Washington, we began frantically phoning our families. Maya answered at our house and was crying. "We're all right, Daddy," she assured me, "but please come home. This is too awful to describe." We all took the next flight back.

Before we left the hotel, Dennis Ross came to see us off. He, too, was shaken by the news and shared my concern that the peace process was in genuine jeopardy. He told me that after holding a phone conversation with Peres, President Clinton had decided to call an international antiterror conference in Egypt, which he would cohost with President Mubarak. The region, and especially Israel, needed a resounding international commitment to a coordinated fight against terrorism, a rescue mission on behalf of peace. Just before we parted, I asked Ross whether he had spoken to Moualem.

"Yes, I did," he said. "He sends you his personal wishes, understands why you must leave, and hopes the talks will resume soon."

My reaction to that message was bitter. I knew that the Syrians, situated somewhere between the forces trying to build a better future and those bent on stopping them, had, at best, done very little to prevent these attacks. It was exactly this ambivalence that made the Syrians so important in the peacemaking. For, once they decided to join the peace camp, they could draw the more hesitant regimes in their wake. In the meantime, however, by a process of default, they were aiding the forces of destruction. And after a week of repeated acts of terror, those forces seemed to have gained the upper hand. Peace had been struck a severe blow.

Immediately upon returning to Israel, I met with Prime Minister Peres, who seemed to have aged ten years since our last meeting, ten days before. Four times that week he had visited the sites of the bombings and had walked among the victims as a choir of rage and hatred lashed at him. The public had lost its self-confidence and its faith in the peace process. Peres had to take measures to restore them both—and they weren't always in line with our basic peace strategy. The political landscape had also changed dramatically, and the polls now showed Peres and Netanyahu running neck and neck (down from a 20-point lead for Peres). The radical right emerged from the shelter it had taken after the Rabin assassination and again took over the streets. While Netanyahu prudently expressed support for the government's antiterror actions (such as the full closure imposed on the territories), some of his associates denounced Peres's policies as the source of the terror. Extremism had again become legitimate.

The public's response was also much stronger in this latest round of the battle of nerves. Fear turned almost into a collective phobia that some expressed through near hysteria and others through withdrawal into silence. Our famous resilience seemed to have been weakened, and the effect of the collective anxiety was to indeed make terrorism into a strategic weapon. We were reacting just as the terrorists wanted us to, as they drove a wedge between us and our peace partners. And there were those in Israel who contributed to this trend by lumping Hamas and Arafat in the same category. We knew that Arafat had to act with greater vigor, yet a delegitimized Arafat was a weaker match for the fundamentalists, which would threaten the balance of peace. The man who intervened to restore the equilibrium was President Clinton.

On March 13, 1996, eight days after the Dizengoff bombing, Clinton orchestrated the dramatic conference at Sharm el-Sheikh "to advance the peace process, security, and the fight against terrorism." Dubbed "The Conference of Peace Makers," it brought together the host, President Mubarak; King Hussein; the prime minister of Morocco; the foreign ministers of Saudi Arabia, Tunisia, Algeria, Kuwait, the Gulf Emirates, and Yemen; the crown prince of Bahrain; the prime minister of Mauritania; representatives of Qatar and Oman; and of course Shimon Peres and Yasser Arafat. The presence of leaders from outside the region was no less impressive: Chancellor Helmut Kohl of Germany, President Jacques Chirac of France, Prime Minister John Major of Great Britain, UN Secretary-General Boutros Boutros-Ghali, the president of the European Union, the prime ministers of Norway, Spain, and Italy, and the foreign minister of Japan.

All told, thirty national leaders, half of them from the Middle East, came to say no to terrorism. In the concluding photo opportunity, by the pool of the Möewenpick Hotel, they all joined and raised their hands in an act of solidarity with peace. They were actually joining hands in support of one man: the prime minister of Israel.

Israel had been under attack for most of its existence. But now thirteen Arab leaders—most of whom had joined or supported the attacks in the past—stood at its side in a moment of crisis. A common interest had been created to protect the fledgling peace and curb the forces of extremism. For a few minutes I saw a happy Shimon Peres, whose vision of a coalition for peace was becoming a reality in defiance of all its enemies. Even Arafat, under pressure to step up his antiterror efforts, declared before the participants: "We will root out and smash [the terrorists]. We will work hard to face up to the extremists like Hamas and the Islamic Jihad." Israel intended to hold him to his word. We told him bluntly that he could have done more to combat terrorism. But we also knew that it was the agreements we had negotiated with him that had engendered the transformation in the region. Our only course was to deal with his shortcomings while remembering his essential contribution to the process.

Peres, who placed the blame for the terrorism directly on Tehran—"an Iranian hand orchestrates terror inside our country and on our borders"—took the opportunity to discuss with President Clinton both an antiterror treaty between the United States and Israel and the intensification of international pressure on Iran. The two leaders also decided that the peace process must be resumed at the earliest possible date. Their strategy was to strike the proper balance between tactical measures to combat terrorism and pursuit of the peace strategy.

After the conference ended, Clinton accompanied us back to Israel to help soothe the pain of a sad, frightened, and angry nation. He discussed antiterror policies with ministers and experts. He visited the grave of his friend Yitzhak Rabin, holding the hand of the slain leader's widow. The high point of his visit was his speech to the young generation. Meeting with over one thousand teenagers in Israel's opera house in Tel Aviv, he encouraged them to "overcome fear, don't give in to it, don't give up hope, don't let the terrorists win." Where others might have practiced demagoguery, Clinton practiced pedagogy with a strong human touch. Terror, he knew, is best fought with a combination of force, courage, and peace.

On the way to the airport to bid the president good-bye, Peres profoundly thanked Clinton for his support of Israel in another hour of trial and for his efforts to rescue the peace process. As we stood by the steps of Air Force One, the president embraced me with one arm and Dennis Ross with the other and said softly, "Uri, I hope I've helped somewhat."

"More than I can express to you, Mr. President," I said.

Many of my American friends regarded Clinton as a master of political manipulation and politesse. But in all of his encounters with us, he proved both his passion for peace and a sincere empathy with those working to make it, more than any president I had met before.

Air Force One was barely off the ground, however, when we found ourselves facing the next onslaught, by another arm of Iranian-backed fundamentalism: the Hezbollah. The Arab-Israeli-Western coalition against terror posed a threat to Iran and a challenge for Syria (as long as it refused to join such a coalition). Thus since the Sharm el-Sheikh conference, the Hezbollah—instructed and armed by Iran and not deterred by Syria—had been shelling Israel's northern border with Katyusha rockets. Daily attacks also continued on IDF positions in the south Lebanon security zone. When Israel retaliated by bombing Hezbollah positions, a cycle of escalation began. And as the rocket fire continued, public pressure mounted in Israel to stop it by striking a heavy blow to the Hezbollah.

The resolution of the "Lebanese problem"—namely, the protracted miniwar in the security zone between the Hezbollah and Israeli troops deployed to protect our population along Israel's northern border—could be achieved only as part of a broader peace settlement with Syria, leading to a peace treaty with its client state, Lebanon. We had no other interest in keeping our forces in south Lebanon. But our options were limited as long as the Hezbollah continued to operate out of Lebanese territory. The key to solving this imbroglio was Syria, the de facto ruler in Lebanon. Yet the Syrians had no intention of neutralizing the Hezbollah before a Syrian-Israeli peace had been secured.

On March 18 the United States began trying to persuade Syria to curb the guerrilla attacks. Peres decided to give American diplomacy time to act, but Washington's pleas remained unheeded, despite assurances from Syrian Foreign Minister Farouk al-Sharaa to Secretary of State Christopher that Syria would intervene with the Hezbollah. As the Hezbollah attacks and Israeli retaliations deteriorated into a routine, Peres was forced to respond. On the advice of the military, he proposed to the cabinet a military operation based on air force strikes against targets deep in Lebanon, including terrorist headquarters in Beirut. After the cabinet had approved the operation, I passed a note to Yossi Beilin expressing concern that the cycle of violence would play into the hands of those in Israel who advocated solutions by force. The problem, as I saw it, was that, after having sustained so many casualties, Israel was becoming a victim of its own vulnerability to terror. It was clear that we had to act, yet we could be drawn into the kind of deep military engagements that were not necessarily in our long-term interests but appeared unavoidable in the absence of an immediate alternative to our deeply ingrained belief that there is a military solution to every problem. The fundamentalists now had us playing their game on their court. This was the vulnerability of a peace process still in the making, and Peres understood it well. Yet he felt compelled to deal vigorously with the violence first and return to peacemaking afterward. He was in a particularly sensitive position, as he faced the formidable challenge of conducting a military operation, rescuing a peace strategy, and fighting an election campaign all at once.

On April 3 the IDF mounted a surgical strike against terrorist headquarters in Beirut. For a brief moment this raised morale by restoring pride in the IDF's unique abilities. But Katyusha rockets continued to land inside Israel, forcing its citizens to remain in their shelters. Israel also fought back by shelling Hezbollah positions in the south, causing Lebanese civilians to flee the area. As Operation Grapes of Wrath dragged on, Israel hoped that the Lebanese government would pressure Assad to end the turmoil and staunch the flight of tens of thousands of refugees northward by curtailing the Hezbollah. But the Syrian president was not one to heed pressure.

Then catastrophe stuck. On April 17 an IDF artillery unit came under attack and struck back at the source of fire, a Hezbollah unit located near a UN position by the village of Kafr Kana. What the artillery unit did not know was that hundreds of Lebanese had taken refuge in the UN position, and about one hundred innocent people had been killed by our fire with many more wounded. Peres was deeply shocked. So was most of the IDF command. The UN spokesman in Lebanon publicly blamed the Hezbollah for using the UN camp as a cover while firing on Israeli troops. Yet the world's outrage was directed at Israel. The Hezbollah had trapped us, and Lebanese had paid with their lives.

At first Peres contemplated halting Operation Grapes of Wrath, but he soon concluded that the impression that it had ended in defeat would simply strengthen the Hezbollah and encourage it to provoke Israel again. The only course was to continue fighting until the parties could reach a political understanding that would stabilize the situation on the Lebanese border. When I met with Peres just after the Kafr Kana disaster, I found him deeply saddened. Most politicians view tragedy from the vantage of its effect on their own political fortunes. But on that evening, at least, I sensed that Peres was honestly in pain. "I will not flee from responsibility," he said. In the televised press conference held after that meeting, he indeed expressed his sorrow and took full responsibility for the IDF's actions. But he placed the blame for the terrible loss of life squarely on the Hezbollah, and the military operation went on.

What concerned me most at that hour was that our own public, put on the defensive by the world's angry reaction, was so busy denouncing Hezbollah that little sorrow was expressed, or perhaps even felt, for the deaths of one hundred civilians by Israeli fire. In conflict, each side claims a monopoly on suffering.

As it was clear that Syria held the key to extricating the sides from the stalemate, Secretary Christopher, Dennis Ross, and the American peace team arrived in the region on April 20 for ten days of intensive talks in Damascus and Jerusalem, but Assad was in no hurry to restore calm. However, after a series of nerve-racking delays and round-the-clock negotiations, we succeeded in working out a new set of understandings, whereby civilian areas on both sides would be placed out of bounds as both shelters from and targets of attack. Two mechanisms suggested by Peres were established as a result of the American mediation: one to monitor the security situation in southern Lebanon (with the participation of Israel, Lebanon, Syria, France, and the United States), the other to help in the rehabilitation and development of the Lebanese economy (to be led by France and the United States). The final paragraph of the understandings stressed that peace negotiations between Israel and Syria and Israel and Lebanon were the only means of solving the problem in southern Lebanon and that they should be renewed in an atmosphere of stability.

Having faced and contained fundamentalist terror by force—at least in part and temporarily—we turned back to developing the only truly lethal weapon against these enemies of peace: peace itself. Peres concluded with Christopher, and through him with Assad, that the Wye Plantation talks would resume after the Israeli elections.

Within the space of two months, we had faced the Syrians twice on very different ground: first in talks on planning peace and economic development, then against the backdrop of a violent clash with the Hezbollah. The sharp difference between the circumstances illustrated that the peace process was caught between the future and the past, between the thrust toward creating a different region and a new era and the forces trying desperately to block it. Each of the partners to the peace process had to contend with these forces within its own camp: the Palestinians with Hamas, Syria with its fundamentalist allies, and Israel with the fanatics who had inspired the murder of its prime minister. The choice before them seemed clear: to stand up to internal challenges, confront common threats, or return to confronting one another. In this sense, in the spring of 1996 the struggle for peace was testing our resolve as well as our identities.

10

OLD-NEW LANDS

MARCH AND APRIL 1996 WERE THE PEAK OF THE FUNDAMENTALIST onslaught on the peace process and took a heavy toll on Israel. As in earlier periods of profound crisis, some Israelis pronounced the Oslo process dead. It wasn't. But we did have to steer it back onto the right track, which meant working quietly with our Palestinian partners to greatly strengthen their antiterror policy and our security cooperation. We faced the most critical crisis of the Oslo process just weeks before Israel was to decide on its future government and prime minister.

After returning from Wye Plantation and Sharm el-Sheikh, I met my friend Abu Ala. He had run as a candidate for the Palestinian Council in the elections that took place at the end of January and were a watershed in Palestinian attempts at political self-expression, as well as a resounding success for the Palestinian Authority. Yasser Arafat won 90 percent of the vote for the chairmanship of the Palestinian Authority, and his Fatah Party won more than 80 percent of the vote for the legislative council. Some Hamas representatives were elected despite the movement's call to boycott the elections, as were some independents generally close to the Palestinian Authority. Abu Ala came in first in the Jerusalem District, was elected the first speaker of the Palestinian Council, and devoted all his time to laying the foundations of the new parliament and playing a leading role in the nation-building process.

While we were happy to see each other after a relatively long hiatus, our mood was gloomy. Abu Ala expressed his shock and regret over the Hamas terror actions and told me that his whole family was deeply upset. While I was still at Wye Plantation, his children had been in close touch with Aliza and Maya and shared their sadness.

Abu Ala advised me to leave all other issues aside and devote myself exclusively to rescuing the Oslo process. "Palestinians are opposed to what has happened," he said. "For the first time, there were demonstrations in Gaza against terrorism." In his new capacity as speaker of the council, he was not supposed to conduct negotiations directly, but we decided to maintain close contact and consult informally on how to proceed.

The heads of our security establishment were convinced that the reason for the Palestinian Authority's failure to prevent the wave of violence was the lack of a cogent antiterror policy. It was the policy of the authority's security apparatus to thwart planned terror actions while attempting to convince Hamas to become a purely political force, but little was being done to pursue and arrest the Hamas leaders responsible for terrorism or to dismantle the organization's terrorist infrastructure. No serious effort was made, for example, to confiscate weapons from Hamas's followers.

Like fundamentalist movements elsewhere, Hamas was recruiting followers by answering their basic needs. Social and welfare institutions, educational facilities, mosques, hospitals, and training centers supplied Palestinians with food, work, health services, and rehabilitation after imprisonment. Many intellectuals found in fundamentalist Islam an outlet for their nostalgia for a more glorious Muslim past and a bulwark against the intrusion of Western culture. All these institutions were used to indoctrinate Palestinians in a political dogma that equates compromise with surrender, and they served as recruitment centers for candidates to be trained for terrorist activities. Fundamentalism exists to some degree or another in most Islamic societies today, as a force that attempts to influence the very nature of society. Yet in the cities, villages, and particularly the refugee camps of Gaza and the West Bank, it thrived vigorously on the economic hardship and on the struggle against humiliation associated with the

Israeli occupation. Therefore the Oslo process was perceived as a threat to the movement.

Arafat understood this situation and the dangers it posed for his own regime. From his standpoint, it made sense to grapple with the Hamas movement by using the tactic at which he was most accomplished: divide and rule. He tried to win over some parts of the Hamas leadership in Gaza by holding out the promise of a share in power while keeping others at arm's length. But he failed to give sufficient attention to the activities of the most extreme of the fundamentalist elements, who were determined to undermine his agreements with Israel through terror. I had met alone with Arafat in Gaza ten days before the suicide bombing in Jerusalem and found him to have an exaggerated sense of control over the volatile situation. "Tell the prime minister that every day I do everything that's necessary," he said on February 18. The bombings confronted him with an open challenge to his rule, and he finally began to appreciate that the outcome of the struggle would shape the very identity of Palestinian society and thus of a future Palestinian state.

It was mainly for this reason that Arafat decided to act comprehensively against Hamas. We wanted to ensure that he would do so effectively and continuously. Arafat met an angry and demanding Chief of Staff Amnon Shahak and also received a strong message from Prime Minister Peres conveyed by Yossi Genosar, who was again recruited as a secret liaison between the prime minister and the chairman (replacing Res. Gen. Shlomo Gazit, who had been the secret liaison for Peres until then). In these meetings Israel categorically demanded that the Palestinian Authority strike deep into the Hamas infrastructure, confiscate illegal arms, arrest terror suspects and place them on trial, and turn these measures into a lasting policy. At the same time, a hermetic closure was imposed, cutting the West Bank and Gaza off from Israel and various cities in the West Bank off from their surroundings. Peres also established an antiterror team that would integrate all appropriate elements in Israel. The team was headed by Ami Ayalon, head of the General Security Service, and was mandated to recommend more effective antiterror measures.

For the first time since the Oslo Agreement, Peres expressed his frustration with Arafat, publicly blaming him sharply for not doing his utmost to prevent terror. His public criticism stemmed from the need for a show of strength, but it also contributed to the delegitimization of Arafat in the eyes of the Israeli public and helped intensify the anti-Oslo propaganda of the Israeli right. Once again, it seemed, the fundamentalists had cornered us. Yet Peres never lost sight of who the real enemy was; he knew he had to find a way to revive the peace process with Arafat. Both Rabin and Peres never saw in Arafat an example of integrity. Yet he clearly was perceived as the most important partner, who had the ability to take critical and often unpopular decisions, and constituted a bridge to regional peace. Peres therefore sent Genosar to set up with Arafat a new secret channel of negotiations. It was to be led by Abu Mazen and myself and to include the officers and other officials in charge of security and counterterror activity on both sides. Six months after the signing of the Interim Agreement, the structures we had created for cooperation were facing a grave test.

Between March 23 and April 17, the secret channel met ten times, mostly in Jerusalem and the coastal city of Ashkelon, to work out new understandings on counterterror activity, cooperation on security, and the resumption of the peace process. Much of the discussion in these sessions was directly between the security officers. Abu Mazen and I saw our role as analyzing the mistakes of the past and creating an effective structure for security cooperation in the future. I found him to be a candid and serious partner. He admitted that the Palestinian Authority had erred in believing that it could co-opt Hamas through the extensive dialogue being conducted with its political leadership in Gaza and the Sudan. Consequently, Arafat had issued directives to deal Hamas and the Islamic Jihad a fatal blow. Abu Mazen spoke to me of hundreds of arrests together with the closing of many Hamas-supported social, religious, and academic institutions. Through interrogations of the detainees and the material collected in the course of these operations, the Palestinian Authority concluded that the real target of Hamas's wide-ranging activities was the Authority itself; violence against Israelis was a tool in an internal Palestinian struggle.

At the same time, our Palestinian interlocutors placed much of the blame for the strength of Hamas in the Palestinian street squarely on us. Hassan Asfour, who took active part in these talks, was as sharp as ever in his criticism. "Your closure policy, from the time of Oslo onward, has created the unemployment, bitterness, and despair that have driven thousands of Palestinians into the arms of Hamas," he charged. "Even so, after the outrage of the suicide bombings, people in Gaza shouted: 'Yes to peace, no to terrorism!' Then, after the tightening of the closure, they shouted: 'Yes to peace, no to terror, no to closure!' And now, with the deterioration in the economic situation, they are crying: 'No to occupation, no to closure!' Before long, these shouts could turn into 'No to peace!' Your policies are shortsighted, and you're not seeking real cooperation."

Asfour also argued that Arafat had been unable to engage in an all-out battle against Hamas because he had so little to offer his people as long as the closure policy prevailed. Indeed, we tended to be so focused on the performance of the Palestinian leadership that we often failed to see Palestinian society as a community of needs and aspirations that its leaders must serve and reflect. The result was an exaggerated view of Arafat's power. He, in turn, failed to appreciate the influence of public opinion on the way Israel conducted its side of the peace process. Thus the leaders of both sides were extremely sensitive to pressures on them from below but lacked awareness of what was going on in their partners' constituencies.

Still, this was not the time to pause and get to know each other better. I told Arafat that we had to come up with swift and effective remedies and that they had to crush the violent opposition as a first step to revive the peace process. While the security officials continued to deal with the concrete details of the counterterror struggle, Abu Mazen and I worked on creating a new structure of cooperation, in which (1) pertinent intelligence would be shared in real time; (2) we would be given a greater degree of information on the Palestinians' counterterror activities; and (3) the two sides would cooperate as equals (since the Palestinians complained that we tended to give them orders rather than treat them as partners).

In the days and weeks that followed, the Palestinian Authority waged an all-out battle against Hamas and the Islamic Jihad, while cooperation between our respective security services vastly improved.

Hundreds of Hamas activists were arrested, arms were confiscated, militant religious and academic figures were dismissed from their posts, civilian institutions and even mosques were raided. Arafat and his men were fighting to rescue not only the peace process but their own authority. While our officers still received warnings of possible suicide bomb attacks, they expressed growing satisfaction with the fundamental change in Arafat's policies. The basic Israeli-Palestinian partnership and ability to work together under difficult circumstances proved to be strong. Oslo was more durable than many had imagined, and six weeks after the bombing outside Dizengoff Center, the Palestinian-Israeli peace process reached three milestones.

On April 17 Arafat and Peres approved an informal document on antiterror cooperation between the two sides' security authorities (whose content was obviously never disclosed). At the same time, they announced the renewal of the peace process and the reactivation of all the committees on cooperation that had been established by the Interim Agreement. Preparations also continued on the redeployment of Israeli troops in Hebron (which was rescheduled, by agreement between Abu Mazen and myself, to take place on June 15, after the Israeli elections).

After these understandings were reached, we moved on to one of the most extraordinary meetings ever to take place in the conference room of an Israeli military facility. Prime Minister and Defense Minister Peres arrived accompanied by the top brass of the security establishment: the chief of staff, the head of the Shabak, the head of Military Intelligence, and so forth. Arafat arrived accompanied by the heads of the Palestinian security and intelligence apparatus. An array of uniforms mingled in the room, which echoed with casual conversations in Hebrew, Arabic, and English. After lunch, the Palestinians reviewed their activities since the February and March suicide bombings, with Mohammed Dahlan addressing us in Arabic for the benefit of his boss, while a Shabak man translated his presentation into Hebrew. I never imagined that I would witness a meeting at which a PLO security chief who had spent several years in Israeli jails would brief our generals on how his people were systematically fighting terrorism. We were developing a new routine that signaled a profound change in the nature of our relationships. After that, the heads of security on both sides assured each other of their intention to increase and improve cooperation, and then Peres and Arafat announced to the press their basic resolutions on increased antiterror cooperation and on the resumption of the peace process.

The second milestone was reached on April 24, the day Israel was celebrating its forty-eighth Independence Day. In the evening, as Peres was on his way to the annual reception hosted by the minister of defense, he received a message from Arafat that the Palestinian Council, which was meeting in Gaza, had voted by a margin of 504 to 54 to nullify the articles in the Palestinian Covenant that called for the destruction of Israel. The vote was the fulfillment of the obligation made in Arafat's letter to Prime Minister Rabin on September 9, 1993, as part of the exchange on mutual recognition. In secret contacts between Abu Mazen and Yoel Singer, the Palestinians had shown us the wording of the pertinent resolution to ensure that it was congruent with their commitment. Yoel confirmed for us that it was.

Though the PLO had obviously recognized Israel from every practical point of view by then, the council decision was nonetheless of historic significance. For the council is the equivalent of the pan-Palestinian parliament. It also represents Palestinians living beyond the West Bank and Gaza and includes factions, such as the Democratic and Popular Fronts, that had opposed the Oslo accords and were still not prepared to formally recognize Israel's existence. Thus Arafat had to fight a tough political battle to ensure a majority for amending the Palestinian Covenant. "We made a peace of the brave, now we have to be brave enough to change the covenant," he said on that occasion. As the covenant was replete with rejection and enmity, the council decided to have a committee of lawyers draft an entirely new basic document. Abu Ala, who was actively involved in the council meeting, expressed his view that that document will probably be the constitution of the future Palestinian state.

Gathered on the Defense Ministry's lawn that evening, together with the diplomatic corps, was Israel's political, economic, and military elite. When Peres informed his guests of the Palestinian Council's decision, calling it "a change of historic magnitude," there was an outburst of applause. "Who would ever have thought that we'd be celebrating a PNC decision on Independence Day!" a young colonel standing near me remarked. Indeed, throughout its existence Israel had fought for acceptance in the region against a coalition that demanded blanket rejection. The Palestinian Council's decision that day was, at last, recognition of our independence by the most bitter of former enemies.

President Clinton issued an enthusiastic response in Washington, applauding it as "a major step on the road to peace."

On May 5, 1996, as a result of the efforts to renew the peace process with the Palestinians, I found myself in the familiar setting of the Taba Hilton Hotel, where several months earlier we had concluded the Interim Agreement. Now Palestinians and Israelis had returned to open formally the permanent-status negotiations that would lead to the historic reconciliation. Abu Mazen and I headed our respective delegations, made up mostly of Oslo and Taba veterans. After arriving at the hotel, I sat in my room on the eighth floor polishing my speech. "Yes, our peoples must separate," I added to the draft prepared earlier. "Separation will serve to encourage cooperation. . . . As we lay the foundation of this essential separation, we will clarify that each of us is responsible for our respective identities."

I walked out onto the balcony and, gazing at azure sea and pink mountains, reflected on the three years that had passed since I'd met Abu Ala in Oslo. There, in several months of negotiations, we had drawn up a prescription for the future. Since then we had lived through a mixture of promise and agony. The process we had embarked on had withstood formidable tests and fierce enemies and brought us, on schedule, to the day when we would begin negotiating the final chapter of our agreement. The two sides would probably never have been able to tackle the difficult issues now on the table— Jerusalem, the borders, the Palestinian refugees, and the Israeli settlements—had it not been for the arduous road they had traveled together. We had created a dynamic process in which the alternative to moving forward would always be detrimental to *both* sides. Standing on the balcony that day, I felt satisfaction tinged with anxiety. I was reminded of the night of May 20, 1993, when I had stood on Terje Larsen's balcony in Oslo, grasping how momentous was the opportunity facing us, and feared that it would be missed.

Then I packed up my papers and went to Abu Mazen's suite. We had agreed to show each other the speeches we would give at the opening ceremony a short while later. There was no question that on every issue to be deliberated in the future talks, there were yawning gaps between our positions. Yet we were in absolute agreement on the goal of the process: the kind of reconciliation, reached through a commitment to equality and mutual respect, that would ensure peace, security, and economic cooperation. Abu Mazen was preparing to say, "We are determined to put an end to decades of confrontation and to live in peaceful coexistence, mutual dignity, and security."

The opening event was fairly dull; only signing ceremonies create drama. But it did serve a purpose, for we established working groups on all the issues and a steering committee to direct the talks. In a tête-à-tête, Abu Mazen and I decided to form what had become almost a routine feature in our negotiations: a secret back channel where we hoped real progress would be made.

After returning to Jerusalem, I met with Abu Ala and told him about the event at which his presence had been missed (his relations with Abu Mazen were strained at the time).

"It's much too early for me to get involved," he said and then inquired as to how I intended to proceed with the talks.

"I don't think we should set out from the situation in 1996," I responded, "or even from the issues to be resolved by May 1999. I believe we should start by describing what our common goals will be in the year 2000—a year after the permanent-status agreement is signed—for what is at stake is the essential character of our future relationships. We should attempt to define what our desired political, security, and economic ties should be."

Abu Ala agreed. "All along I've believed in the principle of profound cooperation between us," he said. "It is the only way, and it will add to our respective strengths."

"We also have to make sure that in signing the permanent-status agreement, we finally bury the conflict," I added. "I am going to suggest a kind of alliance between our two peoples that will be a genuine security partnership against common enemies, remove economic barriers between us, as well as between our two economies and Jordan's, and create a political partnership that should encourage regional cooperation. Only when we've achieved a written agreement on our future relations would I start to tackle the tough issues."

"Well, Uri, I see you don't need me now." Abu Ala laughed. "Call me in 1998, when it comes to the crunch." He had lost none of his appetite for the negotiating process.

When we parted that day, it didn't occur to me that this meeting would be my last with Abu Ala, or any other Palestinian partner, in my official capacity as Israel's chief peace negotiator. All told, from day one in Oslo until that chat in May 1996, 1,100 days of negotiating peace had passed. I was busy planning for many more, on the assumption that Peres would be returned to office.

When I reported to him about my recent talks with the Palestinians, he instructed me to prepare for the resumption of negotiations with both Syria and the Palestinians in June. When he approved the approach I had outlined with Abu Mazen and Abu Ala, I told Peres that on March 2 I had reached a similar understanding with Walid Moualem. We had agreed that he, Dennis Ross, and I would each present our vision of the Middle East in the year 2005 to the rest of the group at Wye Plantation. But that session never took place, as the talks were broken off the next day, following the Jerusalem and Dizengoff bombings. Yet I still felt that trying to envision future relationships together would be a helpful prelude to shaping compatible strategic goals.

The Middle East in 2000 or 2005 could find itself in one of two basic situations: either enjoying political stability, regional security, and economic cooperation based on a mutuality of interests; or experiencing chronic violence spawned by fundamentalism and economic retardation. Stalemate is an illusion; the region would be drawn in one or the other of these directions. The main lesson of the Oslo process was that it was up to the countries in the region to determine the destiny they wanted to forge, not up to destiny itself or super-powers. In Israel we especially had learned that much depended on our own decisions. We had, maybe for the first time, developed a proactive peace policy. Peres firmly believed in our ability to contribute to a "new Middle East," which would link itself to global trends, and pursuing that vision was the strategy he had set for the coming four years. But first we had to get through the Israeli elections.

Peres was busy simultaneously running the country and an election campaign. With the ministers so busy campaigning, it seemed that Avi Gil; Peres's media adviser, Aliza Goren; and I were the only civilians around him who assisted him on the first of these two tasks. Peres had created a campaign structure that was hampered by poor personal relations among key players. He himself directed most of his attention during the period leading up to the elections to the fighting against fundamentalist terror and to a rescue of the peace process. The Israeli government knew that Iran had an interest in seeing a change of power in Israel, in the belief that it would bring the peace process to a halt. Tehran had therefore instructed the terror organizations to continue the violence against Israelis. This was not Labor Party propaganda; it had been corroborated publicly by the IDF's chief of Military Intelligence. We also received a similar reading of Iran's intentions from Palestinian security sources, based on information gathered from Hamas detainees. On March 14 a short-range missile that was to be launched against an Israeli embassy in Europe was discovered by the Belgian security services aboard a ship anchored in Antwerp that had sailed out of an Iranian port. I put all our European embassies on full alert, and in the weeks to come Peres was in close contact with President Clinton, President Chirac, and Chancellor Kohl, all three of whom warned the Iranians against pursuing any such plans.

The Israeli electoral contest was thus strongly bound up with the dramatic struggle for peace and against its violent opponents. Israel was essentially split into two camps: those who appreciated and supported the successes of the peace process and those who regarded the violence against it as evidence that the process was fundamentally misguided and naïve.

Binyamin Netanyahu, at forty-seven the youngest man ever to run for the prime ministership in Israel, led an aggressively negative campaign that daily repeated the same basic message: Oslo was a surrender to the PLO, a notorious terrorist organization, and entrusting our security to a terrorist leader could only result in further bloodshed. Showing video clips of the suicide bombings, the Likud reiterated the same slogan night after night in its television ads: "There is no peace; there is no security; there is no reason to vote for Peres."

The Labor campaign showed the achievements of the peace revolution: advancing the region toward political reconciliation as the only path to long-term security. Labor's video clips showed a vibrant, future-oriented Israel whose leader offered its younger generation hope. They dwelled on the theme of optimism, on ending Israel's political isolation, on raising the standard of living, on developing science and technology, and on pursuing peace as the key to all this progress. The process begun by Rabin and Peres, it stressed, deserved to be allowed to continue, whereas Netanyahu would bring it to a halt.

But the schism in Israeli society ran deeper than a division over politics. One part of the country took part in the peace revolution and saw the walls crumbling around Israel as its salvation. The other saw the same process as a nightmare. What one half of Israel viewed as the opening of new horizons and opportunities the other saw as leaving the nation defenseless against violence and the penetration of foreign values. Israel, in this reading, was surrounded not by neighbors but by implacable enemies. This was the "Jewish condition" and had been so for centuries; we were "a people that dwells alone." Trusting others meant delivering ourselves into their hands. The picture most repeated in the Likud propaganda was that of Arafat and Peres walking hand in hand. What symbolized for some a necessary act of reconciliation was interpreted by others as being led to disaster. In the Likud's television ads, this picture shattered like glass, dissolving into flashbacks of the scenes of terrorist attacks.

Netanyahu was able to unify a variety of camps that shared this general outlook. At first he brought together the secular right that had been weakened by the competition among its own leaders. Then he brought under his banner the self-styled champion of the underprivileged, former Foreign Minister David Levy, who was lured into the alliance by the promise of political spoils. A third element was the religious and ethnically Sephardi–oriented Shas Party, led by Rabbi Ovadiah Yosef, a moderate on peace and a fundamentalist on religion. The political sentiment of Shas's constituency tended toward the right, but its voters deferred to the rabbi's judgment.

The Shas campaign was a reflection of a different mind-set and actually of a different age. While other parties distributed literature on their electoral platforms, its activists distributed amulets blessed by a popular mystic, Rabbi Kadoorie, that contained a benediction for a better life and almost anything one could wish for, from personal health and national security to victory for one's favorite soccer team. The implied message accompanying the amulets was that the way to make them work was to vote for Shas. While the distribution of these charms was eventually curbed (because their use in election campaigns is prohibited by law), the spell they had cast on Shas's voters was potent. There was a strong feeling among them that Labor's Israel—a modern Israel that allied itself with the secularist Meretz Party, Yasser Arafat, and Western culture—was antagonistic to Jewish tradition. Many Shas supporters saw a vote for Peres as a vote against the traditional structure of Jewish society, in which the rabbis played a dominant role, and traditional family values. These feelings were joined by an abiding anger against the country's prosperous, predominantly Ashkenazi elite. A link existed in the minds of Shas voters between the social and cultural "threat" to their traditional outlook and the threat posed by Labor's peacemaking efforts, which required openness and trust toward "outsiders." A safe Israel, this reading implied, was necessarily an insular one. Toward the end of the campaign, when Rabbi Kadoorie gave Netanyahu his personal blessing, the party's electoral message, though technically neutral, was clear.

Netanyahu was also able to gather two other constituencies under his banner: the modern-Orthodox followers of the National Religious Party and the Ashkenazi ultra-Orthodox population. The first were a natural ally of the right, as many of them, and especially their leaders, were identified with the settler movement. Since the Six-Day War, they had developed a radically nationalistic interpretation of Ju-

daism that saw in the return to the historic Land of Israel the fulfillment of its ideology and that portrayed the Palestinians not as men
and women endowed with inalienable rights who had a political dispute with Israel but as an alien and subordinate people living in a land
promised exclusively to the Jews. The extreme fringe of this movement had bred the incitement that led to the Hebron massacre and
the assassination of Yitzhak Rabin. While many adherents of the
national-religious doctrine did not condone such violence, they har-
bored a strong aversion to anyone perceived as "catering to Arab interests." And as Arabs were delegitimized, so were their interests.
That, in their eyes, was what "Oslo" was all about.

The Ashkenazi ultra-Orthodox population, like their Sephardi
counterparts, were more focused on religious issues and hoped to
strengthen their institutions and influence through new religious legislation. Yet they also felt at ease with Netanyahu's message, and after
receiving his promises to help them in their cause, they joined his
new alliance. During the closing days of the campaign, these forces,
upon command of their rabbis, papered the streets of Israel with the
ultimate campaign slogan: "Bibi is good for the Jews," implying, of
course, that Peres was good for the Arabs.

The May 1996 election was thus as much a sociocultural referen-
dum as a rational choice between peace and its alternative. It seemed
to me, as it had during the three years of the peace talks, that the
focus of energy and fighting spirit in Israel had shifted to the religious
right. It had a gospel to spread and organized itself to do so as a
movement of popular struggle. By contrast, with its parties in power,
the secular left had become complacent. It believed that the positive
course set by the government's decisions would carry the nation in its
wake, despite difficulties and setbacks. In this sense, the left behaved
as though it already lived in a postpeace era, while the right was en-
trenched in eternal conflict.

The confidence of the left was encouraged by the polls that
showed a three-to-five-point edge for Peres almost up to election
day. Peres's own pollster had predicted a narrow victory throughout
the campaign. I myself was concerned by the complacency I sensed
around me. Yet I found it difficult to believe that the historic drive

toward peace could be halted. The Hamas terrorists, as well as Yigal Amir, had tried to do that, but the process continued to move forward. Toward the end of the campaign, a pro-Peres ad appeared in the papers showing a smiling Amir above the appeal "Wipe that smile off his face."

On election day, May 29, Peres invited Aliza Goren, Avi Gil, and me for lunch at a restaurant in Herzliya. He was optimistic and talked about the renewal of the peace process in the days to come. Yet he was angered by the aggressive dissemination of the banners and posters reading, "Bibi is good for the Jews," by a virtual army of ultra-Orthodox young people and complained about their racist overtones. Driving back home, I could see that the streets had been inundated by these posters. But that wasn't Labor's only problem. When Peres visited the party's election headquarters in the afternoon, he discovered that its organizational efforts were weak and that the turnout wasn't what it should have been, especially among Israel's Arab voters. The late predictions were of a very close race.

I was at home with Aliza and Maya at 10:00 P.M., when Israel's two television channels announced the results of their exit polls. Channel One reported a slight lead for Peres: 50.5 to 49.5 percent. Channel Two showed an identical exit poll but also published an independent public-opinion survey giving Peres a five-point lead. The mood in our living room ranged from relief to sheer joy, because election night projections were rarely wrong. Soon friends began offering their good wishes.

One of the first to call was Abu Ala. "May one say congratulations?" he asked.

"Well, it looks good, but it's not over yet," I replied cautiously.

I hesitated to call Peres and congratulate him before the exit polls were confirmed by the trend of the vote count. At 1:30 A.M., when the predictions had not altered, celebrations were already in progress at the Labor election headquarters, and members of the Knesset were speculating about the composition of the next cabinet. I decided to make the call.

"Mazel tov, Shimon," I said. "It seems you've made it."

"Yes," he replied, "I just had a call from Channel Two informing me that the vote count shows the gap has widened to 2.5 percent. I

think I'll go to sleep for a few hours and visit the campaign headquarters in the morning. I've asked Leah Rabin to join me there. At
eight-thirty I want to meet with you, Beilin, and Gil to plan where we
go from here."

Since I was anticipating a full day ahead, I can't explain why, but
at 2:00 A.M. I was still glued to the television. It was at about that
time that the figures under Peres's and Netanyahu's portraits began
to change, first to a fifty-fifty tie and within minutes to 51 to 49 percent in Netanyahu's favor. As the crowd still gathered in the Likud's
election headquarters exploded into chants of joy, I phoned Moshe
Te'umim, Peres's longtime friend and his informal adviser on public-
opinion-related issues, who had inside information from the TV analysts charting the returns. In a broken voice, he told me that the
count had already turned dramatically in Netanyahu's favor. The
reason for the initial mistaken predictions, on both channels, was
that many of the Shas and ultra-Orthodox voters had refused to participate in the exit polls.

"We've lost," Te'umim told me. "There's no longer any doubt
about it."

It turned out, when all the ballots had been counted, that Netanyahu had beaten Peres by less than 1 percent of the vote.

After I'd finished talking with Te'umim, Avi Gil called. Since Peres
had gone to sleep believing he had won, Avi had asked Peres's daughter, Zikki, and her husband, Rafi, a physician, to break the news to
him when he awoke. At 8:30, when we reported to his office as directed, we met a very sad yet very strong man. He was planning a
smooth transition of power and kept consoling those who had come
to comfort him by explaining that he would go on fighting for peace.
Peres seemed to be the only Israeli who was not taken in by the widespread portrayal of him as the tragic figure of Israeli politics. Politics
had repeatedly dealt him unpromising hands. Yet he played each one
in a way that led him to the highest offices in government and enabled him to achieve some of his country's greatest accomplishments,
even though he lost four elections.

The analysis of these returns proved that voters adhered to their
camps out of deep sociopolitical identification. The election was virtually an expression of tribal politics. A 29,457 plurality of Israelis be-

longed to those "tribes" that believed in defending our interests and traditional structure and beliefs behind a wall of suspicion erected against eternal enemies. The second "tribe" believed in the need to protect our interests by destroying the walls of hatred and creating new relationships, based on common interests, with former enemies and to adapt our society to a changing modern world. The result was close (and would probably have gone the other way if not for the wave of terror in February and March), and therefore the battle over the nature and soul of Israel was bound to continue. Now, however, it would be under a new leadership, with a new ideology, intent on following different policies.

Yet Oslo had created a new reality, which obliged Netanyahu to maneuver in constant dissonance among his beliefs, his political support, and the reality created by the process.

Binyamin Netanyahu put together the most right-wing government in Israel's history. In his victory address, to an audience of delirious Likud supporters, he announced: "Israel embarks today on a new path of hope, unity, security, and peace. The first peace must be at home."

On June 18, the day the new government was formed, I tendered my resignation as director-general of the Foreign Ministry to the new minister, David Levy. I felt that he should be able to work with a man who could wholeheartedly implement his policies. A few weeks later, with a heavy heart, I also left the foreign service, which had been my career for twenty-one years and, since it had also been my father's career, one that I had been born into. But having been so closely identified with a process that was repudiated by the parties now in power, I felt that my place lay elsewhere.

"We still need you and Mr. Peres," Abu Ala told me during a private talk soon after the Netanyahu government had been installed. "Peres is regarded by Palestinians as a world leader and a man of peace. And you must continue what we started."

"We'll fight for our beliefs through other channels," I told him. "Peres and I have decided to create a peace center dedicated to fostering cooperation between our two peoples. But the course of the diplomatic process is up to the new government and its prime minister."

"Yes, I heard his speech," Abu Ala murmured. "We Palestinians are very worried. On the one hand he speaks about the peace process continuing, while on the other he talks about expanding the settlements. The two don't go together. We don't yet know how to handle this new situation. It took us by surprise."

"All I can say is that I'd advise you to do your best to make peace with the new government. The Oslo process has created a dynamic that poses a great dilemma for it. The right may have won the elections, but it has lost its ideological platform. There is no 'Greater Israel' anymore. Netanyahu has also promised peace and security, and he can't deliver either without you. Remember we used to say that Oslo is stronger than its opponents? Well, you have to help ensure that. Hamas had a lot to do with the outcome of the Israeli elections, but extremists can't be allowed to carry the day."

"That would be a catastrophe for the whole region," Abu Ala reflected. "People don't understand what's at stake here."

"It's important to remember that if you make peace with a right-wing government, eighty to ninety percent of the Israeli people will support it. So you can't give up."

Abu Ala tried to smile as he shook my hand. "I'll go on trying as long as I live, and I believe you will too," he said. Then he let out a loud laugh, adding, "I think this is our curse."

Neither Abu Ala nor I could really imagine the peace process being destroyed. I can't say whether that's because we had invested so much of ourselves in it or because we understood its deeper meaning and strength. Oslo is not just a pragmatic effort at peacemaking after having exhausted all other alternatives. It is—with all its setbacks—a revolutionary development that implies a reversal of historical, social, and cultural trends within both Israeli and Palestinian societies. Shaking hands and building a partnership meant not only the renunciation of past hostility but a break with traditions deeply ingrained in each of our societies.

Jewish life has long been held together by strong social and cultural defensiveness—traits that helped preserve the Jews through centuries of diaspora life. At its best, this tradition is what moved the nascent State of Israel to absorb hundreds of thousands of immigrants in a just a few years. At its worst, in a state that has had to harden itself to win wars of survival, it can be distorted into an ugly kind of ethnocentrism and xenophobia. Given our heritage, it seems it is no easier to deal out of strength than out of weakness. Secular Zionism intended to create a modern state that would modernize and normalize Jewish life by, among other things, opening itself up to new relations with the non-Jewish world. Israel was to understand that sovereignty and strength would be translated into coexistence with the world. The Oslo process was largely a fulfillment of that vision.

Arab nationalism tried to develop a modern Arab identity and build a united front against foreign occupiers—past and present—with other victims of colonialism. Whether linked to religion, socialism, or monarchy, however, Arab nationalism advocated closed and conservative social systems. A succession of revolutionary trends in the late 1980s and early 1990s—the collapse of the Soviet Union, the fragmentation of Arab unity as a result of the Gulf War, and the globalization of the economy—greatly challenged our Arab neighbors. For them, as well as us, Oslo spelled a bridge to the world and thus a challenge to traditional assumptions, identities, and social structures.

The peace process grew out of the courage of three leaders—Rabin, Peres, and Arafat—in assessing respective prospects and risks and taking bold, sometimes unpopular decisions. But its main strength was that it addressed a basic need, in both societies, resulting from weariness with the seemingly endless struggle and violence and aspiring to a resolution of the conflict, leading to freedom, economic development, and security. While Israelis and Palestinians who shared this view remained suspicious of each other, they knew that these goals could be achieved only through common efforts.

The process, in fact, created a basic interdependence on the ground that made it impossible for either side to ignore or dismiss the other without suffering consequences. A quasi-independent Palestinian government was responsible for its people, for the first time in their history, yet it depended upon Israel for their well-being. An Israel that had relinquished its full control over the Palestinians was dependent upon their cooperation to maintain one of its key interests: security. The economic prosperity of both sides also depended on peace.

The gradual nature of the process, which has drawn so much criticism over the years, is perhaps Oslo's greatest strength. For given the basic condition of interdependence, stalemate became very costly to both sides. The process virtually forced the parties to advance continually.

The greatest weakness of the three-year negotiation effort was that its messages did not filter down enough to the people. The decision makers often had to respond to internal criticism by claiming that the peace process was the best way to achieve traditional aims: security for Israel, statehood for the Palestinians. There was little talk of reconciliation, even less of the other side's predicaments. While the key decisions were motivated by values, such as a desire to end the occupation and replace rejection with cooperation, these were often obscured in favor of pragmatic arguments.

For the Netanyahu government, Oslo is a problematic legacy that contradicts its ideology on the Land of Israel, its perception of constant hostility toward us, and its conviction that peace can be achieved only by deterrence. Thus the new prime minister found himself trapped between pragmatic necessities and norms he rejected. The result was a zigzag policy that would veer toward Oslo and then away from it but always lacked its underlying spirit and values. Netanyahu swerved from the redeployment in Hebron to a provocative construction project in East Jerusalem (Har Homa), from blaming Arafat for terrorism and suspending the negotiations to trying to resuscitate them again. During the first year and a half of Netanyahu's tenure, last rites were repeatedly chanted over the Oslo process, but few were willing to pronounce it dead and even fewer had a viable alternative. The destiny of the peace process will ultimately be determined by what Israelis and Palestinians want most for themselves.

The Palestinians are engaged in a nation-building process plagued by contradictory forces. They have approached this task with a degree of political pluralism despite a tradition of centralized rule. They are struggling to develop their economy despite evidence of high-level corruption and the damaging effects of the closures. Their society is evolving somewhere between a paradigm of modernism and powerful fundamentalist trends. The Palestine that will emerge in the future depends largely upon the outcome of these struggles, as well as the resulting attitude toward the peace process.

The Oslo process has led Israel to a necessary historic struggle. Shimon Peres once defined this struggle to me as the second stage of the Zionist revolution, an effort to remove the ghetto from the Jewish ethos decades after it had disappeared from Jewish history. The Passover Hagaddah we read every year to celebrate our liberation from slavery in ancient Egypt includes a song that reminds us: "In every generation, [our enemies] rise up to destroy us, and the Almighty saves us from their hand." This song the Jews have sung for centuries and still do. Yet at the end of the twentieth century, the leaders of the State of Israel acted on the premise that enemies may not be eternal; that we may be strong enough to transform them into partners; that we need not be perpetual victims; and that we may even, because of our mistakes, become victimizers.

Not that all our enemies have vanished from the face of the earth. It was the perception of the threat posed by Iranian fundamentalism and the proliferation of nonconventional weapons in the hands of fanatic governments such as in Iraq or even terrorists that encouraged the Oslo decision makers—Rabin and Peres—to start building new coalitions against common enemies. We had to learn to ignore imaginary dangers and work with our neighbors on the basis of mutual understanding and interests. We were now a modern nation-state, not an institutionalized ghetto. It was up to us to forge a different future by influencing the trends and attitudes in our region. Since 1993, when peace with the Palestinians moved from the drawing board to the ground, it has been testing our identity, as well as that of our neighbors. This has now become an ongoing struggle. Life in this part of the world will never be the same as it was before the Oslo process.

I celebrated the Passover seder in 1997 at the home of the former American ambassador Martin Indyk. Around the table were many Israeli, American, Australian, and South African Jewish friends of the Indyks. The two surprise guests at the ceremonial dinner were Mohammed Basyouni, for fifteen years Egypt's ambassador to Israel, and

Abu Mazen of the PLO. Reading the Hagaddah aloud, we recited, with some embarrassment considering the presence of our Egyptian friend, the ten plagues brought down upon Egypt for persecuting the Children of Israel. But Basyouni rescued us from our discomfort by announcing, "That was a different Egypt you're talking about." Abu Mazen, meanwhile, carefully followed the English translation of the Hagaddah and finally said, with his kind smile: "I like the text. It is against oppression."

At the end of the Hagaddah, when we reached the line looking forward to "next year in Jerusalem," I was sure that there were many interpretations of its meaning around that table. Yet it was an exceptional evening, reflecting the bridge that can be built between tradition and universal values by people desiring to be neither oppressors nor oppressed. Such a bridge and such values were also the basis of the partnership that was born with the peace process, withstood severe tests, and will face even greater challenges in the future. It may be fraught with contradictions, but it is ultimately a partnership between people, as I had learned at my very first meeting in Oslo with my partner Abu Ala.

11

ANOTHER ENCOUNTER

NOT LONG AGO I AGAIN MET WITH THE MAN TO WHOM I HAD FIRST
been introduced in Oslo on May 20, 1993, as my "Enemy Number
One."

I still maintain close personal contact with a number of people
from the Oslo days: Terje Larsen and Mona Juul, who have returned
to Oslo but are always drawn back in our direction; and Dennis Ross
and Martin Indyk, who continue to sustain the threads of the process.
And I go on sharing a strong bond with Abu Ala. He is still the
speaker of the Palestinian Council, still fighting for the betterment of
Palestinian society and a future Palestinian state, still a great believer
in peace and in the process he calls "ours." We talk by phone almost
every day and meet almost every week. A while ago, during one of the
deep crises that have occurred since May 1996, the two of us encountered a senior official of the Netanyahu government. He turned to us
with great curiosity, plus a touch of sarcasm, and said, "So tell me,
how did you do it?"

I smiled at Abu Ala. "Tell him how we really did it."

"We didn't do it," Abu Ala replied. "Don't you remember? We
were completely against it!"

We shared yet another laugh; humor still binds us.

"Look," I told the man from the present government, "you see
here two friends who conducted the most stubborn and brutal negotiations possible. They lurched from crisis to crisis. They were be-

sieged by a harsh atmosphere, violent enemies, and a multitude of skeptics. But the most important thing happened right at the beginning, when we created a partnership based on the decision of our leaders and the relationship between us."

"Yes, Uri was my partner," said Abu Ala. "He's also my friend. We agreed about almost nothing, except for the most important thing: that if we go forward together, our peoples will be strong, because each can contribute to the other and create a new reality. If we don't, both of us will suffer."

"That's not a matter of naïveté," I explained. "It means overcoming hard feelings and—most important—not giving in to enemies and violence."

"In Oslo I told Uri that both sides would make a lot of mistakes—and that they certainly did. After all, we had reached the point of dialogue after years of bitter conflict, bloodshed, hatred, and little experience of peace. You need a lot of patience for this kind of challenge—patience, faith, and tenacity."

"And everything must flow from a sense of equality," I added. "People are driven by motivation, not by orders. It was our understanding from the start that partnership creates the substance of an agreement, not vice versa."

"And by remembering that the alternative is dreadful, tragic. So it is our duty to the next generation, to our children, to offer a life different from the one we had known. In that we are partners."

"Precisely, Abu Ala."

There was an embarrassing pause after that. Abu Ala gave the official one of his wicked looks, and I feared what might come next. But then his face softened and all he said was "Understand?"

Index